INTERPRETING
THE PSALMS

INTERPRETING
THE PSALMS

An Exegetical Handbook

Mark D. Futato

David M. Howard Jr.
SERIES EDITOR

KREGEL
ACADEMIC

Interpreting the Psalms: An Exegetical Handbook

© 2007 by Mark D. Futato

Published by Kregel Publications, a division of Kregel Inc., 2450 Oak Industrial Dr NE, Grand Rapids, MI 49505.

Library of Congress Cataloging-in-Publication Data
Futato, Mark David.
  Interpreting the Psalms: an exegetical handbook / by Mark D. Futato; David M. Howard Jr., editor.
    p. cm.
  Includes bibliographical references.
  1. Bible. O.T. Psalms—Criticism, interpretation, etc. I. Howard, David M.

II. Title.

  BS1430.52.F86   2007   223'.206—dc22   2007026923

ISBN 978-0-8254-2765-7

Printed in the United States of America

9 10 11 12 / 26 25 24 23 22 21

To my parents,
Rudolph D. Futato and June E. Futato,
for all of their love and support through the years.

CONTENTS IN BRIEF

CONTENTS

SERIES PREFACE

AN APPRECIATION FOR THE RICH diversity of literary genres in Scripture is one of the positive features of evangelical scholarship in recent decades. No longer are the same principles or methods of interpretation applied across the board to every text without regard for differences in genre. Such an approach can, however, lead to confusion, misunderstanding, and even wrong interpretations or applications. Careful attention to differences in genre is, then, a critical component of a correct understanding of God's Word.

The Handbooks for Old Testament Exegesis series (HOTE) offers students basic skills for exegeting and proclaiming the different genres of the Old Testament. Because there is no one–size–fits–all approach to interpreting Scripture, this series features six volumes covering the major genres in the Old Testament: narrative, law, poetry, wisdom, prophecy, and apocalyptic. The volumes are written by seasoned scholar-teachers who possess extensive knowledge of their disciplines, lucid writing abilities, and the conviction that the church and the world today desperately need to hear the message of the Old Testament. These handbooks are designed to serve a twofold purpose: to present the reader with a better understanding (principles) of the different Old Testament genres, and provide strategies (methods) for preaching and teaching these genres.

These volumes are primarily intended to serve as textbooks for graduate-level exegesis courses that assume a basic knowledge of Hebrew. There is no substitute for encountering God's Word in its original languages, even as we acknowledge the limitations of language in plumbing the depths of who God is. However, the series is also accessible to those without a working knowledge of Hebrew, in that an English translation is always given whenever Hebrew is used. Thus, seminary-trained pastors for whom Hebrew is a distant memory, upper-level college students, and even well-motivated laypeople should all find this series useful.

Each volume is built around the same six-chapter structure as follows:

1. The Nature of the Genres
2. Viewing the Whole
3. Preparing for Interpretation
4. Interpreting the Text
5. Proclaiming the Text
6. Putting It All Together

Authors are given freedom in how they title these six chapters and in how best to approach the material in each. But the familiar pattern in every volume will serve students well, allowing them to move easily from one volume to another to locate specific information. The first chapter in each handbook introduces the genre(s) covered in the volume. The second chapter covers the purpose, message, and primary themes in the individual books and canonical sections under consideration. The third chapter includes such diverse matters as historical and cultural backgrounds, critical questions, textual matters, and a brief annotated bibliography of helpful works. The fourth chapter sets forth guidelines for interpreting texts of the genre(s) under consideration. The fifth chapter details strategies for proclaiming such texts. The final chapter gives one or two hands-on examples of how to move through different stages of the interpretive process, in order to demonstrate how the principles discussed previously work out in practice. Each volume also includes a glossary of specialized terms.

The Scriptures themselves remind us in many ways about the importance of proper interpretation of God's words. Paul encouraged Timothy to "do your best to present yourself to God as one approved by him, a worker who has no need to be ashamed, rightly explaining the word of truth" (2 Tim. 2:15 NRSV). In an earlier day, Ezra the scribe, along with the Levites, taught God's Word to the postexilic community: "So they read from the book, from the law of God, with interpretation. They gave the sense, so that the people understood the reading" (Neh. 8:8 NRSV). It is my prayer, and that of the authors and publisher, that these handbooks will help a new generation of God's people to do the same.

Soli Deo Gloria.

—DAVID M. HOWARD JR.
Series Editor

PREFACE

THE BOOK OF PSALMS IS perhaps the most frequently used book of the Old Testament. We read psalms in public worship and private devotion. We sing them, pray them, and contemplate their application to our lives. In the psalms we encounter God, others, and ourselves in life's joys and sorrows, tragedies and triumphs. The psalms capture our imaginations, engage our thoughts, stir our emotions, and move our wills. They also present interpretive challenges. Their poetic form has few if any points of contact with English poetry. Their images come from a world quite different from our own. Their ethics at times seem to go against the grain of the teachings in the New Testament. How to interpret the psalms in order to use them effectively in our own lives and in the lives of others is the focus of this volume.

Upon successful study of this volume, you will be able to (1) understand the nature of Hebrew poetry and use this understanding as a key tool for interpreting the psalms, (2) understand the purpose and message of the Psalms as a literary whole, so that you can interpret specific psalms in their proper literary context, (3) understand the primary categories of psalms so that you can interpret specific psalms in their proper generic context, and (4) understand how to shape your interpretation of the psalms, so that you can present your understanding with clarity and conviction.

Part of the interpretive process involves the use of English translations of the Hebrew text. Unless otherwise indicated, the translation used in this volume is the NIV. I also use the NLT quite often and for the most part cite the second edition (2004); on a few occasions I prefer the first edition (1996) and indicate this with NLT 1.0.

The verse numbers in the Hebrew text and English translations often differ by a verse (or two), because the titles are counted in the versification of the Hebrew text but not in English translations. So, for example, Psalm 3:1 in English is Psalm 3:2 in Hebrew. The English versification is given first with the Hebrew in brackets—for example, Psalm 3:1 [2].

Technical terms have been kept to a minimum. When used, all such terms are marked with bold font the first time they occur in a given chapter and are included in the glossary at the end of the book. I use italics when I provide my own definition for terms and when I wish to draw attention to key terms in Scripture quotations. All abbreviations used are given in the abbreviations list that follows this preface.

While this volume is focused on interpreting the book of Psalms, many of the principles apply to other portions of the Old Testament, especially those principles discussed in chapter 1. Chapter 1 deals with the poetry of the Psalms. Poetry is found in many other places in the Old Testament: the wisdom books (Job, Proverbs, and Ecclesiastes) are predominantly poetic, as are Lamentations and the Song of Songs. Isaiah and the Minor Prophets (minus Jonah) are also predominantly poetic. In addition, poems are scattered throughout numerous prose texts (e.g., Exodus 15, Judges 5, 2 Samuel 18). The principles for interpreting the poetry of the Psalms apply equally to interpreting these other poetic texts.

I am grateful for all of the authors from whom I have learned much about the psalms over the years, for the many students with whom I have studied the psalms, and especially for my wife and children with whom I have lived the psalms. I also want to thank David M. Howard Jr. for his patient and painstaking editing of the manuscript, which has been greatly improved through his efforts.

ABBREVIATIONS

ABD	*Anchor Bible Dictionary*. Edited by D. N. Freedman. 6 vols. New York: Doubleday, 1992.
AOTC	Abingdon Old Testament Commentaries
BASOR	*Bulletin of the American Schools of Oriental Research*
BDB	Brown, F., S. R. Driver, and C. A. Briggs. *A Hebrew and English Lexicon of the Old Testament*. Oxford: Clarendon, 1974.
BETL	Bibliotheca ephemeridum theologicarum lovaniensium
CHALOT	Holladay, William L. *A Concise Hebrew and Aramaic Lexicon of the Old Testament*. Grand Rapids: Eerdmans, 1988.
CTA	*Corpus des tablettes en cunéiformes alphabétiques découvertes à Ras Shamra-Ugarit de 1929 à 1939*. Edited by A. Herdner. Mission de Ras Shamra 10. Paris: Geuthner, 1963.
DBI	*Dictionary of Biblical Imagery*. Edited by Leland Ryken, James C. Wilhoit, and Tremper Longman III. Downers Grove, IL: InterVarsity Press, 1998.
DCH	*Dictionary of Classical Hebrew*. Edited by David J. A. Clines. 8 vols. projected. Sheffield: Sheffield Academic Press, 1993—.
EBC	*Expositor's Bible Commentary*. Edited by Frank E. Gaebelein. Vol. 5. Grand Rapids: Zondervan, 1991.
ESV	English Standard Version
FOTL	Forms of the Old Testament Literature

HALOT	Koehler, L., W. Baumgartner, and J. J. Stamm, *The Hebrew and Aramaic Lexicon of the Old Testament*. Leiden: E. J. Brill, 2000.
HKAT	Handkommentar zum Alten Testament
Int	*Interpretation*
JSOTSup	Journal for the Study of the Old Testament: Supplement Series
KTU	*Die keilalphabetischen Texte aus Ugarit*. Edited by M. Dietrich, O. Loretz, and J. Sanmartín. Neukirchen-Vluyn: Kevelaer, 1976. 2nd enlarged ed. of *KTU: The Cuneiform Alphabetic Texts from Ugarit, Ras Ibn Hani, and Other Places*. Edited by M. Dietrich, O. Loretz, and J. Sanmartín. Münster, 1995 (= *CTU*)
LXX	Septuagint
MT	Masoretic Text
NAB	New American Bible
NAC	New American Commentary
NASB	New American Standard Bible
NCBC	New Century Bible Commentary
NIB	*The New Interpreter's Bible*
NICNT	New International Commentary on the New Testament
NICOT	New International Commentary on the Old Testament
NIDOTTE	*New International Dictionary of Old Testament Theology and Exegesis*. Edited by W. A. VanGemeren. 5 vols. Grand Rapids: Zondervan, 1997.
NIV	New International Version
NIVAC	The NIV Application Commentary
NKJV	New King James Version
NLT	New Living Translation, 2004
NLT 1.0	New Living Translation, 1996
NRSV	New Revised Standard Version
OTG	Old Testament Guides
OTL	Old Testament Library
RevExp	*Review and Expositor*
SBLDS	Society of Biblical Literature Dissertation Series
TDOT	*Theological Dictionary of the Old Testament*. Edited by G. J. Botterweck and H. Ringgren. Translated by J. T. Willis,

	G. W. Bromiley, and D. E. Green. 8 vols. Grand Rapids: Eerdmans, 1974–2004.
TLOT	*Theological Lexicon of the Old Testament.* Edited by E. Jenni and C. Westermann. Translated by M. E. Biddle. 3 vols. Peabody, MA: Hendrickson, 1997.
TNK	Tanakh: The Holy Scriptures—The New JPS Translation According to the Traditional Hebrew Text, 1985.
TOTC	Tyndale Old Testament Commentaries
TWOT	*Theological Wordbook of the Old Testament.* Edited by R. L. Harris, G. L. Archer Jr., and B. K. Waltke. 2 vols. Chicago: Moody, 1980.
TZ	*Theologische Zeitschrift*
WBC	Word Biblical Commentary
WTJ	*Westminster Theological Journal*

1

APPRECIATING THE POETRY

Beautiful words stir my heart.
I will recite a lovely poem about the king,
for my tongue is like the pen of a skillful poet.
(Ps. 45:1 NLT)

DO YOU APPRECIATE POETRY? You may or may not. Not everyone does. I didn't appreciate poetry very much until I began to study Hebrew poetry a good number of years ago. If you're like me, this chapter may open up a new world for you. What is a "lovely poem" in your estimation, and who is a "skillful poet"? Which, if any, of the following do you appreciate?

Once upon a midnight dreary, while I pondered, weak and weary,
Over many a quaint and curious volume of forgotten lore,
While I nodded, nearly napping, suddenly there came a tapping,
As of someone gently rapping, rapping at my chamber door.
"'Tis some visitor," I muttered, "tapping at my chamber door;
Only this, and nothing more."[1]

---

1. Edgar Allan Poe, "The Raven," in *The Collected Works of Edgar Allan Poe—Volume I: Poems* (Cambridge: Belknap Press of Harvard University Press, 1969), 364–65.

✧

September tenth . . . the year starts home.
Morning broke clear today
no fog . . . no rain
only a clear cold September morning.
It's autumn all right.
You can feel it
with the taste of summer still in my mouth
my lungs breathe autumn.[2]

✧

coffee
in a paper cup—
a long way from home[3]

✧

The metered rhyme of Poe, the free verse of McKuen, and the haiku of Hotham are just three of many styles of English poetry. Yet as great as the difference is between the poetry of Poe, McKuen, and Hotham, even greater is the difference between these English poets and the poets who wrote the psalms.

To appreciate a lovely poem found in the Psalms and written by a skillful Hebrew poet requires at least a basic knowledge of what makes Hebrew poetry poetry. And the more you appreciate the *poetry* of the psalms, the more you will get their *message*. So one key to interpreting the psalms is understanding and appreciating their poetic features. This is the task of chapter 1.

Before getting into the specific characteristics of Hebrew poetry, let's look at a brief definition: *Hebrew poetry is a type of literature that communicates with terse lines employing* **parallelism** *and* **imagery** *in high fre-*

---

2. Rod McKuen, "September 10," in *And Autumn Came* (Hollywood: Cheval Books, 1969), n.p.

3. Gary Hotham, "Coffee," in *Breath Marks: Haiku to Read in the Dark* (Moscow: Canon Press, 1999), 20.

quency. Major sections of this chapter will go into detail on the nature of parallelism and imagery. For now, let it be said that Hebrew prose can also contain parallelism and imagery, so it is the consistent and sustained use of these features that characterize Hebrew poetry and distinguish it from prose.

You may have wondered why this definition contains no reference to either rhyme or meter. We tend to think of rhyme and meter as the essence of poetry, because since childhood we've been exposed to poems like, "Jack and Jill went up the hill. . . ." There is almost universal agreement, however, that rhyme is not a feature of Hebrew poetry. On occasion we detect apparent rhyming as in Psalm 121:3 (author's translation appears below):

אַל־יִתֵּן לַמּוֹט רַגְלֶךָ

'al-yittēn lammôt <u>ragĕlekā</u> ("he will not permit <u>your foot</u> to slip")

אַל־יָנוּם שֹׁמְרֶךָ

'al-yānûm <u>shōmĕreka</u> ("<u>your guardian</u> will not sleep.")

But this apparent end rhyme is accidental, resulting from the form of Hebrew words with pronoun suffixes rather than to a sustained effort to rhyme.

The presence of meter, on the other hand, is debated. Two main proposals have been offered for recognizing meter in Hebrew poetry. Some scholars follow a system of counting syllables, while others count accents. Many other scholars, of which group I include myself, believe that neither system does justice to all the data. What we can say with confidence is that poetic lines in Hebrew are terse and relatively equal in length, even though we have no instrument for measuring this terse length with precision.[4] A glance at, for example, the prose account of Deborah's victory in Judges 4 and the poetic account of that same victory in Judges 5 demonstrates the terse nature of Hebrew poetry.

This terseness is related to a number of grammatical features that occur less often in Hebrew poetry than in Hebrew prose. Hebrew

---

4. James L. Kugel, *The Idea of Biblical Hebrew Poetry: Parallelism and Its History* (New Haven: Yale, 1981), 71.

poetry employs the *waw*-relative imperfect,[5] the direct-object marker, the relative pronoun, and the definite article with far less frequency than does Hebrew prose. The minimal occurrence of these grammatical features in poetry adds to the terseness of the poetic line. The following chart shows the statistics on these grammatical features as they occur in the prose account of Creation in Genesis 1 and the poetic account of Creation in Psalm 104.

	Genesis 1	Psalm 104
Waw-relative Imperfect	50	1
Direct-object Marker	26	2
Relative Pronoun	9	2
Definite Article	79	27

Since terseness, parallelism, and imagery are relative measuring tools, the boundary between poetry and prose at times will be fuzzy.[6] We are, after all, dealing here with literature in general and poetry in particular, and not with algebraic equations. So we need to give the poets sufficient space to be creative within the parameters of their own literary conventions. The poetic lines of Psalm 1, for example, do not scan with anything like the regularity of the lines in Psalm 2. Poetry and prose thus are better viewed as types of literature occurring *on a continuum* rather than *in isolated boxes*.[7]

ANALYZING THE PARTS

While we could begin with a study of Hebrew phonology (sounds) and morphology (words) as the basic building blocks of poetry, we will

---

5. Also known as the "*waw*-consecutive plus imperfect" construction, this grammatical feature, along with the others listed here, is not accessible in English translation.

6. Kugel, *Idea of Biblical Hebrew Poetry*, 59–95, for example, denies the distinction for all practical purposes.

7. David L. Petersen and Kent Harold Richards, *Interpreting Hebrew Poetry* (Minneapolis: Fortress, 1992), 13–14.

instead start at a higher level, the level of the poetic line.[8] Then we will look at how poets batch lines together to form strophes and how they, at times, go on to batch strophes into stanzas.

The Line

A **line** can be viewed as the basic unit of Hebrew poetry. A line is not to be confused with a sentence in English, because many lines contain more than one complete sentence. Psalm 117:1 is a case in point.

> Praise the LORD, all you nations.
> Extol him, all you peoples.

Also a line is not to be confused with a verse in the Bible, because many verses contain more than one line, as is the case in Psalm 47:9.

> Line 1: The rulers of the world have gathered together
> with people of the God of Abraham.
> Line 2: For all the kings of the earth belong to God.
> He is highly honored everywhere.
>
> (NLT)

This one verse contains two lines and three sentences. What, though, comprises a line?

Before defining a line, I will describe one. The most frequent line in Hebrew poetry is made up of two halves. Each half line is called a **colon**,[9] so the basic line is called a **bicolon**. Look at Psalm 92:1 for example.

> It is good to give thanks to the LORD,
> to sing praises to the Most High.
>
> (NLT)

---

8. For a discussion of the role that sound plays in Hebrew poetry, see L. Alonso Schökel, *A Manual of Hebrew Poetics*, Subsidia Biblica (Rome: Pontifical Biblical Institute, 1988), 11:20–33.
9. Many scholars, but not all, distinguish line and colon as I do. Others, such as Michael O'Connor, *Hebrew Verse Structure* (Winona Lake, IN: Eisenbrauns, 1980), 32, do not.

Notice that the cola (plural of colon) correspond: "to give thanks to the LORD" corresponds with "to sing praises to the Most High." This correspondence is the essence of parallelism, which is discussed in detail below. For now, we can define a line as one complete parallelistic expression of thought.[10]

While most lines are made up of two cola, some contain three. We call such a line a **tricolon**. Psalm 112:9–10 provides two clear examples.

> They [the righteous] share freely and give generously
>   to those in need.
>   Their good deeds will be remembered forever.
>   They will have influence and honor.
> The wicked will see this and be infuriated.
>   They will grind their teeth in anger;
>   they will slink away, their hopes thwarted.
>
>   (NLT)

Sometimes a line can contain four cola. We call such a line a **tetra-colon** or a **quatrain** as in Psalm 29:1–2 and Psalm 96:11–12.

> Honor the LORD, you heavenly beings;
>   honor the LORD for his glory and strength.
> Honor the LORD for the glory of his name.
>   Worship the LORD in the splendor of his holiness.
>
>   (NLT)

> Let the heavens be glad, and let the earth rejoice!
>   Let the sea and everything in it shout his praise!
> Let the fields and their crops burst forth with joy!
>   Let the trees of the forest rustle with praise!
>
>   (NLT 1.0)

On occasion, a psalm contains the somewhat anomalous "**mono-colon**," of which the expression הַלְלוּ־יָהּ ("Praise the LORD!") is

---

10. Tremper Longman III, *How to Read the Psalms* (Downers Grove, IL: InterVarsity Press, 1988), 96.

one example. This Hebrew expression occurs twenty-three times in the book of Psalms and only at the beginning or ending of a poem.[11] Hebrew הַלְלוּ־יָהּ is best understood as an opening and closing exclamation, as indicated by the exclamation point used in the NLT.

Numerous modern translations, like the NIV and NLT, use a series of indentations to indicate the cola in a line. The first colon (colon A) will be on the left margin. The second colon (colon B) will always be differentiated by one indentation, as in the examples above. Tricola will keep the second and third cola at the same level of indentation. Sometimes a third level of indentation is employed, meaning simply there was not enough room in the column to get the entire colon on one line of print, so the publisher wrapped that colon down to the next line. Thus, a single column edition makes for a more aesthetically pleasing presentation of the poetic lines of Hebrew poetry, since it virtually eliminates the need for this third level of indentation.

The basic unit of a poem, then, is the line, usually made from two cola, but sometimes made from one, three, or four.

The Strophe

When writing prose, we group related sentences together to form a paragraph. When writing poetry we group related lines together to form a **strophe**. A strophe is in poetry what a paragraph is in prose.

Numerous modern translations indicate the division between strophes by placing extra space between them. This extra space functions like the indentation that marks the beginning of a new paragraph in English prose.

The primary basis for grouping lines into a strophe is sense. A strophe is a group of lines that focus on a common theme; one idea holds the verses in the strophe together. In the NLT of Psalm 13, for example, extra space appears between verses 2–3 and verses 4–5, indicating three strophes: verses 1–2, 3–4, and 5–6. Note that verses 1–2 focus on the question, "How long?" Verses 3–4 make specific requests: "Turn," Restore," "Don't let," "Don't let." Verses 5–6 are united by the note of confidence they express: "But I trust," "I will rejoice," "I will sing."

---

11. The one exception is Psalm 135:3, but here הַלְלוּ־יָהּ is followed by a כִּי ("for") clause and is, therefore, not used absolutely as in the other occurrences.

Hebrew poets used other techniques for grouping lines into strophes. One technique is the alphabetic acrostic. An alphabetic acrostic uses the letters of the alphabet to structure a poem. Psalm 119 is an eightfold acrostic: each group of eight lines is joined together by the use of the same letter of the alphabet as the first letter in the first word of each line. So, for example, the first word in each line of verses 1–8 begins with *aleph* (the first letter of the Hebrew alphabet), the first word in each line of verses 9–16 begins with *beth* (the second letter of the Hebrew alphabet), and so on through verses 169–176, where the first word in each line begins with *tav* (the last letter of the Hebrew alphabet).

A poet can also use grammar to group lines into strophes, as in Psalm 148. This psalm is naturally divided into two strophes: verses 1–6 and verses 7–14. (Note that the NLT puts extra space between v. 6 and v. 7.) The theme of verses 1–6 is found in verse 1a: "Praise the LORD from the heavens!" The theme of verses 7–14 is found in verse 7a: "Praise the LORD from the earth." The universe is often pictured as two-layered in the Old Testament: heaven above and earth beneath (see Gen. 1:1). Corresponding to this division, the poet divides this poem into two strophes. In the first, the poet invites the heavens to praise the Lord, and in the second he invites the earth to do so. In addition to the unity of subject matter, the poet employs **head linkage** to mark the beginning of each strophe. Head linkage is the literary technique of marking the beginning of two sequential sections by repeating grammar or vocabulary:

(v. 1a) הַלְלוּ אֶת־יְהוָה מִן־הַשָּׁמַיִם
Praise the LORD from the heavens.

(v. 7a) הַלְלוּ אֶת־יְהוָה מִן־הָאָרֶץ
Praise the LORD from the earth.

In both strophes, a variety of subjects are called upon to praise the Lord (vv. 2–4 and vv. 8–12). The poet then shifts from the imperative to the jussive[12] in verse 5 and verse 13:

---

12. The *jussive* is a form of the Hebrew verb that is used to express the will of the speaker with regard to the third person, e.g., "Let him go up." See Paul Joüon and T. Muraoka, *A Grammar of Biblical Hebrew* (Rome: Pontifical Biblical Institute, 1991), §46a.

(v. 5a) יְהַלְלוּ אֶת־שֵׁם יְהוָה

Let them praise the name of the LORD.

(v. 13a) יְהַלְלוּ אֶת־שֵׁם יְהוָה

Let them praise the name of the LORD.

Each of these shifts to the jussive is then followed by a reason clause:

(v. 5b) כִּי הוּא צִוָּה וְנִבְרָאוּ

for he commanded and they were created

(v. 13b) כִּי־נִשְׂגָּב שְׁמוֹ לְבַדּוֹ

For his name alone is exalted

The following lines each begin with a *waw*-relative imperfect verb:

(v. 6a) וַיַּעֲמִידֵם

He set them

(v. 14a) וַיָּרֶם

He has raised up

In Psalm 148 the poet has used repeated grammatical structures to create a **parallel pattern**, which, taken together, summons the whole universe to praise the Lord. Paying attention to the strophic structure of Hebrew poems, then, is a key to following the poetic thought, and keeps the interpreter from getting lost in the forest of trees/verses.

The Stanza

Some poems, in particular longer ones, will have two or more strophes that focus on the same theme. We call a group of closely related strophes a **stanza**.

Psalm 139, for example, is comprised of two stanzas—verses 1–18 and verses 19–24. The first stanza focuses on the nature of God and is divided into four strophes. Verses 1–6 reflect on God's knowledge.

Note how the poet uses the repetition of words (reflected in the NLT) to focus our attention on God's knowledge: "know" (v. 1b), "know" (v. 2a), "know" (v. 2b), "know" (v. 3c), "know" (v. 4a), "knowledge" (v. 6a). Verses 7–12 reflect on his presence: "I can never escape from your spirit" (v. 7a), "I can never get away from your presence" (v. 7b), "you are there" (v. 8a), "you are there" (v. 8b), "even there" (v. 10a), "I cannot hide from you" (v. 12a). Verses 13–16 reflect God's care: "You made . . . my body" (v. 13a), "and knit me together" (v. 13b), "You watched me" (v. 15a), "You saw me" (v. 16a). Verses 17–18 conclude this stanza by repeating its themes: "How precious are your thoughts" (v. 17a) and "you are still with me" (v. 18b).

In the second stanza the poet responds to this reflection in two strophes. Verses 19–22 are a request for the elimination of evil by eliminating "the others." Verses 23–24 are a request for the elimination of evil from "me."

One other technique employed by this poet is called **inclusion**.[13] An inclusion is the use of the same or similar grammar or content at the beginning and end of a poem or stanza or strophe. In the first verse of the first strophe the poet says,

> O LORD, you have examined my heart
> and know everything about me.
>   (NLT)

And in the first verse of the last strophe the poets says,

> Search me, O God, and know my heart;
> test me and know my anxious thoughts.
>   (NLT)

This repetition of the examination motif provides a sense of closure and shows that the overarching concern of the poem is an ever deepening relationship between the poet and God. This theme is underscored in the concluding verse.

---

13. Also referred to as an *inclusio*.

> Point out anything in me that offends you,
>   and lead me along the path of everlasting life.
>   (NLT)

As with strophes, so with stanzas: segmenting a poem into stanzas helps us to better understand the flow of the poet's thought and thereby helps us to better understand the poem.

It is clear that understanding the parts of a poem (lines, strophes, and stanzas) is basic to understanding Hebrew poetry. We can now build on this foundation by taking a closer look at how Hebrew poets expressed their thoughts in parallel lines.

PENETRATING THE PARALLELISM

Hebrew poets expressed their thoughts in poems comprised of lines, strophes, and, at times, stanzas. We have seen how strophes and stanzas are put together, but what comprises a line? Since Hebrew poetry has no apparent meter or rhyme, what makes a line a line? At the heart of the answer to this question is "parallelism." In a line there is a particular relationship between the cola, a certain flow of thought from one colon to the next. We call this flow of thought or relationship "parallelism."

What Is Parallelism?

Correspondence

At its core, parallelism is *correspondence*. Adele Berlin has said that correspondence is the very essence of parallelism.[14] Similarly, Tremper Longman has said that "parallelism refers to the correspondence which occurs between the phrases of a poetic line."[15] We can say, then, that parallelism is a relationship of correspondence between the cola of a poetic line.[16]

---

14. Adele Berlin, *The Dynamics of Biblical Hebrew Parallelism* (Bloomington: Indiana University, 1985), 2–3.
15. Longman, *How to Read the Psalms*, 95.
16. Mark D. Futato, *Transformed by Praise: The Purpose and Message of the Psalms* (Phillipsburg, NJ: P & R Publishing, 2002), 35–36.

The correspondence between the cola can occur on a number of levels. It may occur, for instance, on the level of grammar or on the level of meaning. Since English grammar and Hebrew grammar are quite different, appreciating grammatical parallelism requires knowledge of basic Hebrew grammar. Correspondence on the level of meaning, however, can be appreciated to a large extent by those reading Hebrew poetry in translation. Let's take a look at both levels.[17]

Correspondence in Grammar

At times the degree of correspondence on the grammatical level is so high that the grammar of each colon is identical. Psalm 103:10 is an example.

לֹא כַחֲטָאֵינוּ עָשָׂה לָנוּ

Not according to our sins has he done to us.

(author's translation)

וְלֹא כַעֲוֹנֹתֵינוּ גָּמַל עָלֵינוּ

Not according to our iniquities has he repaid upon us.

(author's translation)

Both cola are comprised of the identical grammar: negative adverb + preposition governing a noun with pronoun suffix + verb + preposition with pronoun suffix. This example should not lead us, however, to equate grammatical parallelism and *grammatical identity*.

More often than not grammatical parallelism is expressed through *grammatical equivalence*, that is, the substitution in the second colon of something grammatically different from, but equivalent to, an element in the first colon.[18] Psalm 117:1 provides an example of grammatical equivalence:

---

17. For much more detail on this topic see Berlin, *Dynamics of Biblical Hebrew Parallelism*, 31–102.
18. Ibid., 32.

הַלְלוּ אֶת־יְהוָה כָּל־גּוֹיִם

Praise the LORD all nations.
(author's translation)

שַׁבְּחוּהוּ כָּל־הָאֻמִּים

Glorify him all peoples.
(author's translation)

Here, for the divine name in the first colon (יהוה), the poet has substituted the grammatically equivalent pronoun, *him* (הו-) in the second colon. The kinds of substitutions possible are seemingly endless, as there were not only morphological equivalents but also syntactic equivalents at the disposal of the ancient poet.[19] An awareness of grammatical parallelism will enable the student who can read Old Testament poetry in Hebrew to see parallelism that is not evident to one who reads the poetry in English.

The parallel lines in the two previous examples have cola that are seemingly identical in meaning. Sometimes, however, the grammar is identical but the meaning is not. Psalm 103:3 is a good example:

הַסֹּלֵחַ לְכָל־עֲוֹנֵכִי

who pardons all your iniquities
(NASB)

הָרֹפֵא לְכָל־תַּחֲלֻאָיְכִי

who heals all your diseases
(NASB)

Sin and sickness are certainly closely related concepts in ancient Israelite theology, as Psalm 38:3–5 makes clear.

> Because of your anger, my whole body is sick;
>   my health is broken because of my sins.
> My guilt overwhelms me—
>   it is a burden too heavy to bear.

---

19. See ibid., 32–65.

> My wounds fester and stink
> because of my foolish sins.
>   (NLT)

But not everyone who sinned in the Old Testament got sick, and not every sickness was a result of sin, as the book of Job clearly teaches. So sin and sickness are not identical, nor are forgiveness and healing. Thus, the cola in Psalm 103:3 are identical in grammar but not in meaning.

Correspondence in Meaning

Semantic parallelism is the correspondence in meaning that exists between the cola of a poetic line. At times this correspondence amounts to identity in meaning, as in Psalm 92:6 [7].

> Only a simpleton would not know,
> And only a fool would not understand this.
>   (NLT)

Robert Alter refers to this kind of correspondence as "static synonymity."[20] While it may not be fair to call such static lines rare, they are not the rule for how the cola of poetic lines relate on the level of meaning.

The correspondence in meaning is not typically as exact as in Psalm 92:6 [7]. This can be demonstrated from Psalm 92:1[2].

> It is good to give thanks to the LORD,
> to sing praises to the Most High.
>   (NLT)

"To give thanks" obviously corresponds with "to sing praises," as does "LORD," with "Most High." But the meanings of Hebrew יָדָה and זָמַר are by no means identical. Hebrew יָדָה in the Hiphil means to give thanks or to praise in the sense of confessing or acknowledging

---

20. Robert Alter, *The Art of Biblical Poetry* (New York: Basic Books, 1985), 22.

who the Lord is and what he has done,[21] and זָמַר means "to play an instrument, to sing,"[22] which helps to explain the references to instruments in verse 3.

> accompanied by the ten-stringed harp
> and the melody of the lyre.
>
> (NLT)

Lines like Psalm 92:15, however, seemingly have very little correspondence at all.

> They will declare, "The LORD is just!
> He is my rock!
> There is no evil in him!"
>
> (NLT)

What kind of correspondence does exist, then, between the cola of a poetic line?

How Does Parallelism Work?

An Older Understanding

C. S. Lewis spoke for the vast majority of students of Hebrew poetry when he defined parallelism as the poetic technique of "saying the same thing twice in different words."[23] Lewis was part of a long stream of scholars that flowed from the headwaters of Robert Lowth's 1753 *Lectures on the Sacred Poetry of the Hebrews*. In these lectures Lowth described parallelism as a technique of poets who "express in many different ways the same thing in different words."[24]

Since, according to Lowth, in parallelism "a proposition is delivered, and a second is subjoined to it . . . equivalent, or contrasted," some

---

21. See *HALOT*, 1:389; and Walter Brueggemann, *The Message of the Psalms* (Minneapolis: Augsburg, 1984), 125.
22. *HALOT*, 2:273–74; see also C. Barth, "זָמַר," in *TDOT*, 4:96–97.
23. C. S. Lewis, *Reflections on the Psalms* (San Diego: Harcourt Brace Jovanovich, 1958), 11.
24. Quoted in Berlin, *Dynamics of Biblical Hebrew Parallelism*, 1.

parallel lines are said to be "synonymous" (saying the same thing twice in different words), while others are said to be "antithetic" (saying the same thing twice with opposite expressions). An example of the former would be Psalm 92:12:

> The righteous will flourish like a palm tree,
>   they will grow like a cedar of Lebanon.

The book of Proverbs has many examples of the latter, Proverbs 1:8 being just one.

> My child, listen when your father corrects you.
>   Don't neglect your mother's instruction.
>
> (NLT)

But there was a third category of parallelism for Lowth—"synthetic." Synthetic parallelism refers to those many lines wherein the second colon does not really say the same thing again in either different or opposite words, but simply adds new information to the first colon. The need for this third category eventually called into question the adequacy of the older understanding of parallelism as "saying the same thing twice in different words." As a result, a new understanding has been formulated in recent years.

A New Understanding

Students of Hebrew poetry have articulated a new understanding of parallelism, one that I think better reflects how parallelism works.[25] I have put it this way: "Parallelism is the art of saying something similar in both cola but with a difference added in the second colon."[26] Usually there is some kind of movement from the first to the second colon, some kind of addition.

Let's look at several examples from Psalm 29, beginning with verse 1.

---

25. See Kugel, *Idea of Biblical Hebrew Poetry*; and Alter, *Art of Biblical Poetry*.
26. Futato, *Transformed by Praise*, 36.

> Honor the LORD, you heavenly beings;
> honor the LORD for his glory and strength.
> (NLT)

The repetition of "honor the LORD" establishes a correspondence between these two cola, which invites us to read the cola together. Having established the correspondence, the poet then adds a difference: the first colon tells us *who* is to give honor to the Lord—the angels—and the second colon adds the idea of *what* the angels are to give honor to the Lord for, namely, his glory and strength. Verse 4 presents a different kind of movement:

> The voice of the LORD is powerful;
> the voice of the LORD is majestic.

Here the difference is the simple change from one characteristic (power) to another (majesty). Verse 5 has yet another kind of movement.

> The voice of the LORD breaks the cedars;
> the LORD breaks in pieces the cedars of Lebanon.

The movement is from "cedars" to "cedars of Lebanon." To the ancients this would be like our saying, "The wind blew down redwood trees, and not just any redwood trees, but those colossal redwoods of northern California." Finally, let's look at verse 10.

> The LORD sits enthroned over the flood;
> the LORD is enthroned as King forever.

The first colon tells us *where* the Lord's throne has been set up—above the forces of chaos that he has vanquished in battle. The second colon tells us *for how long* this is true—forever.[27]

My objective is not to provide a list of the kinds of differences you will find as you reflect on parallel lines. My objective is to acquaint you

---

27. For the "flood" as a reference to God's vanquishing of chaos, see Richard J. Clifford, *Psalms 1–72*, AOTC (Nashville: Abingdon, 2002), 156.

with the principle that *parallelism is the art of saying something similar in both cola but with a difference added in the second colon.* Hebrew poets thus invite us to read slowly, looking for a difference in the second colon, be that difference small or great.

Before leaving this discussion of parallelism, let's look at one more text to illustrate how our understanding of the nature of parallelism affects our interpretation of poetic lines. The Hebrew text of Psalm 150:1 reads,

הַלְלוּ־אֵל בְּקָדְשׁוֹ

Praise God in his sanctuary

הַלְלוּהוּ בִּרְקִיעַ עֻזּוֹ

praise him in his mighty heaven!

In the Old Testament, the Hebrew word קֹדֶשׁ ("holiness") frequently refers to God's sanctuary.[28] In keeping with this, most English translations use the word "sanctuary" here.[29] But does "sanctuary" refer to God's sanctuary in heaven or on earth? If parallelism is saying the same thing twice in different words, the sanctuary is in heaven, given the second colon, "praise him in his mighty heaven." This is the understanding of NLT 1.0, which renders the first colon, "Praise God in his heavenly dwelling." If, however, parallelism is saying something similar in each colon but with a difference in the second colon, it is likely that the sanctuary is on earth.[30] The sense would then be "that worship cannot be confined to a small building in a particular city. The Lord's grandeur can only be adequately praised in the amphitheatre of the cosmos."[31] Whether I am right or wrong on how to read this line is not as important as seeing that the old understanding of how parallelism works has the potential of flattening the text, while the new understanding opens up possibilities for a richer reading.

---

28. *HALOT*, 3:1078.
29. See ESV, NAB, NASB, NIV, NRSV, and TNK.
30. See Hans-Joachim Kraus, *Psalms 60–150: A Commentary* (Minneapolis: Augsburg, 1989), 570.
31. Richard J. Clifford, *Psalms 73–150*, AOTC (Nashville: Abingdon, 2003), 319.

When we read the poetic lines of a psalm slowly and by reflecting on how the second colon adds to the sense of the first, our
understanding of the text deepens and our delight in the text
blossoms. Understanding what parallelism is and how it works
enriches our experience of hearing God speak to us through
the Psalms.[32]

SEEING THE PICTURES

"Images are the glory, perhaps the essence of poetry, the enchanted
planet of the imagination, a limitless galaxy, ever alive and ever chang-
ing," says L. Alonso Schökel.[33] William P. Brown, in his illuminating
work, *Seeing the Psalms: A Theology of Metaphor*, maintains that imagery
is "the most basic building block of poetry."[34] Leland Ryken in a similar vein has said that "poetry is the language of images."[35]

A quick look at the beginning of Psalm 104 supports these assess-
ments, as it yields no less than eight images in the first four verses: God
is clothed with splendor and wrapped in light, stretching out the heavens like a tent, laying foundation beams for his house on the celestial
waters, making clouds his chariots, riding on the wings of the wind,
making winds his messengers and lightning his servants. Nothing
comparable to this is found in prose. Prose certainly employs imagery
but not with the intensity or density of poetry.

Images Touch the Emotions and Engage the Mind

John Calvin called the book of Psalms "an Anatomy of all the Parts
of the Soul."[36] Calvin used this language because he was in touch with
how profoundly the psalms touch our emotions. One of the reasons
why the psalms touch our emotions and have endeared themselves to
the hearts of God's people throughout the centuries is the high frequency of images they employ.

---

32. Futato, *Transformed by Praise*, 39.
33. Schökel, *Manual of Hebrew Poetics*, 95.
34. William P. Brown, *Seeing the Psalms: A Theology of Metaphor* (Louisville: Westminster John Knox, 2002), 2.
35. Leland Ryken, *How to Read the Bible as Literature* (Grand Rapids: Zondervan, 1984), 89.
36. John Calvin, *Commentary on the Book of Psalms* (Grand Rapids: Baker, 1979), xxxvii.

Images often grab our emotions before they engage our minds. We feel their sense before we grasp their meaning. As Brian Gerrish has said, an image "stirs the heart, and then the intellect has to catch up later."[37] As early as the fourth century, Athanasius, in a letter to Marcellinus, showed his awareness of the interplay of the affective and the cognitive in the imagery of the Psalms:

> In the other books one hears only what one must do and what one must not do. . . . But in the Book of Psalms, the one who hears, in addition to learning these things, also comprehends and is taught it in the emotions of the soul, and, consequently . . . he is enabled by this book to possess the image deriving from the words.[38]

Images touch our emotions because they weave vivid pictures from the fabric of ordinary life.

Images Are Pictures of Concrete Actions or Things

"The poets of the Bible constantly put us into a world of water and sheep and lions and rocks and arrows and grass."[39] Ryken's list illustrates why we connect so readily with the psalms: the images are pictures drawn from ordinary life. We can see the picture in our mind's eye when the poet describes the life of the righteous as being "like trees planted along the riverbank, bearing fruit each season" (Ps. 1:3 NLT). When another poet pictures God's Word as "a lamp to guide my feet and a light for my path" (Ps. 119:105 NLT), the mental picture opens before us immediately.

At the same time, Ryken's list points out why biblical imagery at times requires extra work on the part of the modern reader. The poet creates the image from ordinary life, but the ordinary life is that of a people living in a different culture from most contemporary readers of the psalms. The agrarian life of the ancient Israelite who lived in a

---

37. Brian Gerrish, *The Pilgrim Road: Sermons on Christian Life* (Louisville: Westminster John Knox, 1999), 1.

38. Quoted in Brown, *Seeing the Psalms*, 4.

39. Ryken, *How to Read the Bible*, 90.

semidesert climate is not ordinary life for most of us. A contemporary illustration may help at this point. In her passionate song "Turn Me On," Norah Jones says she is waiting for her lover "like a school kid waiting for spring."[40] We all see this picture, at least to a certain extent. But what about the listener who has known only the seasonless climate of Central Florida or Southern California. The image doesn't grab that reader in the same way that it touches the heart of a person who was raised in the Northeast. The northerner can feel the anticipation for that early spring day when the jacket would be shed and the bike would come out of the cellar for the first time in months.

Thus, we see with varying amounts of clarity the images presented in different psalms. In some psalms, we clearly see images. In others we see, but without the clarity of the ancients. In still others we see images as if looking through a window of opaque glass blocks.

As an illustration of images we see, but without great clarity, let's look at the familiar picture painted in Psalm 23:2.

> He makes me lie down in green pastures,
> he leads me beside quiet waters.

Few of us cannot envision this idyllic scene wherein the shepherd provides grass and water to meet the sheep's basic needs. But how many of us feel the pathos of the sheep, who have confidence in the Shepherd, that he will provide in spite of their not having had much to drink or eat for several months, because it is the end of the five-month dry season and the first fall rains have not yet arrived to fill the pools and cause the fresh grass to sprout? We see this image, yet there is more here than immediately meets the eye of a reader who has no knowledge of Israel's climate.

Even less clear for a contemporary reader is the well-known picture in Psalm 23:5.

> You anoint my head with oil.

For most of us "oil" brings to mind either cooking oil or motor oil. Few of us immediately smell the fragrance of a perfumed body lotion.

---

40. Norah Jones, *Come Away with Me*, Blue Note Records, 2002.

And how many of us feel the refreshment that the ancients would have felt, knowing that anointing with oil in this context is analogous to "washing up" after a long trip to partake of a holiday meal?

Probably totally obscure to most readers of psalms is the picture in Psalm 74:13–14.

> It was you who split open the sea by your power;
>   you broke the heads of the monster in the waters.
> It was you who crushed the heads of Leviathan
>   and gave him as food to the creatures of the desert.

How many of us see here a picture of God's work of creation, as verses 15–17 make clear, and how many of us feel the thrill of the Lord's victory over the forces of chaos that these verses portray? In verses 13–14 the poet is using language well known to ancient Israelites, language that was adapted from the creation myths of Israel's neighbors and used as a metaphor for God's work of creation. Without knowledge of these myths, modern readers will be baffled by the Bible's references to "monsters" and to "Leviathan" with its many heads, and might mistakenly try to identify these with any number of marine animals living in the Mediterranean Sea or with prehistoric dinosaurs.[41]

Images Work by Creating Associations

How does an image do its job? Two concepts are helpful in answering this question: source domain and target domain.[42] The source domain is the aspect of ordinary life the poet is drawing from to create the image. The target domain is the subject the poet is speaking of. An image does its job when an aspect of the source domain is transferred to the target domain, thereby creating an association between the two. Psalm 47:9 [10] provides an example:

> The princes of the people have assembled themselves
>   as the people of the God of Abraham,

---

41. For more on this topic, see the excursus on mythopoeic imagery at the end of this chapter (pages 53–55).
42. Brown, *Seeing the Psalms*, 4–7.

> For the shields of the earth belong to God;
> He is highly exalted.
>
> (NASB)

When the poet uses the word *shields*, he is not referring to literal shields. The "shields" correspond to and are an image for the "princes" of the previous line. The source domain is the ancient warrior-king's use of a shield; the target domain is the kings of the nations who have now been subdued by the Lord (see v. 3). The aspect of the shield that is transferred to the king is the shield's use for protection.[43] The poet associates the protective power of the shield with the king, who in the ancient world was viewed as the ultimate source of protection for his people. Now, from the immediate context, we sense more than a touch of irony here, for the shields did not protect the kings and the shields/kings did not protect their nations when they dared to battle against the Lord (v. 3). The reason for this is implicit in Psalm 47:9 [10] ("he is highly exalted") and explicit elsewhere in Psalms: the Lord is the ultimate king and the ultimate shield. For example, Psalm 33:20 says,

> We wait in hope for the LORD;
> he is our help and our shield.[44]

Ultimate protection is found in the Lord alone; he is "the great King over all the earth" (Ps. 47:2 [3]).

Identifying the target domain and studying the source domain are, then, the first two crucial steps in analyzing images. Before fleshing out these steps (see below), let's consider how images can have multiple meanings.

Images Can Have Multiple Meanings

When I say images can have multiple meanings, I mean two separate things. First, a source domain can be used to create different associations in different texts. To be at the "right hand," for example, is to be

---

43. "Shield," in *DBI*, 785.
44. For the Lord as shield, see also Psalms 3:3 [4]; 5:12 [13]; 7:10 [11]; 18:2 [3], 30 [31]; 28:7; 59:11 [12]; 115:9–11; 119:114; 144:2.

in a position of *favor and honor*. Thus, the words, "Sit at my right hand until I make your enemies a footstool for your feet" (Ps. 110:1) gives the messianic king the position of prestige. Note the rendering of this line in the NLT: "Sit in the place of honor at my right hand." Used another way, the "right hand portrays an image of intense *power and strength*,"[45] as in Psalm 138:7:

> Though I am surrounded by troubles,
>   you will protect me from the anger of my enemies;
> you reach out your hand,
>   and the power of your right hand saves me.
>
> (NLT)

Psalm 138:7 must be read in the context of verses like Exodus 15:6.

> Your right hand, O LORD,
>   was majestic in power.
> Your right hand, O LORD,
>   shattered the enemy.

Often an image will make one association in one context and a different association in a different context. So in any given text we must ask, "Which of the possible aspects of the source domain is the poet associating with the target domain?" In Psalm 17:7 does "right hand" evoke an image of honor or of power?

> Show the wonder of your great love,
>   you who save by your right hand
>   those who take refuge in you from their foes.

Power is the association in this context. The right hand is intended to "save" (see Ps. 138:7), which requires power, and is to work for those who "take refuge," which is an image for the weak seeking protection in the strong.[46]

---

45. See "Hand," in *DBI*, 361; see also "Right, Right Hand," *DBI*, 727–28.
46. See "Refuge," in *DBI*, 700–701.

Second, by "multiple meanings," I also mean that a source domain can be used to create multiple associations in a single text. Take, for example, Psalm 84:11 [12]: "For the LORD God is sun" (TNK). The sun is used to create a variety of associations in the Old Testament.[47] Because of its scorching heat, for example, the sun is a malevolent foe from which God protects pilgrims (Ps. 126:6). This association obviously is not in view in Psalm 84:11 [12]. Because life is dependent on the light of the sun, the sun is also an image of the source of life. Malachi draws on the image of the sun as the source of life when he says, "But for you who fear My name, the sun of righteousness will rise with healing in its wings" (Mal. 4:2 NASB). Since the poet in Psalm 84:11 [12] follows "the LORD God is sun" with "He does not withhold His bounty from those who live without blame" (TNK), it is natural to see the Lord as the source of life in this image. But is that all that the poet intends?

Because the dawning of sun dispels the darkness of night, "solar imagery directly 'targets' the protective deity."[48] So the poet prays, "Restore us, O God; make your face *shine* upon us, that we may be *saved*" (Ps. 80:3). That "sun" images God as the source of protection as well as the source of life in Psalm 84:11 [12] can be defended by appealing to the image that the poet joins to that of sun: "For the LORD God is sun and shield" (TNK). "The shield was an ancient Near Eastern warrior's primary defensive weapon. . . . Because of its importance in battle the shield became a metaphor for protection in both biblical and other ancient Near Eastern literature."[49]

I do not presume that "source of life" and "source of protection" exhaust the associations the poet intends to create between the Lord and the sun in Psalm 84. I simply wish to illustrate that imagery is rich and can have multiple meanings not only in multiple texts but also, at times, in a single text.

Images Need to Be Analyzed

Especially because ancient poets drew upon source domains from a distant time and place, their images do not always or immediately grab

---

47. See "Sun," in *DBI*, 827.
48. Brown, *Seeing the Psalms*, 86.
49. See "Shield," in *DBI*, 785.

our emotions and captivate our imaginations.[50] At times, before our imaginations can appreciate the poetry, our minds need to understand the imagery. So to summarize and conclude this study of imagery, I offer three steps for analyzing poetic images.

1. *Identify the target domain.* Most of the time this step is quite easy. When the psalmist says, "The LORD is my Shepherd," the Lord is the obvious target domain. The target domain is not as clear, however, in an image like, "their throat is an open grave" (Ps. 5:9 [10]). Context is the key to identifying the target. In this verse the poet refers to the "word from their mouth" and how "they speak deceit," which points to the enemy's speech as the target domain.

2. *Study the source domain* thoroughly so that you can "experience the image as literally and in as fully a sensory way as possible."[51] The more you learn about the ordinary lives of ancient Israelites, the more clarity you will have in seeing the pictures the ancient poets painted with their words. There is no substitute for the study of the topography, climate, and agricultural practices in ancient Israel, because these three are primary aspects of "ordinary life" the psalmists drew upon to create images.[52] Two reference works deserve special mention for the study of imagery in the book of Psalms. One is the *Dictionary of Biblical Imagery*, which I have drawn upon repeatedly in the foregoing discussion. This volume contains concise and illuminating articles on virtually every image used in the Old Testament and is in my estimation an indispensable tool. A second is *The Symbolism of the Biblical World: Ancient Near Eastern Iconography and the Book of Psalms*.[53]

---

50. See the discussion in the section, "Images Touch the Emotions and Engage the Mind," on pages 41–42.

51. "Introduction," in *DBI*, xiv.

52. One of the best introductions to the geography of Israel is Denis Baly, *The Geography of the Bible: A Study in Historical Geography* (New York: Harper & Brothers, 1957). Although out of print, this volume can still be purchased at Amazon.com. A good, brief introduction is O. Palmer Robertson, *Understanding the Land of the Bible: A Biblical-Theological Guide* (Phillipsburg, NJ: P & R Publishing, 1996). Excellent material can also be found in Bible atlases. My first and second atlas recommendations are Barry J. Beitzel, *The Moody Atlas of the Bible* (Chicago: Moody, 1985); and Carl G. Rasmussen, *Zondervan NIV Atlas of the Bible* (Grand Rapids: Zondervan, 1989).

53. Othmar Keel, *The Symbolism of the Biblical World: Ancient Near Eastern Iconography and the Book of Psalms* (Winona Lake, IN: Eisenbrauns, 1997).

This volume goes a step further by providing drawings of much "ordinary life" in the ancient Near East, along with explanations as to how these ancient graphics bear on the interpretation of images used in Psalms.

3. *Identify the aspect of the source that is associated with the target.* Context once again is the key. Look for clues within the immediate context that support the association(s) you think the poet intends to make. In Psalm 127:4, for example, the poet compares a man's sons to arrows. The key to the image is found in the next verse, which says,

> How joyful is the man whose quiver is full of them!
> He will not be put to shame when he confronts his
>   accusers at the city gates.
>
> (NLT)

The reference to confronting accusers leads to associating arrows with defense. Numerous sons provide ample defense, just as numerous arrows do.

FOLLOWING THE PATTERNS

Hebrew poets used structural patterns in organizing their compositions. Following these patterns deepens our understanding of, and appreciation for, the individual psalms, because patterns add beauty to the poems and communicate meaning. Hebrew poets used patterns on all levels of their poetry—lines, strophes, and entire poems. The following discussion looks at the three basic patterns: linear, parallel, and symmetrical.[54] Poets employed numerous variations on these basic three.

Linear Pattern

The **linear pattern** is the most common pattern and the easiest to follow.[55] In the linear pattern the units follow each other in a

---

54. See David A. Dorsey, *The Literary Structure of the Old Testament* (Grand Rapids: Baker, 1999), 26–35.
55. Ibid., 27.

nonrepeating order: A B C D E (with each letter representing one unit). Psalm 2:6 is an example of a linear line:

וַאֲנִי | נָסַכְתִּי | מַלְכִּי ||
עַל־צִיּוֹן | הַר־קָדְשִׁי

And I | have installed | my King ||
on Zion, | my holy hill.

This line would be represented: A B C || D E (with || indicating the break between the two cola).

Many strophes are arranged in a linear fashion. Take Psalm 104:27–30 as an example:

A. All depend on God (v. 27)
B. God provides (v. 28)
C. God withholds (v. 29)
D. God renews (v. 30)

Psalm 150 provides an example of an entire poem with a linear structure.

A. Call to praise the Lord throughout the universe (v. 1)
B. Call to praise the Lord for his deeds (v. 2)
C. Call to praise the Lord with instruments (vv. 3–5)
D. Call to praise the Lord by all creatures (v. 6)

Parallel Pattern

The **parallel pattern** is quite common in the Old Testament and is typically formed by two cola; the units of the second colon parallel or match the units in the first colon.[56] Given the nature of parallelism in poetry, as discussed above, it is not surprising that the parallel pattern is frequent in poetic lines. Look at Psalm 19:1:

---

56. Ibid., 28–29.

> The heavens | proclaim | the glory of God. | |
> The skies | display | his craftsmanship.
>
> (NLT)

This line would be represented: A B C | | A' B' C'. In addition to its aesthetic beauty and its aid to memorization, the parallel pattern communicates meaning as it invites the reader "to compare, contrast, reiterate, emphasize, explain, and illustrate."[57] For most modern readers "the glory of God" is a rather abstract concept. The parallel pattern helps us to understand that "the glory of God" was quite concrete for the ancient poet; the second colon explains "the glory of God" as "his craftsmanship." We see God's glory when we look at God's creation.[58] Psalm 19:2 has the identical structure:

> Day by day | they pour out | speech. | |
> Night by night | they declare | knowledge.
>
> (Author's translation)

"Day by day" coupled with "night by night" emphasizes the uninterrupted nature of creation's communicative power.

An example of the parallel pattern in an entire psalm is found in Psalm 100.[59]

A   Call to praise the Lord (vv. 1–2)
    B   Reasons to praise the Lord (v. 3)
A'   Call to praise the Lord (v. 4)
    B'   Reasons to praise the Lord (v. 5)

Among other functions, this parallel pattern invites us to wed two concepts: the Lord made us to be his people (v. 3), and the Lord is a good and loving God in his relationship with us (v. 5). We live a life of praise and gratitude because we have a good and loving Creator.

---

57. Ibid., 29.
58. Mark D. Futato, *Creation: A Witness to the Wonder of God* (Phillipsburg, NJ: P & R Publishing, 2000), 3–10.
59. Dorsey, *Literary Structure*, 185. See also our discussion of the parallel pattern in Psalm 148 on pages 30–31.

While the ancients were at home with the repetition involved in the parallel pattern, we are not. Our literary conventions, in fact, eschew such repetition. Modern expositors of these ancient texts will not, therefore, often be able to mirror the structure of the text in the structure of their presentation of the text. A presentation of Psalm 100 would likely have two main divisions: call to praise (combining the content of vv. 1–2 and v. 4) and reasons for praise (combining the content of v. 3 and v. 5).

Symmetrical Pattern

The final pattern is the **symmetrical pattern**.[60] Like the parallel pattern, the symmetrical pattern involves repetition. The difference is that the symmetrical pattern adds the inversion of order to the repetition: A B C || C' B' A'. Psalm 51:2 [4] offers an example of a nice symmetrical line.

> Wash me clean | from my guilt. ||
> From my sin | purify me.
> (author's translation)

To mirror the Hebrew, I had to alter standard English word order in the second colon. No English translation I know of (nor do many texts like this one) replicates the order of the Hebrew text at this point. Instead, the symmetrical pattern will often be obscured in English translations that strive for good English style. Thus, reading the text in Hebrew is obviously the only way to appreciate some of the features of the poetry of the Old Testament.

Often the poet will use a variation of the symmetrical pattern that is not fully symmetrical. Psalm 6:9 [10] is an example.

> Has heard | the LORD | my plea;
> the LORD | my prayer | will answer.
> (author's translation)

---

60. The symmetrical pattern is also referred to as a chiasm or a concentric pattern. In addition, some scholars distinguish the chiastic pattern from the concentric pattern, using *chiasm* for a unit with an even number of subunits (A B B' A') and *concentric* for a unit with an odd number of subunits (A B C B' A'). I use the term *symmetrical* for both patterns.

Again, I had to alter standard English word order. The pattern in Hebrew is A B C || B' C' A'. By placing the two verbs at the beginning and the end, the poet creates the feeling of hope and confidence in moving from "has heard" to "will answer." This movement is underscored by a shift in grammar from the Hebrew perfect (past) in the first verb to the Hebrew imperfect (future).

Psalm 70 in its entirety follows the symmetrical pattern.[61]

A   Hurry to help (v. 1)
    B   Curses on the wicked (vv. 2–3)
    B'   Blessings on the righteous (v. 4)
A'   Hurry to help (v. 5)

The repetitions of "hurry" and "help" in verse 1 and verse 5 provide a sense of closure in this emotional prayer. In addition, the repetitions create hope and confidence: there is a shift in "help" from verse 1 to verse 5—in verse 1 "help" is an imperative, expressing a plea ("help me"); in verse 5 "help" is a noun, expressing confidence in the Lord ("You are my help"). The symmetrical pattern creates a beauty that communicates meaning. All three patterns, in fact, help us not only to feel the poetry but to understand it as well.

EXCURSUS: MYTHOPOEIC IMAGERY

Mythopoeic imagery is a special kind of imagery found in the book of Psalms and elsewhere in the Old Testament. With this term I refer to those texts that use the language of ancient Near Eastern mythology in a figurative way to communicate truth about the God of Israel. L. Alonso Schökel articulates my view on these texts quite well.

> If we take as models the undoubtedly mythological texts of the ancient Near-East . . . it is clear that *the OT has not admitted myths.* . . . The Hebrews do not welcome myths as narratives, but *they have no difficulty in incorporating mythical motifs into their*

---

61. Dorsey, *Literary Structure*, 177.

lyric texts. . . . The most frequent motif is the struggle of God with chaos as he creates or imposes order on the world.[62]

Thus, *mythopoeic*, as used here, refers to a special kind of imagery and not the presence of myth in the biblical text.

The use of mythopoeic imagery can be illustrated by a comparison of Psalm 74:13–14 with *KTU* 1.3 iii 38–42/*CTA* 3. III 36–38, a poetic text from Israel's northern neighbors in Ugarit.[63]

Psalm 74:13–14	*KTU* 1.3 iii 38–42/*CTA* 3. III 36–38
You split the sea [*yām*] by your strength	Didn't I demolish El's Darling, Sea [*yamm*]? Didn't I finish off the divine river, Rabbim?
And smashed the sea monster's [*tannînîm*] heads.	Didn't I snare the Dragon [*tannin*]? I enveloped him,
You crushed the heads of Leviathan [*liweyātān*] And let the desert animals eat him. (NLT 1.0)	I demolished the Twisting Serpent [*lotan*], the monster of seven heads.

In Psalm 74, the God of Israel defeats three foes: sea (*yām*), the monster (*tannînîm*), and Leviathan (*liweyātān*), who has multiple heads. In the Ugaritic text, the goddess Anat[64] defeats the same three foes in the exact same order: Sea (*yamm*), Dragon (*tannin*), and Leviathan (*lotan*), who also has multiple heads. The foes are symbols of the chaos that threatens a well-ordered life in this world. The affirmation of both texts is that deity vanquishes these forces of chaos. The point of the psalm is that the God of Israel is the one who vanquishes chaos, not Anat, or any other ancient Near Eastern deity for that matter.

Psalm 74, and texts like it, thus presents a view of Creation that is somewhat different from, and complementary to, that in Genesis 1, in which God effortlessly creates by word. Here, the poet engages the

---

62. Schökel, *Manual of Hebrew Poetics*, 17 (emphasis added).
63. The English translation is from Bill T. Arnold and Bryan E. Beyer, eds., *Readings from the Ancient Near East: Primary Sources for Old Testament Studies* (Grand Rapids: Baker, 2002), 53. See also Walter Beyerlin, ed., *Near Eastern Religious Texts Relating to the Old Testament,* OTL (Philadelphia: Westminster Press, 1978), 197–98.
64. The *I* is in all likelihood Anat but may possibly be Baal. See Neil H. Walls, *The Goddess Anat in Ugaritic Myth*, SBLDS (Atlanta: Scholars Press, 1992), 175–76.

ancient Near Eastern worldview on its own terms, and affirms that Israel's God is greater than any and all forces of chaos—which certainly existed in the perceived reality of the ancients, if not in ultimate reality—and that he had defeated them.

To summarize, mythopoeic imagery is the figurative use of mythological language for polemical purposes. The biblical writers did not believe the myths themselves, but they used such language in their arguments against those who did believe in such forces and deities.[65]

---

65. See also Elmer B. Smick, "The Mythological Elements in the Book of Job," *WTJ* 40 (1977–1978): 213–28; and idem, "Mythopoeic Language in the Psalms," *WTJ* 44 (1982): 88–98.

2

VIEWING THE WHOLE

Oh, the joys of those who do not
follow the advice of the wicked,
or stand around with sinners,
or join in with mockers.
But they delight in the law of the LORD,
meditating on it day and night.
(Ps. 1:1–2 NLT)

WHEN MY SECOND SON WAS about three years old, he broke something valuable in our home. When his mother asked about the incident, he replied, "I didn't do it by meanly; I did it by accidentally." He meant, of course, that he didn't "mean" to do it; it was an accident. We might ask the same about the composition of the book of Psalms: Was it done "by meanly" or "by accidentally"? Are the psalms a random anthology of prayers and praises or an intentional collection with a clear purpose and unified message?

No doubt Christians have read Psalms in private devotions and in public worship more than any other texts of the Old Testament. Individual psalms have expressed the full gamut of our thoughts and feelings, whether we've been elated or depressed, intentional or confused, ill or well, angry or tranquil. The message of this or that psalm often has been just what we needed in our circumstances.

The individual psalms, though, were written by many different people in many different times and places. Psalm 90, for example, is "A prayer of Moses the man of God," written, to use a round number, in 1400 B.C. At the other end of the continuum, Psalm 137 is an anonymous poem written perhaps around 400 B.C. Thus our use of the psalms as isolated texts is reinforced.

Yet there is more to the book of Psalms than the individual psalms themselves. There is the *book* of Psalms. As is the case with other books in the Bible, the book of Psalms has an overarching purpose. The purpose of a book in the Bible is made explicit on occasion, as when John tells us that he wrote his Gospel "so that you may continue to believe that Jesus is the Messiah, the Son of God, and that by believing in him you will have life by the power of his name" (John 20:31 NLT).[1] But most of the time the overarching purpose of a book is implicit in the text and needs to be drawn out through careful reflection. Such is the case with the book of Psalms. Discovering the overarching purpose and message of the book of Psalms is the intent of the next two main sections.

Where will we find the purpose and message of the book of Psalms articulated? As with many books, the best place to turn is the introduction. Some books of the Bible, although not all, provide clear introductory material at the beginning. Proverbs 1:1–7, for example, forms a clear introduction to the whole book of Proverbs.[2] Ecclesiastes 1:1–11 likewise introduces that whole book.[3] Similarly, Psalms 1 and 2 have been intentionally placed at the head of the Psalms as an introduction to the whole.[4]

First, note that Psalms 1 and 2 are separated from the following psalms. Psalms 3–41 constitute Book 1 (see below) in Psalms, and except for Psalms 1 and 2 all other psalms in Book 1 are designated

1. See also the explicit statement of purpose for the gospel of Luke, stated in Luke 1:1–4.

2. Bruce K. Waltke, *The Book of Proverbs: Chapters 1–15*, NICOT (Grand Rapids: Eerdmans, 2004), 10.

3. Tremper Longman III, *The Book of Ecclesiastes*, NICOT (Grand Rapids: Eerdmans, 1998), 57.

4. So, for example, Gerald H. Wilson, *Psalms Volume 1*, NIVAC (Grand Rapids: Zondervan, 2002), 89; Richard J. Clifford, *Psalms 1–72*, AOTC (Nashville: Abingdon, 2002), 37–38; J. Clinton McCann, *A Theological Introduction to the Book of Psalms: The Psalms as Torah* (Nashville: Abingdon, 1993), 26; Patrick D. Miller Jr., "The Beginning of the Psalter," in *The Shape and Shaping of the Psalter*, JSOTSup, ed. J. Clinton McCann (Sheffield, England: JSOT, 1993), 83–92.

"A Psalm of David."[5] Thus Psalms 1 and 2 stand apart from what follows. Second, note that Psalms 1 and 2 are linked to each other. The repetition of אַשְׁרֵי ("blessed") in 1:1 and 2:12 forms an inclusion for the whole. The repetition of דֶּרֶךְ ("way") and אָבַד ("perish") in 1:6 and 2:12 form a **tail linkage** that further ties the two texts together. Moreover the play on הָגָה in 1:2 and 2:1 contrasts "meditate" and "plot": the righteous "meditate" on God's instruction in order to submit to it, and the wicked "plot" to rebel against God's authority.

While Psalm 1 provides us with insight into the purpose of the book of Psalms, Psalm 2 provides us a window on the message of the whole.

THE PURPOSE OF THE PSALMS

While many of the psalms were originally composed for use in public worship, it cannot be demonstrated that all were.[6] In addition, the function of a given psalm in its original context and the function of that same psalm in the context of the completed book of Psalms are not necessarily the same. For example, many psalms were originally human words to God in prayer or praise. But once included in the canonical book, these texts became God's word to humans to teach us how to pray and praise.[7]

Exactly how the 150 psalms were selected for, and collected into, our book of Psalms is not clear.[8] What is clear is that the final shape of the book of Psalms is significantly influenced by the wisdom tradition.[9]

---

5. There are two other apparent exceptions. Psalm 10 has no title, but it can be argued that Psalms 9 and 10 were originally a single psalm (see Clifford, *Psalms 1–72*, 71). Psalm 33 also has no title but is clearly linked to Psalm 32 by the repetition of vocabulary in 32:11 and 33:1.

6. While it is possible that the wisdom psalms (see pages 171–73), for example, were originally liturgical, it is more likely that they originated outside of a liturgical context, in the nascent synagogue, for example. See C. John Collins, *Introduction to the Hebrew Bible* (Minneapolis: Fortress, 2004), 468–69.

7. McCann, *Theological Introduction*, 48–49.

8. Ernest C. Lucas, *Exploring the Old Testament: A Guide to the Psalms and Wisdom Literature* (Downers Grove, IL: InterVarsity Press, 2003), 27.

9. See Collins, *Introduction to the Hebrew Bible*, 469; Gerald H. Wilson, "Shaping the Psalter: A Consideration of Editorial Linkage in the Book of Psalms," in *The Shape and Shaping of the Psalter*, JSOTSup, ed. J. Clinton McCann (Sheffield, England: JSOT, 1993), 72–82; and idem, *Psalms Volume 1*, 74.

It is no accident that Psalm 1, as the first half of the introduction to the Psalms, has numerous points of contact with the wisdom tradition. "Its terminology and thought and teaching reflect the thought of the Wisdom Literature in general and the book of Proverbs in particular."[10] For example, the opening word of the Psalms (אַשְׁרֵי ["blessed"]) is wisdom vocabulary,[11] and the contrasting of the way of the righteous and the way of the wicked is a wisdom motif.[12] Wisdom literature is didactic at its heart, its purpose being to teach: "Listen, my son, to your father's instruction and do not forsake your mother's teaching" (Prov. 1:8). Psalm 1, then, has been set at the beginning of the book of Psalms to show us the purpose of the book. The book of Psalms is, as I will discuss below, an instruction manual or "guidebook along the path of blessing."[13]

Instruction

The joy/blessings (v. 1) and prosperity/success (v. 3) held out in Psalm 1 are for those who delight in and meditate on "the law of the LORD" (v. 2). Just what is meant by "the law of the LORD"?

The Hebrew word translated "law" is תּוֹרָה (tôrāh). This word can mean (1) instruction or teaching, (2) an established instruction or law, or (3) the summation of God's law.[14] The more common meaning in wisdom texts is "instruction or teaching."[15] Proverbs 1:8, for example, says, "Listen, my son, to your father's instruction and do not forsake your mother's teaching [תּוֹרָה]." Psalm 78:1–3, with language reminiscent of the book of Proverbs, uses תּוֹרָה in the same way:

---

10. Peter C. Craigie, *Psalms 1–50*, WBC (Waco: Word, 1983), 58.

11. See Proverbs 3:13; 8:34; 20:7; 28:14.

12. The word *way* (דֶּרֶךְ) occurs seventy-five times in the book of Proverbs. Compare, for example, Proverbs 2:12 ("the ways of wicked men") and 2:20 ("the ways of good men").

13. Brevard S. Childs, *Introduction to the Old Testament as Scripture* (Philadelphia: Fortress, 1979), 513. See also J. Clinton McCann, "Psalms," in *NIB* (Nashville: Abingdon, 1996), 4:665.

14. *CHALOT*, 388; see also *HALOT*, 4:1710–12.

15. Out of the thirteen occurrences in the book of Proverbs the NASB translates תּוֹרָה with "instruction" or "teaching" eight times (Prov. 1:8; 3:1; 4:2; 6:20, 23; 7:2; 13:14; 31:26) and "law" five (Prov. 28:4 [twice], 7, 9; 29:18). The NASB translates the sole occurrence in Job (22:22) with "instruction."

O my people, listen to my instructions [תּוֹרָה]
Open your ears to what I am saying,
    for I will speak to you in a parable.
I will teach you hidden lessons from our past—
    stories we have heard and known,
    stories our ancestors handed down to us.

(NLT)

Given these wisdom connections, it seems natural to understand תּוֹרָה in Psalm 1:2 as "instruction."[16] This sense seems to be confirmed by the antithesis of תּוֹרָה, which is "the advice [עֲצַת] of the wicked" (v. 1), not their legal commands.[17]

Yet the word תּוֹרָה does not occur in isolation in Psalm 1:2. It occurs in the phrase תּוֹרַת יְהוָה ("the instruction of the LORD"). How does this affect our understanding of the word and the purpose of the book of Psalms?

While precision is not possible, it is safe to say that the book of Psalms was substantially in the form as we know it by the end of the fourth century B.C.[18] This is the same time as the writing of Chronicles and Ezra and Nehemiah. When we turn to these late books, we get a clear picture of the meaning of תּוֹרַת יְהוָה ("the instruction of the LORD"). In 2 Chronicles 34:14 it is recorded that Hilkiah "found the Book of the Law of the LORD [תּוֹרַת יְהוָה] that was written by Moses" (NLT). In Ezra 7:6 we read that Ezra was "well versed in the Law of Moses [תּוֹרַת מֹשֶׁה], which the LORD, the God of Israel, had given to the people of Israel" (NLT). It seems that at the time of the writing of Ezra and Chronicles the תּוֹרַת יְהוָה, given through Moses, was identical to the תּוֹרַת מֹשֶׁה, given by the Lord, and that both refer to the Five Books of Moses.[19] So the תּוֹרַת יְהוָה in Psalm 1 naturally refers to the Five Books of Moses.

When we combine the sense of תּוֹרָה as "instruction" with יְהוָה תּוֹרַת as the Five Books of Moses, we conclude that the book of Psalms

---

16. See Wilson, *Psalms Volume 1*, 96; and McCann, "Psalms," 4:684.
17. Clifford, *Psalms 1–72*, 40.
18. So Lucas, *Exploring the Old Testament*, 28; and Craigie, *Psalms 1–50*, 31.
19. See G. Liedke and C. Petersen, "תּוֹרָה," in *TLOT*, 3:1421; and H. G. M. Williamson, *1 and 2 Chronicles*, NCBC (Grand Rapids: Eerdmans, 1982), 402. See also J. A. Thompson, *1, 2 Chronicles*, NAC (Nashville: Broadman & Holman, 1994), 376.

invites believers to meditate on the Five Books of Moses as a source of instruction for experiencing the joy/blessings (v. 1) and prosperity/success (v. 3) held out in Psalm 1. And there is more.

The book of Psalms itself is divided into five sections: Book 1 (1–41), Book 2 (42–72), Book 3 (73–89), Book 4 (90–106), and Book 5 (107–150). This fivefold division is embedded in the ancient text, as each book ends with a doxology.

> Praise be to the LORD, the God of Israel,
>   from everlasting to everlasting.
> Amen and Amen.
>   (Ps. 41:13 [14])

> Praise be to the LORD God, the God of Israel,
>   who alone does marvelous deeds.
> Praise be to his glorious name forever;
>   may the whole earth be filled with his glory.
> Amen and Amen.
>   (Ps. 72:18–19)

> Praise be to the LORD forever!
> Amen and amen.
>   (Ps. 89:52 [53])

> Praise be to the LORD, the God of Israel,
>   from everlasting to everlasting!
> Let all the people say, "Amen!"[20]
>   Praise the LORD.
>   (Ps. 106:48)

Psalms 146–150 constitute the doxology to Book 5 and to the whole book of Psalms, as each psalm in this last group begins and ends with the exclamation, "Praise the LORD!" Why a fivefold division? Why not four or six divisions?

An ancient Jewish tradition points us in the right direction, con-

---

20. The word *amen* occurs only in these doxologies in the book of Psalms.

necting the Five Books of the Psalms with the Five Books of Moses: "As Moses gave five books of laws to Israel, so David gave five books of Psalms to Israel."[21] The convergence of this ancient tradition, plus the wisdom influence on the book of Psalms and the meaning of "instruction" for תּוֹרָה, lead us to the conclusion that, in the final canonical form, the book of Psalms is in five sections because the Five Books of the Psalms are just like the Five Books of Moses: the Five Books of the Psalms are fundamentally תּוֹרָה ("instruction") to be meditated on.

Therefore, as the opening psalm, Psalm 1 teaches us that the purpose of the book of Psalms is, in one word, "instruction."[22] And as we will now see, this instruction has two inseparable foci: instruction for happiness and instruction for holiness.[23]

Instruction for Happiness

People as ideologically far apart as Sigmund Freud and C. S. Lewis agree that happiness is a universal human pursuit.[24]

> No aspect of life is more desired, more elusive, and more perplexing than happiness. People wish and strive for what they believe will make them happy—good health, attractive looks, an ideal marriage, children, a comfortable home, success, fame, financial independence—the list goes on and on. Not everyone who attains these goals, however, finds happiness.[25]

But what is happiness? And how can people attain this most desired treasure? Psalm 1 and the book of Psalms provide answers to these questions.

The answer to the first question is found in the opening word of

---

21. William G. Braude, *The Midrash on Psalms* (New Haven: Yale University, 1959), 5.

22. Collins, *Introduction to the Hebrew Bible*, 469.

23. In the Reformed tradition happiness and holiness are closely related concepts. The connection finds clear articulation in Question and Answer #21 of *First Catechism: Biblical Truth for God's Children* (Suwanee: Great Commission Publications, 1996), 6. Question: "In what condition did God make Adam and Eve?" Answer: "He made them holy and happy."

24. Armand M. Nicholi, *The Question of God: C. S. Lewis and Sigmund Freud Debate God, Love, Sex, and the Meaning of Life* (New York: Free Press, 2002), 97–125.

25. Ibid., 97.

Psalm 1, אַשְׁרֵי (*'ašĕrê*). Hebrew אַשְׁרֵי has traditionally been translated "blessed" (KJV), and a number of modern English translations maintain this tradition (NKJV, NASB, NIV, ESV). Others use the word "happy" (TNK, NRSV, NAB); the NLT is similar: "Oh, the joys of . . ." The choice is more a matter of style than meaning, since "blessed" means "blissfully happy."[26] The major Hebrew dictionaries give "happiness" as the English gloss for אַשְׁרֵי.[27] But what does אַשְׁרֵי in the sense of happiness mean?

We can define אַשְׁרֵי from its use in both Psalm 1 and the book of Psalms as a whole. Our first insight into the meaning of אַשְׁרֵי comes from the image of the tree (v. 3). This is a complex image, as those who are אַשְׁרֵי are not simply like trees, but

> They are like trees planted along the riverbank,
> bearing fruit each season.
> Their leaves never wither . . .
>
> (NLT)

The poet creates at least three associations with this image. (1) To be אַשְׁרֵי is to be characterized by *life*. The tree is alive, whereas its counterpoint, chaff, is dead.[28] (2) To be אַשְׁרֵי is to be characterized by *endurance*. The tree is planted and its leaves never wither, whereas its counterpoint, chaff, is withered by definition and also "scattered by the wind" (v. 4 NLT). (3) To be אַשְׁרֵי is to be characterized by *significance*. The tree bears fruit, fulfilling the primary, meaningful purpose for its existence, whereas its counterpoint, chaff, is good for nothing.

That chaff is good for nothing leads to our second insight from Psalm 1 into the meaning of אַשְׁרֵי: אַשְׁרֵי as is the opposite of perishing. Hebrew אַשְׁרֵי is the first word in the poem, and it starts with *aleph*, the first letter in the Hebrew alphabet. The last word in the poem is תֹּאבֵד ("perish"), and it starts with *tav*, the last letter of the Hebrew

---

26. *Random House Webster's Unabridged Dictionary* (2005), s.v. "blessed." *Blessed* does, however, have a religious ring to it that *happy* does not.

27. *DCH*, 1:437; *HALOT*, 1:100; *BDB*, 80; F. Zorell, *Lexicon hebraicum et aramaicum Veteris Tesamenti* (Rome: Pontifical Biblical Institute, 1963), 87, glosses אַשְׁרֵי with *beatitudo* ("happiness").

28. Note the use of the "tree of life" image in the wisdom tradition (Prov. 3:18; 11:30; 13:12; 15:4).

alphabet. Just as the first word and last word are at the opposite ends of
the poem, and just as *aleph* and *tav* are at opposite ends of the alphabet,
אַשְׁרֵי and תֹּאבֵד are opposite in meaning.

Among other meanings, Hebrew אָבַד means "cease, vanish, fade
away."[29] This meaning fits the context of Psalm 1—as chaff vanishes
in the wind, the way of the wicked will vanish, not literally but metaphorically. In contrast to the way of the righteous, which results in
"fruit," the way of the wicked is "fruitless." It goes nowhere; it "comes
to nothing." A number of translations recognize in other texts this
sense of "comes to nothing" for Hebrew אָבַד. Take for example the
final **colon** in Psalm 112:10.

תַּאֲוַת רְשָׁעִים תֹּאבֵד

the longings of the wicked will come to nothing (NIV)
the desires of the wicked come to nothing (NRSV)
the desires of the wicked come to nothing (NAB)
the desire of the wicked shall come to nothing (TNK)

It is interesting to note that Psalm 112, like Psalm 1, not only ends
with the word תֹּאבֵד but also begins with אַשְׁרֵי (after the opening
"Praise the Lord!"). This positioning strengthens the opinion that the
positioning of אַשְׁרֵי and תֹּאבֵד at opposite ends of Psalm 1 is not accidental but intentional, especially in light of the other correspondences
between Psalm 112:1 and Psalm 1.[30] Such positioning also supports the
opinion that the sense of תֹּאבֵד in Psalm 1:6 is "comes to nothing," as
is the case in Psalm 112.

Moreover, several wisdom texts in Proverbs use the verb אָבַד with
this same sense.

The prospect of the righteous is joy,
but the hopes of the wicked *come to nothing*.[31]
(Prov. 10:28)

---

29. *DCH*, 1:99.
30. See the use of הָאִישׁ ("the man") with אַשְׁרֵי in Psalms 1:1 and 112:1 and the use of חָפֵץ
    ("delight") in Psalms 1:2 and 112:1.
31. See also the NRSV and the NAB.

> When a wicked man dies, his hope perishes;
>   all he expected from his power *comes to nothing*.[32]
>   (Prov. 11:7)

That אַשְׁרֵי is the opposite of "comes to nothing" fits well with אַשְׁרֵי being compared to a tree: אַשְׁרֵי refers to a life of enduring significance that truly amounts to something. And there is more.

We have already seen connections between Psalm 1 and Psalm 112. Psalm 112, though, paints a more detailed picture than does Psalm 1 of what the life of those who are אַשְׁרֵי looks like. In short, it is a life of well-being. Those who are אַשְׁרֵי experience well-being in their families (v. 2), in their finances (v. 3a), in their spirituality (vv. 3b–6), and in their emotions (vv. 7–8). This list is representative and not exhaustive[33] and is intended to teach that אַשְׁרֵי is well-being in every area of life. As Bruce Waltke has said, "Sages reserve the laudatory exclamation *blessed ('ašrê)* for people who experience life optimally, as the Creator intended."[34]

Hebrew אַשְׁרֵי not only refers to a state of well-being; it also has an emotional component. The word is joined with feelings of satisfaction (Ps. 65:4 [5]), joy (Ps. 89:15 [16]), and delight (Ps. 112:1). Hebrew אַשְׁרֵי thus is a rich term that refers to a state of well-being and its attendant feelings of joy and satisfaction.

In answering, then, "What is happiness?" the English language may not suffice. This is because the English word *happiness* is often used in a purely emotional sense, which is probably why some translations steer away from this word as a translation of אַשְׁרֵי. This is not the only sense, however, that *happiness* has. Happiness is also "a state of well-being." As one dictionary says, happiness refers to "1: state of well-being characterized by emotions ranging from contentment to intense joy 2: emotions experienced when in a state of well-being."[35] In neither definition is the emotional side of happiness divorced from the state of

---

32. See also the NRSV, NAB, and the TNK.
33. So, for example, well-being in body and spirit is the point of Psalm 32:1–5.
34. Waltke, *Proverbs: Chapters 1–15*, 256.
35. WordNet 2.0, s.v. "happiness," http://www.cogsci.princeton.edu/cgi-bin/webwn2.0?stage=1&word=happiness (accessed November 23, 2004). See also *Random House Webster's Unabridged Dictionary* (2005), s.v. "happiness": "Happiness results from the possession of or attainment of what one considers good."

well-being. Perhaps "truly happy" captures the richness of אַשְׁרֵי better than either "blessed" or simply "happy."[36]

The frequent appearance and placement of Hebrew אַשְׁרֵי presents inescapable evidence. It is not only the opening word of the opening psalm, but it also occurs twenty-eight times in the book of Psalms. It occurs at least once in each of the Five Books of the Psalms and is most heavily concentrated in Book 1 and Book 5.[37] We are thus led to conclude that the book of Psalms is an instruction manual for living a truly happy life.

Instruction for Holiness

The book of Psalms holds out the prospect of attaining that which the human heart longs for, true happiness. Having seen that Psalms is an instruction manual for guiding readers to a truly happy life, we now ask the question, "How is this happiness attained?" The answer is, in a word, "holiness."

A holy life, according to the book of Psalms, results in a happy life. A holy life, as I am using the term, is simply a life lived in keeping with God's instructions (תּוֹרָה). Psalm 1:1–2 says, for instance, that happiness results from delighting in and meditating on God's instruction (תּוֹרָה). This same connection between happiness (אַשְׁרֵי) and God's instruction (תּוֹרָה) is made elsewhere in the book of Psalms.

> Happy [אַשְׁרֵי] are those whom you discipline, O LORD,
> and whom you teach out of your law [תּוֹרָתְךָ].
> (Ps. 94:12 NRSV)

> Happy [אַשְׁרֵי] are those whose way is blameless,
> who walk in the law [תּוֹרַת] of the LORD.
> (Ps. 119:1 NRSV)

---

36. See the excellent and concise discussion of the pros and cons of "blessed" and "happy" and the defense of "truly happy" in M. Brown, "אַשְׁרֵי," in *NIDOTTE*, 1:571.

37. Book 1 (10x): 1:1; 2:12; 17:5; 32:1, 2; 33:12; 34:8 [9]; 40:2 [3], 4 [5]; 41:1 [2]; Book 2 (1x): 65:4 [5]; Book 3 (5x): 73:2; 84:4 [5], 5 [6], 12 [13]; 89:15 [16]; Book 4 (2x): 94:12; 106:3; Book 5 (10x): 112:1; 119:1, 2; 127:5; 128:1; 137:8, 9; 144:15 (2x); 146:5.

This connection between happiness and holiness is typical in wisdom literature. Although the book of Proverbs does not explicitly connect אַשְׁרֵי and תּוֹרָה, it does connect אַשְׁרֵי with following wisdom or godly instruction. Proverbs 16:20 says, for example, "Those who listen to instruction will prosper; those who trust the LORD will be happy [אַשְׁרָיו]" (NLT 1.0).[38]

Holiness, then, according to Psalm 1, begins with study. Those who are truly happy study or meditate on God's instruction (Ps. 1:2). Meditation in our current culture is often characterized by silence. To meditate is to silence speech and thought. Ancient Israelite meditation was quite different. The Hebrew word translated "meditate" in Psalm 1:2 (הָגָה) is used for low animal sounds like the cooing of a dove (Isa. 38:14) or the growl of a lion (Isa. 31:4). This word is also used for human speech, whether articulate (Ps. 35:28) or not (Isa. 16:7). So the Hebrew word הָגָה in texts like Psalm 1:2 does not describe a silent activity but means to "read in an undertone" or to "mutter while meditating."[39]

Not only is the voice engaged in meditation, so is the mind. Hebrew הָגָה is at times a parallel term with other cognitive terms like "remember" (Pss. 63:6 [7]; 143:5) or "think/consider" (Pss. 63:6 [7]; 77:12 [13]). The NAB captures this cognitive side of הָגָה, translating Psalm 1:2b, "God's law they *study* day and night."

While it is true that many individual psalms were originally composed for and used in public worship at the temple, Psalms in its final form is fundamentally a book to be meditated on. Years before the current interest in Psalms as instruction rose to the fore, E. J. Young wrote,

> Moreover, we are mistaken when we regard the entire Psalter as designed for the usage of the Temple. That some Psalms were so used cannot be denied, but it is interesting to note that liturgical directions are lacking for many of the Psalms. The Psalter, rather, is primarily a manual and guide and model for the devotional needs of the individual believer. It is a book of

38. See also Proverbs 3:13; 8:32, 34; 14:21; 20:7; 28:14.
39. *HALOT*, 1:237.

prayer and praise, to be meditated upon by the believer, that he may thereby learn to praise God and pray to Him.[40]

I would only add, ". . . and experience a truly happy life."

In ancient Israel, meditation was not, though, an end in and of itself. Meditation or study was to be followed by living out that which was learned. This is clear from Joshua 1:8, which has striking parallels to Psalm 1:2–3.

> Do not let this Book of the Law [הַתּוֹרָה] depart from your mouth; meditate [וְהָגִיתָ] on it day and night, so that you may be careful to do everything written in it. Then you will be prosperous [תַּצְלִיחַ][41] and successful.

It is not simply study but study coupled with following God's instruction that results in prosperity and success—a truly happy life.

In the book of Psalms, holiness, or following God's instruction, is not conceived of as drudgery. On the contrary, God's instruction is a delight to the psalmist: "they delight [חֶפְצוֹ] in the law [תוֹרַת] of the LORD" (Ps. 1:2 NLT). Another psalmist says of himself,

> I delight [חָפַצְתִּי] to do Your will, O my God;
> Your Law [וְתוֹרָתְךָ] is within my heart.
> (Ps. 40:8 [9] NASB)

A synonym of חָפֵץ is שַׁעֲשֻׁעִים (delight), and this word is used repeatedly in the psalm that most celebrates God's instruction, Psalm 119.[42] Take, for example, Psalm 119:77.

> Surround me with your tender mercies so I may live,
> for your instructions [תוֹרָתְךָ] are my delight [שַׁעֲשֻׁעָי].
> (NLT)

---

40. E. J. Young, *An Introduction to the Old Testament* (Grand Rapids: Eerdmans, 1958), 309.

41. This is the same Hebrew word that is used in Psalm 1:3.

42. See Psalm 119:24, 77, 92, 143, 174.

Nor is holiness or following God's instruction conceived of as a mechanical keeping of commandments. The ideal was for this instruction to be in the heart. "Your Law [וְתוֹרָתְךָ] is *within* my heart," says one psalmist (Ps. 40:8 [9] NASB), and another says of the righteous, "The law [תוֹרַת] of their God is *in their hearts*" (Ps. 37:31 NRSV). Still another poet prays,

> Give me understanding and I will obey your instructions [תוֹרָתֶךָ];
> I will put it into practice *with all my heart.*
>
> (Ps. 119:34 NLT)

Such a view of God's instruction explains why the poet can say things like,

> How *I love* your teaching [תוֹרָתֶךָ], LORD!
> I study it all day long.
>
> (Ps. 119:97 NAB)

> How I delight in your commands!
> How *I love* them!
>
> (Ps. 119:47 NLT)

One final note: the holiness of the book of Psalms, or living in keeping with God's instruction, is not a legalistic approach to life but is actually a life of faith. Texts like Psalm 119:1 could lead to a legalistic approach to life, if taken out of context.

> Happy are those whose way is blameless,
> who walk in the law [בְּתוֹרַת] of the LORD.
>
> (NRSV)

One could conclude that perfect obedience is required for experiencing a truly happy life, but this would be a misunderstanding. As John Calvin has said with regard to this verse,

> But it may be asked, whether the prophet excludes from the hope of happiness all who do not worship God perfectly? Were

this his meaning, it would follow, that none except angels alone would be happy, seeing that the perfect observance of the law is to be found in no part on the earth. The answer is easy: When uprightness is demanded of the children of God, they do not lose the gracious remission of their sins, in which their salvation alone consists. While, then, the servants of God are happy, they still need to take refuge in his mercy, because their uprightness is not complete. In this manner are they who faithfully observe the law of God said to be truly happy.[43]

Calvin continues, supporting his contention by referring to Psalm 32:2. Verses 1–2 say,

> Oh, what joy [אַשְׁרֵי] for those
>   whose disobedience is forgiven,
>   whose sin is put out of sight!
> Yes, what joy [אַשְׁרֵי] for those
>   whose record the LORD has cleared of guilt,
>   whose lives are lived in complete honesty!
>
> (NLT)

In context, "complete honesty" refers to the confession of sin rather than the hiding of it. The truly happy life is experienced by those who know and confess their sin and experience God's forgiveness.

In keeping with this idea of the truly happy life are the texts that pronounce "happy" (אַשְׁרֵי) those who "trust" in God.

> O LORD of Heaven's Armies,
>   what joy [אַשְׁרֵי] for those who *trust* in you.
>   (Ps. 84:12 [13] NLT)

> Oh, the joys [אַשְׁרֵי] of those who *trust* the LORD,
>   who have no confidence in the proud,
>   or in those who worship idols.
>   (Ps. 40:4 [5] NLT)

---

43. John Calvin, *Commentary on the Book of Psalms* (Grand Rapids: Baker, 1979), 317.

As might be expected, the wisdom tradition's advice for attaining the truly happy life is the same.

> Those who listen to instruction will prosper;
> those who trust the LORD will be joyful [אַשְׁרָיו].
>
> (Prov. 16:20 NLT)

Psalm 119:165 probably sums up the purpose of the book of Psalms as an instruction manual for living a truly happy life as well as any one verse can.

> Those who love Your teaching enjoy well-being;
> they encounter no adversity.
>
> (TNK)

THE MESSAGE OF THE PSALMS

Having gleaned the purpose of the book of Psalms from Psalm 1, we can now turn to the second half of the introduction, Psalm 2, to discover the overarching message of the Psalms. What message assures us that living in keeping with divine instructions will issue in a truly happy life? It is simply this: "The Lord reigns!"[44]

> While Psalm 1 orients the reader to receive the whole collection as instruction, Psalm 2 makes explicit the essential content of the instruction—the Lord reigns![45]

The next section, "Other Themes of the Psalms," surveys several of the major theological themes in the book of Psalms. This section traces the dominant **theme** of the book—the kingship of God. We will first look at the teaching that our God is King, then we will discover that our destiny is glory, and finally we will uncover the **eschatological** hope that our King is coming.

---

44. Mark D. Futato, *Transformed by Praise: The Purpose and Message of the Psalms* (Phillipsburg, NJ: P & R Publishing, 2002), 101.

45. McCann, "Psalms," 4:688. McCann goes on to say, "The entire Psalter will be about the 'happy'/'blessed' life, and it will affirm throughout that this life derives fundamentally from the conviction that God rules the world" (689).

Our God Is King

By referring to God as "He who sits in the heavens" (Ps. 2:4 NASB, ESV, NRSV), the poet declares with simple profundity God's sovereign reign over the universe. Hebrew יָשַׁב is a word used for ordinary "sitting,"[46] like כִּסֵּא is a word for an ordinary "chair"[47] and בַּיִת is a word for an ordinary "house."[48] If, however, a king sits on the chair, we call it a "throne,"[49] and if a king lives in the house we call it a "palace."[50] So the NIV, NAB, and TNK capture the sense of Hebrew יָשַׁב in Psalm 2:4 by using the English word "enthroned," and the NLT makes explicit what is implicit in יָשַׁב when it renders Psalm 2:4 with "the one who *rules* in heaven." The message of Psalm 2 is simply this: The Lord reigns!

This picture of God reigning from his throne appears throughout the book of Psalms. In Psalm 29:10 the poet tells us that the Lord reigns over all the forces that threaten a well-ordered world and, therefore, a truly happy life.

> The LORD sits enthroned [יָשַׁב] over the flood;
> the LORD sits enthroned [וַיֵּשֶׁב] as king for ever.
>
> (NRSV)

The "flood" (מַבּוּל) is not a direct reference to the flood in the days of Noah, even though Hebrew מַבּוּל is used only in Psalm 29:10 and the Genesis flood story. In Psalm 29:10 מַבּוּל is a mythopoeic[51] reference to the chaotic waters of the sea that threaten a well-ordered world but that the Lord has vanquished.[52] These waters have been alluded to

---

46. See, for example, Genesis 18:1, "The LORD appeared to Abraham near the great trees of Mamre while he was *sitting* [יֹשֵׁב] at the entrance to his tent in the heat of the day."
47. See, for example, 2 Kings 4:10, "Let's make a small room on the roof and put in it a bed and a table, a *chair* [וְכִסֵּא] and a lamp for him."
48. See, for example, Deuteronomy 6:7, "You shall teach them diligently to your children, and shall talk of them when you sit in your *house* [בְּבֵיתֶךָ]" (ESV).
49. See, for example, Esther 5:1, "On the third day of the feast, Esther put on her royal robes and entered the inner court of the palace, just across from the king's hall. The king was sitting on his royal *throne* [כִּסֵּא], facing the entrance" (NLT).
50. See, for example, 1 Kings 7:1, "Solomon also built a *palace* [בֵּיתוֹ] for himself, and it took him thirteen years to complete the construction" (NLT).
51. See the excursus at the end of chapter 1 and the detailed discussion of this text in chapter 6.
52. See Clifford, *Psalms 1–72*, 156; and Wilson, *Psalms Volume 1*, 507.

earlier in the psalm (v. 3) in the reference to the מַיִם רַבִּים ("mighty waters"), which, according to Psalm 93:4, were vanquished at the time of Creation.[53]

> Mightier than the thunder of the great waters [מַיִם רַבִּים],
>   mightier than the breakers of the sea—
>   the LORD on high is mighty.

Another poet tells us in Psalm 47:8 [9] that the Lord reigns over the nations.

> God reigns over the nations;
>   God is seated [יָשַׁב] on his holy throne.

Psalm 55:19 [20] affirms that the Lord has reigned from time immemorial, referring to him as "the one who sits [וְיֵשֵׁב] enthroned from of old" (NASB). Psalm 102:12 [13] extends this reign as far into the future as the mind can imagine: "But you, O LORD, will sit [תֵּשֵׁב] on your throne forever" (NLT). Psalm 2, then, as well as the book of Psalms as a whole, declares unequivocally that the Lord reigns—over the cosmos and over the nations and from everlasting to everlasting.

Psalm 2 goes on to teach that, as King, our God reigns through his "anointed one" (v. 2). "Anointed one" translates Hebrew מָשִׁיחַ, from which we get the word *messiah*. Hebrew מָשִׁיחַ refers to individuals[54] who have been anointed with oil as a symbol of, among other things, the outpouring of the Holy Spirit to empower them for their calling.[55] David's anointing in 1 Samuel 16:13 is illustrative.

> So Samuel took the horn of oil and anointed [וַיִּמְשַׁח] him in the presence of his brothers, and from that day on the Spirit of the LORD came upon David in power.[56]

---

53. See Richard J. Clifford, *Psalms 73–150*, AOTC (Nashville: Abingdon, 2003), 110; and McCann, "Psalms," 4:1054.

54. The noun/adjective מָשִׁיחַ is used in reference to priests (Lev. 4:3) and kings (1 Sam. 2:10). The verb מָשַׁח ("to anoint") is used in reference to prophets (1 Kings 19:16). Psalm 105:15 applies מָשִׁיחַ to the patriarchs, who are also designated "prophets."

55. V. Hamilton, "מָשַׁח," in *TWOT*, 1:530.

56. The Hebrew word translated "came in power" is צָלַח, a word used for the Holy Spirit's empowering of the Judges (see Judg. 14:6, 19; 15:14).

As is the case in the Old Testament in general, מָשִׁיחַ is used in the book of Psalms predominantly for the anointed king.[57] The king is David and, as Psalm 18:50 [51] makes clear, his descendants.

> He gives his king great victories;
>> he shows unfailing kindness to his anointed [לִמְשִׁיחוֹ],
>> to David and his descendants forever.

The reign of our God through his Anointed One does not, however, go uncontested in Psalm 2. The poet paints a picture of other kings on the earth who want to rebel against the rule of our God and his Anointed One (Ps. 2:2–3). This picture presumes the ancient Near Eastern **suzerain/vassal** treaty, wherein vassal kings lived in submission to the Great King.[58] The vassal, for example, would bring the Great King a certain amount of tribute each year, and the Great King, for example, would provide military protection for the vassal king. The picture in Psalm 2 presumes that all the kings of the earth are vassals of our God and the Davidic monarch, and that the kings are plotting to free themselves from this dual lordship.

Since there was never a time when God ruled all nations of the earth through the Davidic monarchy, we are not to interpret this text as a description of some particular *historical* situation. Rather, this text paints an *ideological* picture[59] of God's intention for the nations of the world against the backdrop of historical reality. God's intention for the nations is that they *all* experience the truly happy life articulated in the final line of Psalm 2: "But what joy [אַשְׁרֵי] for *all* who take refuge in him!" (NLT).[60] God's intention is that David and his descendants serve as the mediators of this truly happy life. So the kings of the nations are invited to a life of wisdom (v. 10), which includes living in fear of the Lord (v. 11) and in submission to David and his descendants (v. 12).

---

57. Hamilton, "מָשַׁח," 1:530; and K. Seybold, "מָשַׁח," in *TDOT*, 9:45. The use of מָשִׁיחַ in reference to the patriarchs in Psalm 105:15 is the only exception in the book of Psalms.

58. For a brief introduction to these treaties, see Raymond B. Dillard and Tremper Longman III, *An Introduction to the Old Testament* (Grand Rapids: Zondervan, 1994), 97–99. For a more extensive discussion, see Meredith G. Kline, *Treaty of the Great King* (Grand Rapids: Eerdmans, 1963).

59. See Wilson, *Psalms Volume 1*, 109.

60. This theme will be developed in chapter 3.

Such a life of wisdom naturally issues in a truly happy life, as Proverbs 3:13 says,

> Joyful [אַשְׁרֵי] is the person who finds wisdom [חָכְמָה],
> the one who gains understanding.
>
> (NLT)

But God's intention and historical reality did not meet in the days of the Davidic monarchy. The reality was that the Davidic kingdom was often at war with surrounding nations and at times was subject to foreign powers. Psalm 2 is thus profoundly eschatological in two senses. First, I am using *eschatological* in the sense of "the proclamation of God's universal reign amid circumstances that seem to deny it and belie it."[61] In ancient Israel, as well as in our own world, there was much evidence that seemed to belie the teaching that a good God was in control of the world. The message of Psalm 2, and the book of Psalms, is that our God is in control, in spite of what circumstantial evidence might indicate. The book of Psalms called ancient Israelites, and calls us, to live a life of faith in the reign of God—to believe that a truly happy life is possible not just for "us" but for "*all* who take refuge in him" (Ps. 2:12).

Second, I am using *eschatological* in the sense of that which pertains to the destiny of the world. The outcome of continued opposition to God's rule is not in doubt. God laughs (v. 4) at the prospect of the nations freeing themselves from his rule. The Davidic king is on the throne in Jerusalem (v. 6), and because the Davidic king is the vice-regent of God (v. 7), he will inevitably rule the nations (v. 8). The nations will be brought to submission (v. 9), so they are warned against their futile rebellion (v. 10b), which will be met with anger (v. 11) rather than issuing in a truly happy life. The final note of the psalm is not, however, "he will become angry, and you will be destroyed" (v. 12a NLT), but "what joy for all who take refuge in him" (v. 12b NLT). According to the eschatology of the book of Psalms, our destiny is a truly happy life, that is, in a word, glory.

---

61. McCann, "Psalms," 4:668.

Our Destiny Is Glory

Given the teaching of Psalm 1, which promises blessing and prosperity, and Psalm 2, which affirms that God is in control and ready to mediate the truly happy life to everyone through God's Anointed One, we are surprised when we read the title and opening words of Psalm 3 (vv. 1–2 [1–3]).

> *A psalm of David, regarding the time*
> *David fled from his son Absalom.*
> O LORD, I have so many enemies;
>   so many are against me.
> So many are saying,
>   "God will never rescue him!"
>   (NLT)

Where is the truly happy life? Where is the powerful David who is to be taking possession of the nations as his inheritance? And Psalm 3 is not alone, as is clear from the following examples:

> Answer me when I call to you,
>   O my righteous God.
> Give me relief from my distress;
>   be merciful to me and hear my prayer.
>   (Ps. 4:1)

> Give ear to my words, O LORD,
>   consider my sighing.
> Listen to my cry for help,
>   my King and my God,
>   for to you I pray.
>   (Ps. 5:1–2 [2–3])

> O LORD, do not rebuke me in your anger
>   or discipline me in your wrath.
> Be merciful to me, LORD, for I am faint;
>   O LORD, heal me, for my bones are in agony.

My soul is in anguish.
How long, O LORD, how long?
> (Ps. 6:1–3 [2–4])

O LORD my God, I take refuge in you;
   save and deliver me from all who pursue me,
or they will tear me like a lion
   and rip me to pieces with no one to rescue me.
> (Ps. 7:1–2 [2–3])

Why, O LORD, do you stand far off?
   Why do you hide yourself in times of trouble?
> (Ps. 10:1)

In the LORD I take refuge.
   How then can you say to me:
   "Flee like a bird to your mountain.
For look, the wicked bend their bows;
   they set their arrows against the strings
to shoot from the shadows
   at the upright in heart.
When the foundations are being destroyed,
   what can the righteous do?"
> (Ps. 11:1–3)

Help, LORD, for the godly are no more;
   the faithful have vanished from among men.
> (Ps. 12:1 [2])

How long, O LORD? Will you forget me forever?
   How long will you hide your face from me?
How long must I wrestle with my thoughts
   and every day have sorrow in my heart?
   How long will my enemy triumph over me?
> (Ps. 13:1–2 [1–3])

The contrast between these psalms and Psalms 1 and 2 is most striking. Perhaps even more striking is the contrast between this predominantly negative note at the beginning of the book of Psalms and the high note of praise that closes the book:

> *A psalm of praise. Of David.*
> I will exalt you, my God the King;
>   I will praise your name for ever and ever.
> Every day I will praise you
>   and extol your name for ever and ever. . . .
> My mouth will speak in praise of the LORD,
>   Let every creature praise his holy name
>   for ever and ever.
>
> (Ps. 145:1–2, 21)

> Praise the LORD. . . .
>   Praise the LORD.
>   (Ps. 146:1, 10)

> Praise the LORD. . . .
>   Praise the LORD.
>   (Ps. 147:1, 20)

> Praise the LORD. . . .
>   Praise the LORD.
>   (Ps. 148:1, 14)

> Praise the LORD. . . .
>   Praise the LORD.
>   (Ps. 149:1, 9)

And in case we haven't gotten the point, we are called to praise the Lord thirteen times in Psalm 150. Further, the last line brings in the universal intention of God (also articulated in Pss. 2:12; 12:7; 145:21): "Let everything that has breath praise the LORD." Moreover, the book of Psalms as a whole ends with the exclamation, "Praise the LORD," quite a different mood than that experienced at the front end of the book of Psalms!

Claus Westermann was the first scholar to draw attention to this movement in the macro-structure of the book of Psalms, a movement from lamentation to praise, from suffering to glory. The David who is repeatedly oppressed at the beginning of the Psalms is the David who leads "everyone on earth" (145:21 NLT) and, more than that, "everything that breathes" (150:6 NLT) in the praise of our "God and King" (145:1 NLT). This macro-structure teaches us that, while the truly happy life held out in the teaching of Psalm 1 and guaranteed by the reign of God in Psalm 2 may not be experienced at every point along the path of life, the truly happy life is certainly the destiny of Israel and the nations. Our destiny is glory.

Our King Is Coming

Both the placement of Psalms 1 and 2 at the head of the book of Psalms and the movement from lamentation to praise indicate that the book of Psalms is not a random anthology. The psalms have been purposefully arranged.[62] In addition to the movement from lamentation to praise, the macro-structure of the book of Psalms reflects another construct—one that dovetails with the movement we have just seen.

Two pillars in ancient Israelite faith were the temple and the Davidic monarchy. It is difficult for us to imagine the crisis of faith that many would have experienced when the temple was destroyed and the Davidic monarch was taken into captivity by the Babylonians in 586 B.C. Likewise, we can only guess at the great joy that accompanied the dedication of the rebuilt temple by the postexilic community (see Ezra 6:16). No comparable joy, however, was experienced at a re-enthronement of a Davidic king, for this pillar continued to lie in ruins throughout the postexilic era. How were ancient Israelites in the postexilic community to live with one pillar of their faith back in place while the other was nowhere to be found? The book of Psalms can be read as a manual for instructing ancient Israelites, and us, how to live in

---

62. For a brief history of the study of the arrangement of the book of Psalms, see David M. Howard Jr., "Recent Trends in Psalms Study," in *The Face of Old Testament Study: A Survey of Contemporary Approaches*, ed. David W. Baker and Bill T. Arnold (Grand Rapids: Baker, 1999), 332–44; or idem, *The Structure of Psalms 93–100*, Biblical and Judaic Studies, ed. William Henry Propp (Winona Lake, IN: Eisenbrauns, 1997), 5:1–19.

the absence of the Davidic king, who was promised the nations as his inheritance in Psalm 2.

While the psalms found at the beginnings and the endings of Books 1–3 (Pss. 1–89) trace the contours of the rise and demise of the Davidic monarchy, the dominating themes in Books 4–5 (Pss. 90–150) provide insight into how to respond to the apparent failure of the promises made to David and his descendants.

As we have seen, the book of Psalms opens with wonderful promises being made to David.[63] The psalms immediately following make us wonder if these promises will be fulfilled. How can David subdue the nations if he cannot even subdue his son Absalom?[64] In spite of struggles along the way, the final psalm in Book 1—Psalm 41—indicates that the promises to David are in the process of being fulfilled.

Note that the opening word of Psalm 41, אַשְׁרֵי ("Oh, the joys" NLT), forms an inclusion with the opening word of Psalm 1, אַשְׁרֵי ("Oh, the joys" NLT). Psalm 41 is thus intentionally linked to the introduction to the book of Psalms—Psalms 1 and 2. While Psalm 41 acknowledges that inheriting the promises of Psalm 2 involved David in struggles with his enemies (vv. 5–9 [6–10]), the psalm celebrates David's victories over those enemies.

> I know that you are pleased with me,
>> for my enemy does not triumph over me.
>> (v. 11 [12])

The Hebrew word translated "pleased" is חָפֵץ, the same word used in Psalm 1:2, which says the righteous "delight [חֶפְצוֹ] in the law of the LORD" (NLT). Since David delighted in the Lord *à la* Psalm 1, the Lord is pleased with David, and this pleasure is experienced in David's triumphing over his enemies. By the end of Book 1, David is inheriting the nations, just as Psalm 2 promised he would.

These promises were given not only to David but also to his sons (2 Sam. 7:11–16; Ps. 89:3–4). The transition in leadership, however, was by no means a smooth one, and who would be the first successor

---

63. Although Psalm 2 has no title, the New Testament attributes this psalm to David. See Acts 4:25–28.

64. The title of Psalm 3 sets this poem at the time of David's flight from Absalom.

of David was not obvious. First came the coup of Absalom (2 Sam. 15:1–12), followed by the conspiracy of Adonijah (1 Kings 1:5). In the end, Solomon succeeded his father on the throne of Israel (1 Kings 1:28–53). This transition from David to Solomon is embedded in the unfolding story of the Psalms when we turn to the end of Book 2. The title to Psalm 72 is simple: "A psalm of Solomon."[65] By the end of Book 2, the kingship with its promises has been effectively transferred to Solomon, in keeping with the promises of 2 Samuel 7:11–16. In tracing the fortunes of the Davidic line, Psalm 72 draws several significant connections to previous psalms.

First, in Psalm 72:2 Solomon is the king who is caring for the weak:

> He will judge your people in righteousness,
> your afflicted ones with justice.

This theme is expanded in verses 12–14:

> For he will deliver the needy who cry out,
> the afflicted who have no one to help.
> He will take pity on the weak and the needy
> and save the needy from death.
> He will rescue them from oppression and violence,
> for precious is their blood in his sight.

Such kindness to the poor characterized David at the end of Book 1. Psalm 41, which is "A psalm of David," begins with the following:

> Oh, the joys of those who are kind to the poor!
> The LORD rescues them when they are in trouble.
>
> (NLT)

As this line from Psalm 41 looks back to Psalm 1, it connects David with the truly happy person of that psalm. As Psalm 72:2 looks back

---

65. Whether this psalm is "of Solomon" in the sense of "by Solomon" (as the author of the psalm) or "for Solomon" (as the king honored in the psalm) need not be decided at this point. In either case, Solomon is the king in view in this psalm.

to Psalm 41, it connects Solomon to David as the truly happy person caring for the weak, and thereby connects Solomon with the truly happy person of Psalm 1. Thus, in Psalm 72 Solomon is the new "David."

Second, in Psalm 72 Solomon's reign is portrayed with floral imagery that recalls the image of the fruitful tree in Psalm 1:

> The mountains will bring prosperity to the people,
>   the hills the fruit of righteousness. . . .
> He will be like rain falling on a mown field,
>   like showers watering the earth. . . .
> In his days the righteous will flourish;
>   prosperity will abound till the moon is no more. . . .
> Let grain abound throughout the land;
>   on the tops of the hills may it sway.
>   Let its fruit flourish like Lebanon;
>   let it thrive like the grass of the field.
>
> > (vv. 3, 6, 7, 16)

As Solomon is now the truly happy person of Psalm 1, so are those living under his rule.

Third, in Psalm 72 Solomon is envisioned as the Great King ruling over the nations of the earth as promised in Psalm 2.

> He will rule from sea to sea
>   and from the River to the ends of the earth.
> The desert tribes will bow before him
>   and his enemies will lick the dust.
> The kings of Tarshish and of distant shores
>   will bring tribute to him;
>   the kings of Sheba and Seba
>   will present him gifts.
> All kings will bow down to him
>   and all nations will serve him. . . .
> Long may he live!
>   May gold from Sheba be given him.

> May people ever pray for him
> and bless him all day long.
> (vv. 8-11, 15)

The ideological portrait of David in Psalm 2 is now repainted in Psalm 72 with Solomon in the foreground. Solomon is experiencing the promises of Psalm 2 and the nations are as well. The nations are blessing Solomon because they are being blessed through his benevolent reign.

> May his name endure forever,
>   his fame continue as long as the sun.
> May all nations be blessed in him;
>   may they pronounce him happy.
> (72:17 NRSV)

The verb translated "pronounce him happy" is from the same root as אַשְׁרֵי ("happy"). The nations are proclaiming that Solomon is the truly happy person of Psalm 1:1 as they have come to experience the true happiness held out to them in Psalm 2:12. By the end of Book 2 Solomon has replaced David as the truly happy person portrayed in Psalm 1, and as God's anointed mediator of true happiness to the nations portrayed in Psalm 2. The program laid out in Psalms 1 and 2 is working.

Psalm 89 brings Book 3 to a close. The positive tone at the beginning of this psalm is striking.

> I will sing of the LORD's great love forever;
>   with my mouth I will make your faithfulness known
>   through all generations.
> I will declare that your love stands firm forever,
>   that you established your faithfulness in heaven itself.
> (vv. 1–2 [2–3])

The psalmist celebrates God's unfailing love and faithfulness by praising God for his uniqueness in the heavens (vv. 5–8 [6–9]) and his protective power on the earth (vv. 9–18 [10–19]). But these verses are surrounded by clear and unequivocal reaffirmations of God's promises to David and his descendants in verses 3–4 [4–5] and verses 19–37 [20–38]. It is as if the psalmist is saying that God's unfailing love and faithfulness should be experienced, more than anywhere else in the world, in the outworking of the promises made to David. That is why what comes in verses 38–51 [39–52] is so shocking.

In light of God's promises, his rejection of the anointed king (מָשִׁיחַ, v. 38 [39]) and his renunciation of the covenant with David (v. 39 [40]) are incomprehensible to the psalmist. The pain is perhaps most intense in verse 49 [50]:

> O Lord, where is your former great love,
>   which in your faithfulness you swore to David?

The biting irony is felt when we realize that the word translated "great love" in this verse is the same word used in verse 1 to celebrate God's "great love."[66] It is difficult to imagine how people living in postexilic Judah would have felt when saying,

> You have broken through all his walls
>   and reduced his strongholds to ruins.
>   (v. 40 [41])

> You have put an end to his splendor
>   and cast his throne to the ground.
>   (v. 44 [45])

The program begun with David in Book 1 and effectively transferred to Solomon in Book 2 seems, at the end of Book 3, to have been aborted. There are two things the psalmist just cannot put together. One is the unequivocal promise to David articulated in verses 33–37 [34–38]:

> But I will not take my love from him,
>   nor will I ever betray my faithfulness.

---

66. The noun is the relatively infrequent plural of חֶסֶד. The plural occurs in the Psalms only seven times, whereas the singular occurs one hundred twenty times.

> I will not violate my covenant
>   or alter what my lips have uttered.
> Once for all, I have sworn by my holiness—
>   and I will not lie to David—
> that his line will continue forever
>   and his throne endure before me like the sun;
> it will be established forever like the moon,
>   the faithful witness in the sky.

The other is the seemingly incontrovertible truth of the postexilic situation: no Davidic descendant sits on the throne, ruling over the nations, and Judah is a poor province in the pagan Persian Empire. How can the community continue in its faith with the apparent broken promises, with so great a gap between doctrine and reality? The answer is found in Book 4 and Book 5.

Books 4 and 5 provide a twofold answer to the crisis of faith raised at the end of Book 3. This answer can be summarized with the words *faith* and *hope*.

Book 4 calls people to live eschatologically, that is, to live with faith in "God's universal reign amid circumstances that seem to deny it and belie it."[67] This eschatological perspective comes out in two ways in Book 4, the first being the Mosaic flavor of that book. "Moses" occurs nine times in the book of Psalms in the NIV, and eight of these occurrences are in Book 4.[68] It is striking that Book 4 opens with the only psalm attributed to Moses: "A prayer of Moses, the man of God." This attribution takes us back before the monarchy, before the covenant made with David and his descendants. And when we get back to that early time, we find God there. While the opening verses of Psalm 90 do not explicitly address God as king, they do so implicitly by referring to him as "our home," or "dwelling place." "Home," as we will see in the next section, is part of the "refuge" metaphor for God, which is clearly a royal metaphor. Many generations lived before David's time, and people in all of those generations found God to be a secure place to live. As faith in God as our royal refuge characterized life then, so,

---

67. McCann, "Psalms," 668; and see earlier discussion on page 76.
68. See the title of Psalm 90 and Psalms 99:6; 103:7; 105:26; 106:16, 23, 32, 33. The other occurrence is in Psalm 77:20.

says the placement of Psalm 90 just after Psalm 89, it can characterize life now. Before David was king, God was our royal refuge. Now that there is no Davidic king reigning on his throne, God is still our royal refuge.

What is implicit in this first eschatological perspective becomes explicit in the second, and is the dominant theme of Book 4: the Lord is King! Psalms 93 and 95–99 are all hymns that celebrate the reign of the Lord. The Lord's reign comes to expression repeatedly in this cluster.

> The LORD is *king!*
> (93:1 NLT)

> For the LORD is the great God,
>   the great *King* above all gods.
> (95:3)

> Declare among the nations, "The LORD is *king!*"
> (96:10 TNK)

> The LORD is *king!*
> (97:1 NLT)

> Make a joyful symphony before the LORD, the *King!*
> (98:6 NLT)

> The LORD is *king!*
> (99:1 NLT)

It is surely no coincidence that this repeated affirmation follows on the heels of the agonizing question raised in Psalm 89:49 [50]:

> O Lord, where is your former great love,
>   which in your faithfulness you swore to David?

Part of the answer to this question in Psalm 89 is simply faith— having faith that the Lord reigns and is still in control in spite of all the evidence to the contrary, especially his seeming failure to keep his promise to David and his descendants. Israel was called to believe and to "declare among the nations, 'The LORD is king'" (96:10 TNK) in spite of Israel's being a poor province in the world-dominating Persian Empire. That is living eschatologically!

In Books 4 and 5, faith that the Lord is king is coupled with hope that the King is coming. And not just an ordinary king is coming. These books teach first that the divine King is coming, and that the messianic King is coming. We will look first at the former teaching and then at the latter teaching.

Two of the kingship psalms found at the heart of the book of Psalms, Psalms 96 and 98, end on a common note: all creation is rejoicing because the Lord is coming to judge the earth.

> Let the heavens rejoice, let the earth be glad;
> > let the sea resound, and all that is in it;
> > let the fields be jubilant, and everything in them.
> Then all the trees of the forest will sing for joy;
> > they will sing before the LORD, for he comes,
> > he comes to judge the earth.
> He will judge the world in righteousness
> > and the peoples in his truth.
>
> (96:11–13)

> Let the sea resound, and everything in it,
> > the world, and all who live in it.
> Let the rivers clap their hands,
> > let the mountains sing together for joy;
> let them sing before the LORD,
> > for he comes to judge the earth.
> He will judge the world in righteousness
> > and the peoples with equity.
>
> (98:7–9)

These psalms articulate a clear hope that the Lord, as divine King, is coming soon. And this hope ignites jubilant celebration throughout the whole created realm.

How, though, are we to understand the imagery reflected in these psalms? The imagery is rooted in the geography of ancient Israel. Israel has two seasons: seven months of rain (October through May) and five months of drought (June through September). Ancient Israelite farmers had no way to irrigate their fields.

> The land you are entering to take over is not like the land of Egypt, from which you have come, where you planted your seed and irrigated it by foot as in a vegetable garden. (Deut. 11:10)

As a result these farmers in Israel were directly dependent on rain for agricultural success.

> But the land you are crossing the Jordan to take possession of is a land of mountains and valleys that drinks rain from heaven. (Deut. 11:11)

That meant they were dependent on the Lord to provide rain each fall at the end of the dry season and the beginning of the new agricultural year.

> It is a land the LORD your God cares for; the eyes of the LORD your God are continually on it from the beginning of the year to its end. (Deut. 11:12)

In the imagery used by Israelite poets, rain clouds were the Lord's chariot, which he rode to bring the fructifying rains:

> He makes the clouds his chariot
> and rides on the wings of the wind.
> (Ps. 104:3)

> Sing to God, sing praise to his name,
> extol him who rides on the clouds—
> his name is the LORD—
> and rejoice before him.
> (Ps. 68:4 [5])

In the coming of the fall rains, the poets saw the coming of the Lord to bless his people. So thunder is not simply superheated air breaking the sound barrier, but is the Lord's voice.

> The voice of the LORD echoes above the sea.
>   The God of glory thunders.
>   The LORD thunders over the mighty sea.
>   (Ps. 29:3 NLT)

And lightning is proof that the Lord is present.

> The voice of the LORD strikes with lightning bolts.
>   (Ps. 29:7 NLT 1.0)

When the Lord came to bless his people with the fall rains, he came as divine King.

> The LORD rules over the floodwaters.
>   The LORD reigns as king forever.
>   The LORD gives his people strength.
>   The LORD blesses them with peace.
>   (Ps. 29:10–11 NLT)

The creation is jubilant at the prospect of the divine King coming, because the rains come to rejuvenate the earth after five months of drought. "The exultant rejoicing of nature is a metaphor for its blooming and fruitfulness"[69] in the wake of the onset of the rainy season.

These kingship psalms thus articulate a clear and profound hope that the divine King is coming. This was an annual hope for ancient farmers waiting for the fall rains, and it was an eschatological hope for pious Israelites waiting for the Lord to come "to judge the earth" (Pss. 96:13 and 98:9). To "judge" (שָׁפַט) means not only "to pass judgment" but also "to rule/govern."[70] To "judge" means to govern in such a way as to put all things in right order. As one author has said, שָׁפַט "designates

---

69. Clifford, *Psalms 73–150*, 122.
70. *HALOT*, 4:1624, 1625.

an action that restores the disturbed order of a . . . community."[71] The hope of the kingship psalms is that the divine King is coming to put all things in right order, and at this prospect the "whole earth" (Ps. 96:1) and "all the earth" (Ps. 98:4)—Israel, the nations, and the entire creation—"break out in praise and sing for joy!" (Ps. 98:4 NLT).

The Psalms give hope, then, that the divine King is coming. They give hope also that the messianic King is coming. In considering this latter hope, we will examine Psalms 132 and 118.

Psalm 89 brought Book 3 of the Psalms to a close with the agonizing question, "Lord, where is your unfailing love?" (v. 49 NLT). Psalm 132 provides a partial and crucial answer to this question. This psalm can be divided into two stanzas. In the first (vv. 1–10) the psalmist opens with a plea to the Lord.

> O LORD, remember David
> and all the hardships he endured.

This plea does not seem to come from the lips of someone who has given up all hope that a son of David will one day rule the nations. This prayer seems to come from a heart of hope that the promise made to David may yet be fulfilled. Confirmation of this seeming hope comes from the end of the stanza.

> For the sake of David your servant,
> do not *reject* your *anointed one*.
> (v. 10)

We might conclude from Psalm 89:38 that the Lord had rejected David and his descendants once and for all.

> But you have rejected, you have spurned,
> you have been very angry with your anointed one.

But the ancients did not come to this conclusion. They had hope that God would yet show himself faithful to the promises made to David.

---

71. G. Liedke, "שָׁפַט," in *TLOT*, 3:1393.

This hope comes to further expression in the second stanza (132:11–18), which opens with a recitation of the central promise made to David.

> The LORD swore an oath to David,
>   a sure oath that he will not revoke:
> "One of your own descendants
>   I will place on your throne."
>   (v. 11)

And the poet closes out this stanza with this promise from the Lord:

> Here I will make a horn grow for David
>   and set up a lamp for my anointed one.
> I will clothe his enemies with shame,
>   but the crown on his head will be resplendent.
>   (vv. 17–18)

It is evident from the content of Psalm 132, positioned after Psalm 89, that hope remained in the hearts of the pious; in spite of the seeming contradiction between the promise and current circumstances, these people had faith that the Lord, too, would be faithful and the anointed/messianic King would some day come to rule over the nations, just as Psalm 2 promises.

The horn referred to in verse 17 is a common biblical symbol of power. The NLT translates verse 17, "Here I will increase the power of David." The use of "horn" for power is found in texts like Deuteronomy 33:17, where Joseph is described as being as powerful as a bull.

> Joseph has the majesty of a young bull;
>   he has the horns of a wild ox.
> He will gore distant nations,
>   driving them to the ends of the earth.
> This is my blessing for the multitudes of Ephraim
>   and the thousands of Manasseh.
>   (NLT)

The bull with horns will rule the nations with great power. To make a horn grow—the imagery in Psalm 132:17 captured by the NLT—means to "increase the power of David." And according to the New Testament, the Lord kept his promise. At the birth of John the Baptist and in reference to Jesus, Zechariah proclaimed,

> Praise be to the Lord, the God of Israel,
>   because he has *come* and has redeemed his people.
> He has raised up a *horn* of salvation for us
>   in the house of his servant David.
>   (Luke 1:68–69)

Zechariah, and many others in his day, believed that in the coming of the Lord Jesus, the Lord God of Israel had *come,* and his coming had accomplished redemption, and this redemption was accomplished through a *horn* from the house of *David*. Beyond doubt, Zechariah had Psalm 132:17 in his mind and probably Psalm 118:26 as well, when he uttered these words.

Psalm 118:26 says,

> Bless the one who comes in the name of the LORD.
> We bless you from the house of the LORD.
>   (NLT)

Who is this "one who comes in the name of the LORD"? The New Testament identifies this person with Jesus. On one occasion John the Baptist sent his disciples to Jesus with this question: "Are you *the one who was to come*, or should we expect someone else?" (Luke 7:20). This question seems to allude to Psalm 118:26. On the first Palm Sunday, Jesus came riding into Jerusalem on a donkey, and when the people saw him they recognized him as their king and shouted,

> Praise God!
> Blessings on the one who comes in the name of the Lord!
> Hail to the King of Israel!
>   (John 12:13 NLT)

From this quotation of Psalm 118:26 we learn that first-century Jews understood "the one who comes in the name of the Lord" to be the king of Israel, and they saw in Jesus this king. Matthew 21:9 puts it this way,

> Praise God for the Son of David!
> Blessings on the one who comes in the name of the Lord!
> (NLT)

They clearly believed that Jesus was the long-awaited Son of David, the "one who comes in the name of the Lord." Jesus, moreover, also understood himself to be "the one who comes in the name of the Lord," as is clear from the promise that he gave to his disciples:

> For I tell you this, you will never see me again until you say, "Blessings on the one who comes in the name of the Lord." (Matt. 23:39 NLT)

So from Psalms 96, 98, 132, and 118 we discern that Books 4 and 5 teach how Israel is to respond to the apparent decline in the fortunes of the Davidic throne. These books contain clear hope that both the divine King and the messianic King would one day come to fulfill the promises made to David that Israel and the nations might experience the truly happy life that God held out in Psalm 2:12 when he said, "What joy for all who take refuge in him!" (NLT).

Just as the book of Psalms gave hope to the ancient people of God, urging them to look forward to the day when the King would come, so the Psalms give this same hope to us. We live with hope that the King will come into our own lives and world, and establish his reign, which results in truly happy lives. We hope that his kingdom will come "as a present reality that will be fully realized in the future."[72] At that future date, Jesus will put absolutely all things in right order. As Revelation 21:3–4 says,

---

72. Clifford, *Psalms 73–150*, 122.

I heard a loud shout from the throne, saying, "Look, God's home is now among his people! He will live with them, and they will be his people. God himself will be with them. He will wipe every tear from their eyes, and there will be no more death or sorrow or crying or pain. All these things are gone forever." (NLT)

And the book of Revelation closes with Jesus himself saying, "Look, I am coming soon. Blessed are those who obey the words of prophecy written in this book" (Rev. 22:7 NLT).

OTHER THEMES OF THE PSALMS

In studying the purpose and message of the book of Psalms in the previous sections, we discovered that the psalms provide instruction for a holy and truly happy life. We learned, too, that the reign of God and his Anointed One is the dominant theme of Psalms and the prerequisite for a holy and happy life. We also saw in brief that this holy and happy life was not intended for Israel alone, but also for the nations. This latter idea will occupy our attention in this section.

While numerous themes hold significance for understanding the book of Psalms,[73] we will study just two in this section. The first is the theme of the Lord as refuge, and the second is that of blessing for the nations. These two themes rise to the fore in the concluding verse of the Psalter's introduction, "What joy for *all* who take *refuge* in him!" (Ps. 2:12 NLT). Some scholars have argued that this concluding verse was not part of the original form of Psalm 2 and that it was added for a variety of possible reasons. Herman Gunkel, for example, argued that it was added to mitigate the furor of the psalm.[74] More productive is the suggestion of Jerome Creach that this final line "seems to be an addendum perhaps placed to direct the reading of subsequent psalms."[75] Creach's primary argument for understanding this line as an addition

---

73. See, for example, Hans-Joachim Kraus, *Theology of the Psalms* (Minneapolis: Augsburg, 1979).

74. H. Gunkel, *Die Psalmen ubersetzt und erklärt*, HKAT (Göttingen: Vandenhoeck und Ruprecht, 1926), 12.

75. Jerome F. D. Creach, *Yahweh as Refuge and the Editing of the Hebrew Psalter*, JSOTSup (Sheffield, England: Sheffield Academic Press, 1996), 75.

is the apparent incongruity between the way the psalm would both threaten the nations with destruction from the Lord and offer to them a truly happy life through taking refuge in the Lord.[76] While it is possible that this concluding line is an addendum,[77] Creach's arguments are not entirely convincing, nor are they necessary for following his insightful lead in understanding this line as programmatic for the book of Psalms as a whole.

First, the body of Psalm 2 itself expresses the possibility that the nations will experience something other than anger and destruction. Note the commands directed to the kings in verses 11–12.

> Serve the LORD with reverent fear,
>   and rejoice with trembling.
> Submit to God's royal son, or he will become angry,
>   and you will be destroyed in the midst of all your activities.
>
> (NLT)

Implicit in these commands is the offer of an alternative. If there is service and submission, then there will be something other than anger and destruction. The final line makes explicit what this alternative outcome will be for those who cease their rebellion: those who "take refuge" in the Lord will experience a truly happy life. Second, as I will show in this section, both taking refuge in the Lord and blessing for the nations are pervasive themes in the Psalms. Once we grasp the centrality of these two themes, we will no longer be perplexed by their juxtaposition in Psalm 2, the second half of the Psalter's own introduction.

The Lord Is Our Refuge

Jerome Creach attempted "to show that 'refuge' is central to the shape of the Psalter, both in the general sense of the 'thought world' of the book and in the more specific sense of the literary structure."[78]

---

76. Ibid., 75.
77. In my estimation, although the titles to the psalms are canonical and inspired, they are not necessarily original and may have been later additions. Verse 20 is clearly an addition to Psalm 72. The doxologies that end each of the psalms that conclude Books 1–4 also may be additions to these psalms.
78. Creach, *Yahweh as Refuge*, 19.

Creach has, indeed, made a valuable contribution to our understanding of the book of Psalms. In my estimation, the Lord as refuge is, in fact, the second most important metaphor employed in the Psalms, the first being the Lord is King. In this section I will unpack (1) the significance of the refuge metaphor in terms of understanding its meaning and pervasiveness in the Psalms and (2) the relationship between the refuge and kingship metaphors.

The Significance of the Refuge Metaphor

Hebrew poets used many different words to communicate the refuge metaphor. The two primary words are from the root חסה: מַחְסֶה /מַחֲסֶה ("a refuge")[79] and חָסָה ("to seek refuge").[80] The verb is never used in a literal sense in the Hebrew Bible, and the noun is so used only three times:

> The high mountains belong to the wild goats;
>> the crags are a refuge [מַחְסֶה] for the coneys.
>> (Ps. 104:18)

> It will be a shelter and shade from the heat of the day,
>> and a refuge [וּלְמַחְסֶה] and hiding place from the storm and rain.
>> (Isa. 4:6)

> They are drenched by mountain rains
>> and hug the rocks for lack of shelter [מַחְסֶה].
>> (Job 24:8)

These three uses show us that a "refuge" is a "shelter," a place of safety and protection from hostile elements likes the blazing sun or biting rain. "It seems clear that חָסָה has the connotation of 'seek shelter' . . . and מַחְסֶה refers to the shelter itself."[81]

---

79. The two forms are alternate spellings of the same word. See *HALOT*, 2:571; and *DCH*, 5:226.
80. *HALOT*, 1:337; and *DCH*, 3:281–82.
81. Creach, *Yahweh as Refuge*, 25.

The metaphorical sense in relation to the Lord would then be "seek protection in the Lord" and "the Lord is my protection."[82] This is why the first edition of the NLT used the word "protection" to translate the metaphor.

> But what joy for all who find protection [חוֹסֵי] in him!
> (Ps. 2:12 NLT 1.0)

> I come to you for protection [חָסִיתִי], O LORD my God.
> (Ps. 7:1 [2] NLT 1.0)

The pervasiveness of the refuge metaphor is testimony to its central role in the theology of the book of Psalms. This pervasiveness can be seen in two ways. One is the frequency of the primary words (חָסָה and מַחְסֶה): the verb חָסָה occurs twenty-five times[83] in the book of Psalms, and the noun מַחְסֶה occurs twelve times.[84] The other is the large number of words in the "refuge" semantic field.[85] In addition to חָסָה and מַחְסֶה, psalmists use twelve other words to paint the picture of God as refuge:

1. צוּר ("rock" 21x [24x])[86]

> My salvation and my honor depend on God;
>   he is my mighty *rock*, my refuge.
> (62:7 [8])

---

82. Creach, *Yahweh as Refuge*, 51–52. See also "Refuge," in *DBI* 700–701.
83. Psalms 2:12; 5:11 [12]; 7:1 [2]; 11:1; 16:1; 17:7; 18:2 [3], 30 [31]; 25:20; 31:1 [2], 19 [20]; 34:8 [9], 22 [23]; 36:7 [8]; 37:40; 57:1 [2](2x); 61:4 [5]; 64:11; 71:1; 91:4; 118:8, 9; 141:8; 144:2.
84. Psalms 14:6; 46:1 [2]; 61:3 [4]; 62:7 [8], 8 [9]; 71:7; 73:28; 91:2, 9; 94:22; 104:18; 142:5 [6].
85. Moisés Silva, *Biblical Words and Their Meaning: An Introduction to Lexical Semantics* (Grand Rapids: Zondervan, 1994), 219, defines a semantic field as "a defined area of meaning occupied by related words."
86. The first number is the total number of occurrences of the word in reference to the Lord as refuge, and the bracketed number is the absolute total number of occurrences regardless of the referent. In this and the following footnotes, the citations are only of the occurrences in reference to the Lord as refuge. Psalms 18:2 [3], 31 [32], 46 [47]; 19:14 [15]; 27:5; 28:1; 31:2 [3]; 61:2 [3]; 62:2 [3], 6 [7], 7 [8]; 71:3; 73:26; 78:15, 20, 35; 89:26 [27]; 92:15 [16]; 94:22; 95:1; 144:1.

2. מָגֵן ("shield" 16x [19x])[87]

> The LORD is my rock, my fortress and my deliverer;
> my God is my rock, in whom I take refuge.
> He is my *shield* and the horn of my salvation,
>   my stronghold.
>
>   (18:2 [3])

3. מִשְׂגָּב ("fortress" 13x [13x])[88]

> But the LORD has become my *fortress*,
>   and my God the rock in whom I take refuge.
>   (94:22)

4. סֵתֶר ("shelter" 7x [10x])[89]

> I long to dwell in your tent forever
>   and take refuge in the *shelter* of your wings.
>   (61:4 [5])

5. צֵל ("shadow" 6x [10x])[90]

> How precious is your unfailing love, O God!
> All humanity finds shelter
>   in the *shadow* of your wings.
>   (36:7 [8] NLT)

6. מָעוֹז ("stronghold" 7x [9x])[91]

> The LORD is my light and my salvation—
>   whom shall I fear?

---

87. Psalms 3:3 [4]; 7:10 [11]; 18:2 [3], 30 [31], 35 [36]; 28:7; 33:20; 35:2; 59:11 [12]; 84:11 [12]; 89:18 [19]; 115:9, 10, 11; 119:114; 144:2.
88. Psalms 9:9 [10] (2x); 18:2 [3]; 46:7 [8], 11 [12]; 48:3 [4]; 59:9 [10], 16 [17], 17 [18]; 62:2 [3], 6 [7]; 94:22; 144:2.
89. Psalms 27:5; 31:20 [21]; 32:7; 61:4 [5]; 91:1; 101:5; 119:114.
90. Psalms 17:7 [8]; 36:8; 57:1 [2]; 63:8; 91:1; 121:5.
91. Psalms 27:1; 28:8; 31:2 [3], 4 [5]; 37:39; 43:2; 52:7 [9].

> The LORD is the *stronghold* of my life—
>   of whom shall I be afraid?
>
> (27:1)

7. מְצוּדָה ("fortress" 6x [7x])[92]

> I will say of the LORD, "He is my refuge and my *fortress*,
>   my God, in whom I trust."
>
> (91:2)

8. סֶלַע ("rock" 5x [9x])[93]

> The LORD is my *rock*, my fortress and my deliverer;
>   my God is my rock, in whom I take refuge.
> He is my shield and the horn of my salvation,
>   my stronghold.
>
> (18:2 [3])

9. מָעוֹן ("dwelling" 3x [5x])[94]

> If you make the Most High your *dwelling*—
>   even the LORD, who is my refuge.
>
> (91:9)

10. מִגְדָּל ("strong tower" 1x [2x])[95]

> For you have been my refuge,
>   a *strong tower* against the foe.
>
> (61:3 [4])

11. מָנוֹס ("place of safety" 1x [2x])[96]

> But as for me, I will sing about your power.
>   Each morning I will sing with joy about your unfailing love.

92. Psalms 18:2 [3]; 31:2 [3] 3 [4]; 71:3; 91:2; 144:2.
93. Psalms 18:2 [3]; 31:4; 40:3; 42:10; 71:3.
94. Psalms 71:3; 90:1; 91:9
95. Psalm 61:3 [4].
96. Psalm 59:16 [17].

> For you have been my refuge,
>> a *place of safety* when I am in distress.

> (59:16 [17] NLT)

Simply put, the refuge metaphor is a picture of divine protection. Moreover, this dominant metaphor in the book of Psalms dovetails with the kingship metaphor as the primary theme of the Psalter.

The Relationship Between Refuge and Kingship

In the Old Testament world there was a close connection between the office of the king and the role of protection. This connection can be seen in several ways. One is the explicit connecting of the concepts of kingship and refuge in particular texts. Isaiah 30:2 is an example. It shows that in the minds of the Israelites the king of Egypt was a source of protection.

> Who proceed down to Egypt
> Without consulting Me,
> To take refuge in the safety of Pharaoh
> And to seek shelter in the shadow of Egypt!
>> (NASB)

Another text that explicitly connects kingship and refuge is Jotham's fable in Judges 9:7–15. In this fable the trees set out to anoint a king to rule over them. After being turned down by the olive tree, the fig tree, and the grape vine, the trees turn to the thorn bush to see if it would be willing to be their king. The thorn bush replied, "If you really want to anoint me *king* over you, come and *take refuge* [חֲסוּ] in my shade" (emphasis added). Thus, the fable presumes an ever-so-close connection between the office of the king and the role of protection.

This connection between kingship and protection is no doubt one of the reasons why the word "shield" is part of the refuge semantic field, as seen above, and why the word "shield" is used as a metaphor for the king.[97]

---

97. So "Shield," in *DBI*, 785: "Sometimes the shield metaphor appears as a royal idiom, for kings were responsible for protecting their subjects."

> Look upon our *shield*, O God;
>   look with favor on your *anointed one*.
>   (Ps. 84:9)

> Indeed, *our shield* belongs to the LORD,
>   *our king* to the Holy One of Israel.
>   (Ps. 89:18)

Israelite poets explicitly employed this connection between the office of the king and role of protection to speak about God's role in relationship to his people. Notice how in Psalm 5:2 [3] and 11 [12] the poet connects the kingship of God to protection by God.

> Listen to my cry for help,
>   my *King* and my God,
>   for to you I pray. . . .

> But let all who *take refuge* [חוֹסֵי] in you be glad;
>   let them ever sing for joy.
> Spread your protection over them,
>   that those who love your name may rejoice in you.

It is clear, too, that the use of refuge/protection relates to the divine and human kings elsewhere in the Old Testament. Thus, when the poet concludes the introduction to the book of Psalms by saying, "But what joy for all who take refuge in him," we need not choose between the divine king and the human king as the appropriate referent for the pronoun "him."

A second way in which the office of the king and the role of protection are connected is more subtle and artistic. An example from woodworking offers a fitting illustration. Cabinetmakers use a number of techniques to join pieces of wood together. One such joint is called a finger joint because it is like interlocking your fingers together. Hebrew poets used something like a literary finger joint as an "interlocking mechanism" for a group of psalms.[98] One example of this tech-

---

98. Wilson, "Shaping the Psalter, 75.

nique is found in Psalms 45–48.⁹⁹ Psalms 45 and 47 are kingship psalms that are interlocked with Psalms 46 and 48, which are refuge Psalms.

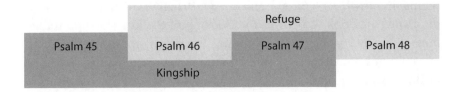

A variation of this technique is found in Psalms 90–99.¹⁰⁰

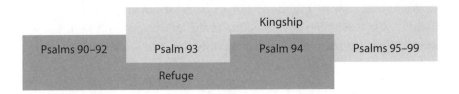

The literary interlocking of kingship and refuge psalms artistically demonstrates the conceptual interlocking of these two motifs. This interlocking of concepts supports the conclusion that the final line of Psalm 2, "But what joy for those who take refuge in him!" (NLT), is integral to the opening kingship hymn of the Psalter.

The Nations Will Be Blessed

The Lord as Israel's refuge is clearly a major theme of the book of Psalms. It is my contention that when the introduction to the Psalms concludes with "Blessed are all who take refuge in him" (Ps. 2:12) this pronouncement extends to the nations, so we ought to be able to trace the theme of blessing for the nations throughout the Psalms. Such is the task of this section.

Blessing for the nations is not found as a dominant theme in Book 1 (Pss. 3–41). This absence, though, is probably owing to the high

99. See Creach, *Yahweh as Refuge*, 87.
100. See Wilson, "Shaping the Psalter," 75. For a detailed analysis of the interlocking of these psalms, see Howard, *The Structure of Psalms 93–100*, 166–83.

frequency of laments at the beginning of the book of Psalms.[101] When we turn to Books 2 and 3, however, the theme of blessing for the nations rises to the fore. Three clusters of psalms in particular accent this theme: Psalms 46–49; 65–67; and 86–87. When we turn to the heart of the Psalter in Book 4, with its interlocking of the kingship and refuge metaphors in Psalms 90–99, blessing for the nations is highlighted several times. Finally, this theme is found in scattered psalms in the rest of Book 4 and in Book 5.

Blessing for the Nations in Book 2 (Pss. 42–72)

We have seen how Psalms 45–48 are interlocked kingship and refuge psalms. When we turn to the second psalm in this group, Psalm 46, we meet the refuge metaphor in the opening line.

> God is our refuge and strength,
>   an ever-present help in trouble.
>   (v. 1)

We then encounter the nations, which are apparently attacking Israel.[102] But because "The LORD Almighty" is Israel's "fortress" (v. 7), the nations are defeated (v. 6).

> Nations are in uproar, kingdoms fall;
>   he lifts his voice, the earth melts.
> The LORD Almighty is with us;
>   the God of Jacob is our fortress.
>   (vv. 6-7)

The poet then invites us to come and see the "works of the LORD," which are then qualified as "the desolations he has brought on the earth" (v. 8). But notice the nature of these "desolations."

---

101. See chapter 2, pages 57–95.
102. See Clifford, *Psalms 1–72*, 229; and Craigie, *Psalms 1–50,* 345.

> He makes wars cease to the ends of the earth;
>   he breaks the bow and shatters the spear,
>   he burns the shields with fire.
>
>   (v. 9)

What is destroyed is the hostility that pits one nation against another. What is destroyed are the weapons used by one nation against another. Because God is our refuge, there is no more war. Because God is our refuge, there is worldwide peace.[103] Because God is our refuge, we can be confident that in the end the nations will be blessed as they come to honor the Lord.

> Be still, and know that I am God;
>   I will be exalted among the nations,
>   I will be exalted in the earth.
>
>   (v. 10)

Since Psalm 46 closes with the nations honoring the God who is our refuge, we are not at all surprised when Psalm 47 invites "all . . . nations" to worship "the great King over all the earth."

> Clap your hands, *all you nations*;
>   shout to God with cries of joy.
> How awesome is the LORD Most High,
>   the great King over *all the earth!*
>
>   (vv. 1–2)

The nations that once fought against the Lord and against his Anointed One have been subdued (v. 3 [4]). The rulers that used to "gather together *against* the LORD and *against* his Anointed One" (Ps. 2:2) now "gather *as* the people of the God of Abraham" to worship the King who "is highly exalted" (Ps. 47:9 [10]).

Psalm 48 focuses our thoughts on the refuge metaphor as it celebrates the fortresslike nature of God, "the Great King" (v. 2 [3]), by celebrating the fortified nature of "the city of the Great King (v. 2 [3]),

---

103. See Wilson, *Psalms Volume 1*, 720–21.

"the city of our God" (v. 8 [9]). After inviting us to tour the fortified city (vv. 12–13 [13–14]), the poet simply says, כִּי זֶה אֱלֹהִים ("for this is God"; v. 14 [15] author's translation). Not only is God *in* the fortified city (v. 3 [4]), but God also *is* the fortified city—at least metaphorically.[104] By inviting worshipers to gaze on the protective walls and towers of Jerusalem, the poet invites them to see another reality, the protective presence of God.

This refuge psalm, like Psalm 47, rehearses the story of the nations' failed attempt to conquer Jerusalem (vv. 4–7 [5–8]). The people of Zion and all those living in Judah rejoice in the strength of the city and the God of the city (v. 11 [12]). And what's more, "the whole earth rejoices to see it!" (v. 2 [3] NLT). Since the divine king is present in the fortified city, he "will be praised to the ends of the earth" (v. 10 [11] NLT). As in Psalms 46 and 47, the nations are no longer fighting against the Lord but are worshiping him throughout the earth.

Psalm 49 follows on the heels of the interlocked 45–48 and is thematically tied to these psalms with its focus on the nations. Note the apparently global focus in the opening colon: "Hear this, *all you peoples*." And in case we think these "peoples" are restricted to Israel, the poet adds, "Listen, *all who live in this world*." This opening invitation to "hear" and "listen" is reminiscent of the wisdom literature, as is the language of "wisdom" and "understanding" (v. 3 [4]) and "proverb" and "riddle" (v. 4 [5]).

The bulk of the psalm (vv. 5–20 [6–21]) is occupied with the wisdom themes of wealth and death in the lives of the wise and the foolish. When read in the context of the universal perspective of Psalms 46–48 and the universal invitation of Psalm 49:1 [2], Psalm 49 is wisdom instruction for the nations that have been subdued by the great King and have become citizens of his kingdom. The nations are here instructed not to trust in wealth (v. 6 [7]), whether they have it or not (v. 2 [3]), because wealth cannot redeem from death (v. 7 [8]). Instead, the nations are to trust in God, who can redeem even from the power of death itself (v. 15 [16]). Implicit in this psalm is the correlation between wisdom and blessedness. As the nations learn to live in keeping with Israel's wisdom tradition, they will experience the blessedness held out in that tradition (see Ps. 1).

---

104. So Craigie, *Psalms 1–50*, 355.

Book 2 contains a second cluster of psalms that focuses on God's blessing for the nations: Psalms 65–67.

The universal scope of Psalm 65 is evident from the beginning, for the psalmist says, "To you all people [כָּל־בָּשָׂר] will come" (v. 2 [3] TNIV). The following verse indicates that "all people" are coming to the God of Israel for the forgiveness of sin, even overwhelming sin. Those who come to receive forgiveness experience deep joy and satisfaction in God's presence (v. 4 [5]). Thus "God our Savior" is hailed in verse 5 [6] as, "the hope of all the ends of the earth and of the farthest seas." The vanquished nations (v. 7 [8]; see also Pss. 46–47) throughout the earth stand in awe of God and shout for joy at his works (v. 8 [9]).

Psalm 66 continues this global focus in the opening line: "Shout with joy to God, all the earth!" And in verse 4 "all the earth" is bowing down to God and singing the praises of his name. Just as we were invited to "come and see" in Psalm 46:8 [9], we are again invited in Psalm 66:5 to "come and see" what God has done. This time we are invited to "come and see . . . what awesome miracles he performs for people!" (v. 5 NLT). The Hebrew phrase translated "people" here is בְּנֵי אָדָם (lit. "sons of man"), a phrase used elsewhere in Psalms for the whole human race.[105] What is it that the God of Israel has done for the benefit of the whole human race?

> He turned the sea into dry land,
>> they passed through the waters on foot.
>>> (v. 6)

The parting of the sea at the time of the Exodus, says the psalmist, was not simply for the benefit of Israel, but ultimately for the benefit of the whole human race. This pivotal step in the history of redemption had the blessings of the nations clearly in view.

Psalm 67 brings this cluster to a close with a matchless simplicity and beauty. "Blessing" forms an inclusion around this psalm: "May God . . . bless" (v. 1 [2]) and "God will bless" (v. 7 [8]). The focus in both cola is on God blessing "us," that is, Israel in the original context. But why is God blessing "us"? The psalmist supplies the answer:

---

105. See Psalms 11:4; 14:2; 53:2 [3]; 89:47 [48]; 90:3.

> That your ways may be known on earth,
> your salvation among all nations.
>
> (v. 2 [3])

The desire of the psalmist is that once God's salvation is made known among the nations, God will be praised by "the peoples," "all the peoples," "the nations" (vv. 3–4a [4–5a]), "the peoples," and "all the peoples" (v. 5 [6]). The psalmist wants the nations to "be glad and sing for joy" as they experience God's just rule and universal guidance (v. 4 [5]). And this guidance (נָחָה) is the same guidance that God's people experienced after the parting of the sea as they wandered in the wilderness.[106]

At the end of the psalm we see a picture of the whole earth[107] yielding its harvest (v. 6 [7]) and God blessing "us" so that "all the ends of the earth will fear him" (v. 7 [8]).

Blessing for the Nations in Book 3 (Pss. 73–89)

Book 3 has two adjacent psalms that focus on the blessing for the nations: Psalms 86–87. This theme is present, although not dominant, in Psalm 86.

> Among the gods there is none like you, O Lord;
>   no deeds can compare with yours.
> All the nations you have made
>   will come and worship before you, O Lord;
>   they will bring glory to your name.
> For you are great and do marvelous deeds;
>   you alone are God.
>
> (vv. 8–10)

Verse 8 might be taken as an affirmation that while the gods of the nations exist they are inferior to the God of Israel. Verse 10 will not permit this interpretation, however, as it confesses that the God of

---

106. See Exodus 13:21; Deuteronomy 32:12; Psalm 78:14, 53.

107. The NIV translates אֶרֶץ here with "land" but is alone in this regard. The global perspective of this psalm requires the English word *earth* here; see the ESV, KJV, NASB, NKJV, NLT, NRSV, and TNK.

Israel alone is God. Since the God of Israel is the incomparable (v. 8) and only true God (v. 10), "all the nations" will eventually come to see this and will worship this one true God (v. 9).

Psalm 87 is a Song of Zion.[108] Yet, as such, the theme of God blessing the nation is not immediately evident. In the Songs of Zion, Jerusalem is the place where God dwells.

> In Judah God is known;
>> his name is great in Israel.
> His tent is in Salem,
>> his dwelling place in Zion.
>> (Ps. 76:1–2 [1–3])

As such, to be in Zion is the ardent longing of God's people, who set their hearts on making pilgrimage to this city.

> How lovely is your dwelling place,
>> O LORD Almighty!
> My soul yearns, even faints,
>> for the courts of the LORD;
> my heart and my flesh cry out
>> for the living God. . . .
> Blessed are those whose strength is in you,
>> who have set their hearts on pilgrimage. . . .
> They go from strength to strength,
>> till each appears before God in Zion.
>> (Ps. 84:1–2, 5, 7 [1–3, 6, 8])

An earlier Song of Zion, Psalm 48, has hinted at the idea that to be in Zion is the longing, too, of the nations, and not just of Israel.

> It is beautiful in its loftiness,
>> the joy of the whole earth.
> Like the utmost heights of Zaphon is Mount Zion,
>> the city of the Great King.
>> (Ps. 48:2 [3])

---

108. For other examples of this category of psalms, see Psalms 46; 48; 76; 84; 122.

Psalm 87 picks up this theme from Psalm 48 by reciting "glorious things" that are true of Zion (v. 3). The "glorious things" are that Egyptians and Babylonians and Philistines and Tyrians and Ethiopians "acknowledge" the God of Israel (v. 4), and they do so not as foreigners but as natural-born citizens of Zion, registered as such by the Lord himself (vv. 4–6). In the final line of this psalm, the nations are singing, "All my fountains are in you" (v. 7). "'Springs' or 'fountains' is a metaphor for the source of life and blessing."[109] Thus, the nations are finding in the God of Zion the blessing the human heart longs for.

Blessing for the Nations in Book 4 (Pss. 90–106)

We have already seen that Book 4 is the heart of the book of Psalms, with its emphasis on the reign of God. Book 4 also contains a substantial cluster of psalms, Psalms 96–100, that join the theme of blessing for the nations to that of God's reign.

We first encounter a global perspective in the opening verse of Psalm 96.

> Sing to the LORD a new song;
>   sing to the LORD, all the earth.

The poet may be portraying the "earth" here in personified terms, or the earth may be a **synecdoche** for the inhabitants of the earth, or both may be in view. Synecdoche is supported by verses 3–10, which mentions the "nations," "all peoples," and "families of nations."

> Declare his glory among the nations,
>   his marvelous deeds among all peoples.
>   (v. 3)

> Ascribe to the LORD, O families of nations,
>   ascribe to the LORD glory and strength.[110]
>   (v. 7)

---

109. Marvin E. Tate, *Psalms 51–100*, WBC (Dallas: Word, 1990), 392.
110. Note that according to the following verse the families of nations are worshiping in the temple courts in Jerusalem.

Say among the nations, "The LORD reigns."
The world is firmly established, it cannot be moved;
he will judge the peoples with equity.

(v. 10)

In the first ten verses of this psalm, the reign of God over the nations results in the worship of God by the nations. In the final verses the nations experience the blessing of God.

In verses 11–13 the "earth" is personified, along with the heavens, the sea, the fields, and the trees. They rejoice, are glad and jubilant, and sing for joy. Why? Because the Lord is coming "to judge" (v. 13). We immediately think in judicial terms when we hear the word "judge," but such was not the case when ancient Hebrews heard the word שָׁפַט. Neither the verb שָׁפַט ("to judge") nor the noun מִשְׁפָּט ("judgment") can be limited to the legal sphere.[111] Broadly speaking, שָׁפַט refers to action that restores a disturbed order.[112] While this restoration of order may involve judicial action with regard to human disputes, such is not the exclusive or even primary sense in Psalm 96. The creation is exuberant with joy at the prospect of the Lord coming to restore its harmony and fertility, along with that of the nations.[113]

> For God's judgment does not, after all, consist only in calling his opponents to account; it serves to restore his order in the world. This order manifests itself as much in the realm of Nature as in that of History; as much in the blessing of the fertility of the earth as in the blessings bestowed upon the nations.[114]

In Psalm 96 the nations and the whole created realm are experiencing blessing in the presence of the divine King.

Psalm 98 is quite similar to Psalm 96, as both open with the same summons: "Sing to the LORD a new song." Psalm 98 goes on to declare that God has made his salvation known among the nations (v. 2)

111. G. Liedke, "שָׁפַט," in *TLOT*, 3:1395.
112. Ibid., 3:1393.
113. Clifford, *Psalms 73–150*, 122.
114. Artur Weiser, *The Psalms*, OTL (Philadelphia: Westminster, 1962), 630.

and that "all the ends of the earth have seen the salvation of our God" (v. 3). The "earth" in verse 4 is primarily the "inhabitants of the earth," who are using song accompanied by musical instruments to celebrate the salvation accomplished by the Lord (vv. 5–6). Like Psalm 96, Psalm 98 closes with the creation rejoicing in anticipation of the Lord's coming to bless the cosmos with restored order.

Psalm 97 opens with the "earth" and "distant shores" rejoicing in the Lord's reign. Sandwiched as they are between Psalms 96 and 98, "earth" and "distant shores" is easy to identify as references to both the creation and the nations. The former identification is supported by the cosmic images in verses 2–5 and the latter is supported by the reference to "the peoples" seeing God's glory in verse 6. Note that verse 6 moves easily between the "heavens" in verse 6a and the "peoples" in verse 6b. We meet this same ease of combination at the opening of Psalm 99.

> The LORD reigns,
>   let the *nations* tremble;
> he sits enthroned between the cherubim,
>   let the *earth* shake.
>
>   (v. 1)

In the following two verses, the nations are praising the Lord, who is exalted over them all. The concluding call to exalt the Lord certainly has the nations in view. The nations, like Israel, are to exalt the Lord because he is to them, as he is to Israel, "a forgiving God" (v. 8). In Psalm 99 the blessing of the nations by the Lord results in the worship of the Lord by the nations.

Psalm 100 brings this cluster to a close with its call to the "earth" to praise the Lord (v. 1) and to serve the Lord (v. 2). The "earth" here refers primarily to the nations, although cosmic overtones certainly can be heard, given the preceding psalms. The nations are included among those whom the Lord has created and who now know the blessings of being part of "his people, the sheep of his pasture" (v. 3). The nations, together with Israel, are summoned to enter the temple to worship the Lord (v. 4), for they too have been experiencing the goodness and the enduring love of God (v. 5).

Psalms 93–100 "are among the most exalted in the Psalter: they proclaim YHWH as King in sustained, joyful outbursts of praise."[115] As such, Psalms 93–100 are arguably the theological heart of the book of Psalms with their sustained emphasis on God's kingship.[116] At the heart of the book of Psalms is the passion of the King of the universe to bless the nations.

Blessing for the Nations in Book 5 (Pss. 107–145)

The theme of blessing for the nations is scattered throughout Book 5 rather than being clustered, as has been the case in Books 1–4. While this motif is not as pronounced in Book 5 as it is in Books 1–4, the motif is present from beginning to end.

The global emphasis found in Books 1–4 comes to expression quickly in Book 5 with, for example, David's expressed intention to praise the Lord among the nations and to sing about the Lord among the peoples (Ps. 108:3). His reason behind this intention is the expansive nature of God's love and faithfulness.

> For great is your love, higher than the heavens;
> your faithfulness reaches to the skies.
> (v. 4)

And it is David's desire that the worship of God be as expansive as the love and faithfulness of God.

> Be exalted, O God, above the heavens,
> and let your glory be over all the earth.
> (v. 5)

As in Psalms 96 and 98, so too here, David's prayer is that the nations, along with the whole cosmic order, be covered with the glory of God.

In Psalm 117, the shortest of all the psalms, it is not Israel but the nations that are invited to praise and exalt the Lord (v. 1). The reason for the invitation is given in verse 2.

---

115. Howard, *Structure of Psalms 93–100*, 22.
116. J. Clinton McCann, "Psalms," in *NIB* (Nashville: Abingdon, 1996), 4:662.

> For great is his love toward us,
>   and the faithfulness of the LORD endures forever.

Does the "us" include the nations or just Israel? On one level the "us" is Israel. As in Isaiah 40–55 the nations are here invited to consider the love and faithfulness of God demonstrated in the history of Israel. This invitation is to the end that Israel will praise and exalt the Lord. In addition "the psalm invites the nations of the world to recognize in one people a pledge of the one Lord's generosity and justice toward all."[117] This "little poem is not about imperialism but about God's desires for the human race."[118] This is the apostle Paul's understanding of Psalm 117, as is clear from his quotation of verse 1 in Romans 15:11, where he is praising God for his inclusion of the nations in the blessings promised to the patriarchs. Thus, even the shortest psalm in the book of Psalms articulates the theme of God's blessing for the nations.

David picks up this theme again in Psalm 138, where he prays that the kings of the earth (who once raged against the Lord [Ps. 2]) will praise the Lord (v. 4a). The occasion is the nations' hearing words from God's mouth (v. 4b). What words would put praise for the Lord on the lips of the kings of the nations if not words like "blessed are *all* who take refuge in him" (Ps. 2:12)?

David continues his prayer with the request that the nations sing about the Lord's ways. His ways include bringing Israel through the sea at the time of the Exodus, which we now know was an act of God carried out on behalf of the whole human race.[119] The reason for this prayer is the greatness of the glory of God (v. 5b). The Lord's glory is so great that it must transcend the boundaries of Israel and encompass the nations (see Ps. 108:5).

Blessing for the Nations in the Final Doxology (Pss. 146–150)

The book of Psalms is brought to a close with a grand collection of doxological psalms—Psalms 146–150. Psalm 148 expresses praise for God on a cosmic scale. This cosmic doxology summons the universe to

---

117. Clifford, *Psalms 73–150*, 204.
118. Ibid.
119. See Psalm 66:5–6 and the discussion on pages 107–8.

praise the Lord, first by extending the call to worship to the "heavens" (vv. 1–6) and then extending it to the "earth" (vv. 7–14). Among those on earth who are called to praise the Lord are the "kings of the earth," "all nations," the "princes [of the earth]," and "all rulers on earth" (v. 11). These are to praise the Lord because of his expansive glory (v. 13) and his blessing of Israel (v. 14). In a psalm so focused on God as Creator, why the shift to his redemptive work in this last verse? In a psalm so focused on the global, why the shift to one nation? It is because God has chosen this one nation as the vehicle through which he will make his entrance into the world in order that his blessings might flow to all and to the whole.[120]

When we arrive at the end of the book of Psalms we encounter for one last time the praise of God in cosmic proportions. After the opening "Praise the LORD" of Psalm 150, those "in his sanctuary" (v. 1a) and those "in his mighty heavens" (v. 1b) are called upon to praise God. Scholars have debated what the psalmist has in view in the reference to God's "sanctuary." Is it the earthly or heavenly sanctuary?[121] Several reasons can be offered for understanding "sanctuary" as a reference to the earthly temple. One is the resultant dramatic movement in the line from earth (v. 1a) to heaven (v. 1b). Another is the human worshipers obviously in view in the verses that follow. Yet another reason is the matching line at the end of the psalm just before the final "Praise the LORD":

Let everything that has breath praise the LORD.

"In the Old Testament vocabulary, 'breath' [*neshama*] more than any other term designates the vitality of the physical life of the human being, the life and breath that comes from God."[122] At the end of the psalm, humans with "breath," then, match up with humans, who are, at the beginning of the psalm, in the "sanctuary." And it is not *some* who have breath but *all* who have breath who, in the final line of the book of Psalms, are called upon to praise God.

---

120. See Genesis 12:3; and Clifford, *Psalms 73–150*, 311.
121. See Leslie C. Allen, *Psalms 101–150*, WBC, rev. ed. (Nashville: Thomas Nelson, 2002), 403, for a survey of opinions.
122. James L. Mays, *Psalms*, Int (Louisville: John Knox, 1989), 450.

Thus, from beginning to end, the book of Psalms has a sustained focus on the heart of God that encompasses the nations. God desires that all peoples on earth take refuge in him and in so doing experience blessing from him, to the end that they, along with the whole cosmic order, might give glory to him.

3

PREPARING FOR
INTERPRETATION

For the director of music.
Of David the servant of the LORD.
He sang to the LORD the words of this song
when the LORD delivered him
from the hand of all his enemies
and from the hand of Saul.
He said:
(Ps. 18)

THE TITLE TO PSALM 18 raises a number of questions for the interpreter of the book of Psalms:

1. What is meant by לַמְנַצֵּחַ? Is it "For the director of music" (NIV)
   or "To the leader" (NRSV) or "For the leader" (TNK)?
2. Does לַמְנַצֵּחַ belong at the beginning of Psalm 18 or at the end of
   Psalm 17?[1]

---

1. Bruce Waltke has persuasively argued that לַמְנַצֵּחַ is a colophon and belongs at the end
   of the preceding psalm rather than where it is currently located in the MT. See Bruce K.
   Waltke, "Superscripts, Postscripts, or Both," *JBL* 110 (1991): 583–96.

3. Does לְדָוִד mean "written by David," "written for David" "written about David," or "collected by David"?
4. Is this historical note a reliable and essential key to the interpretation of this psalm?
5. Does this historical note encourage us to find in the life of David the historical setting of other psalms that have no such information in the title?
6. Who are "the enemies"?
7. What would this psalm have meant to readers in later generations, especially those in the postexilic community?
8. Did the original text read מִיַּד שָׁאוּל ("from the hand of Saul") or מִכַּף שָׁאוּל ("from the palm of Saul" [author's translation])?[2]

The goal of this chapter is not necessarily to answer all of these questions that are related to Psalm 18 in particular. Rather, the goal is to equip interpreters with the tools needed to discover on their own answers to such questions as they arise throughout the book of Psalms. First, we will deal with issues related to the psalms and history: (1) What role does historical setting play in interpreting psalms? (2) Why do the psalms seem timeless in there applicability to life? (3) What is the "historical context" in which to read a psalm? Second, we will deal with issues related to the text of Psalms: (1) How well did the ancients preserve the text of the book of Psalms for us? (2) Is text criticism needed in interpreting the Psalms? (3) What does text criticism in Psalms look like? Third, we will survey some of the resources that can contribute to a proper interpretation of the psalms.

THE ROLE OF HISTORY

It is customary for books on interpreting the Bible to advise students to interpret a text in its original historical context. This is sound advice. The fact that some psalms provide information on their historical setting indicates that this advice is also applicable to the interpretation of the psalms. Yet most psalms seem to defy the best efforts to locate

---

2. The MT here reads מִיַּד שָׁאוּל ("from the hand of Saul"), but multiple manuscripts and the parallel text in 2 Samuel 22:1 read מִכַּף שָׁאוּל ("from the palm of Saul" [author's translation]).

them in history. In addition, the original setting of an individual psalm clearly is not the same as the historical setting of that psalm in the final form of the book of Psalms. The original historical setting of Psalm 90, "A prayer of Moses the man of God" (title of psalm), was somewhere around 1400 B.C., while the setting of this psalm when the book of Psalms reached its final form was some one thousand years later. Which "historical setting" is the context for interpretation? What role does history play in the interpretation of the psalms?

The Historical Setting of a Psalm

Before addressing the specific question about the historical setting of individual psalms, let's address the more general question of the authenticity of the titles. In short, my view is that the titles are canonical although not necessarily original.[3]

It seems that at least some of the titles to individual psalms are not original to the text but were added latter for the following reasons: (1) the titles are written in the third person and thus give the impression of being editorial;[4] (2) only 116 psalms have titles in the MT, while all but Psalms 1 and 2 have titles in the LXX, thus a certain fluidity in the titles appeared at a fairly late stage in the compiling of the book of Psalms;[5] (3) Psalms 14 and 53 are apparently two different versions of the same original psalm.[6] This one original psalm seemingly was adapted to fit two different settings as it circulated in two different collections.[7] The titles are not identical: Psalm 14 reads, לַמְנַצֵּחַ לְדָוִד ("For the director of music. Of David"), while Psalm 53 reads, לַמְנַצֵּחַ עַל־מָחֲלַת מַשְׂכִּיל לְדָוִד ("For the director of music. According to mahalath. A maskil of David").

---

3. Raymond B. Dillard and Tremper Longman III, *An Introduction to the Old Testament* (Grand Rapids: Zondervan, 1994), 214–15, do not entertain this option but seem to allow only an either/or option: either original or not canonical. In a more recent article, Longman views the titles as not original but nevertheless canonical. See Tremper Longman III, "Lament," in *Cracking Old Testament Codes: A Guide to Interpreting the Literary Genres of the Old Testament*, ed. D. Brent Sandy and Ronald L. Giese (Nashville: Broadman & Holman, 1995), 208n. 22.

4. Derek Kidner, *Psalms 1–72*, TOTC (Downers Grove, IL: InterVarsity Press, 1973), 33.

5. Ernest C. Lucas, *Exploring the Old Testament: A Guide to the Psalms and Wisdom Literature* (Downers Grove, IL: InterVarsity Press, 2003), 19.

6. So, for example, Willem VanGemeren, "Psalms," in *EBC*, 388; and Gerald H. Wilson, *Psalms Volume 1*, NIVAC (Grand Rapids: Zondervan, 2002), 287.

7. For the interpretive significance, see VanGemeren, "Psalms," 388–89.

This difference in titles suggests that the titles were added independently and, therefore, that at least one of the two was added after the original composition of the psalm.

Nonetheless, the titles are ancient. Such is indicated because the meaning of a number of the words found in the titles was lost by the time translators of the LXX did their work (after 250 B.C.). For example, the oft-repeated לַמְנַצֵּחַ ("For the director of music")[8] was misunderstood by the translators of the LXX, who rendered it with εἰς τὸ τέλος ("to the end"), apparently thinking it was related to לָנֶצַח ("forever"). It must have taken several centuries for such a loss of meaning to have taken place,[9] so at least some of the titles predate the LXX by a considerable amount of time.

Although ancient but not original, the titles are part of the canonical text for several reasons: (1) The New Testament at times treats the titles as Scripture and builds arguments on this material (see Mark 12:35-37; Acts 2:29–35; 13:35–37). (2) The title to Psalm 18 is embedded in the canonical text of 2 Samuel at 22:1. It seems that the canonical nature of this material in 2 Samuel 22:1 entails the canonical nature of this material in the title in Psalm 18. (3) The standard phrase לַמְנַצֵּחַ ("For the director of music") is embedded in the canonical text of Habakkuk at 3:19. Again, it seems that the canonical nature of לַמְנַצֵּחַ in Habakkuk 3:19 entails the canonical nature of this material in its occurrences in the titles of the various psalms.

With these general comments in mind, we can turn our attention to the role of the historical notes[10] in the titles to various psalms and the implications of this material, if any, for the interpretation of other psalms.

Thirteen psalms contain information that links these psalms to various episodes in David's life.[11]

---

8. This phrase occurs fifty-five times in the book of Psalms and only once elsewhere in the MT: Habakkuk 3:19.

9. See Wilson, *Psalms Volume 1*, 80–81, for a fuller discussion of this point.

10. I am not going to discuss all of the terms that occur in the titles. Students can find adequate coverage of this material in any number of places, e.g., C. Hassell Bullock, *Encountering the Book of Psalms* (Grand Rapids: Baker, 2001), 24–30; Lucas, *Exploring the Old Testament*, 19–25; VanGemeren, "Psalms," 33–39; and Wilson, *Psalms Volume 1*, 78–80.

11. In addition, Psalm 30 is "For the dedication of the temple."

Psalm 3	David flees from Absalom	(2 Sam. 15–16)
Psalm 7	Concerning Cush	(Event unknown)
Psalm 18	David delivered from Saul	(1 Sam. 24 and 26)
Psalm 34	David pretends to be insane	(1 Sam. 21)
Psalm 51	David mourns sin with Bathsheba	(2 Sam. 12)
Psalm 52	David betrayed by Doeg	(1 Sam. 22)
Psalm 54	David betrayed by the Ziphites	(1 Sam. 23)
Psalm 56	David captured by the Philistines	(1 Sam. 21)
Psalm 57	David flees from Saul	(1 Sam. 22)
Psalm 59	David sought by Saul	(1 Sam. 19)
Psalm 60	David fights the Arameans and Edomites	(2 Sam. 8 and 10)
Psalm 63	David hides in the wilderness	(1 Sam. 23–24)
Psalm 142	David flees from Saul	(1 Sam. 22)

While affirming the canonical status of the historical information in the titles, I must admit that this information does not play a major role in my own interpretation of the corresponding psalms for several reasons: (1) the psalm texts generally lack the kind of specific details needed to correlate the psalm with the historical event in 1 and 2 Samuel in any precise way; (2) at least one of the people referred to (Cush the Benjaminite in Ps. 7) and the event in view are completely unknown to us and so can provide no background information for interpreting the details of the psalm; (3) at times there is almost a tension between the event referred to and the content of the psalm. Psalm 3, for example, is about the time when David fled from Absalom. David's attitude toward his adversary in the psalm ("Strike all my enemies on the jaw; break the teeth of the wicked," v. 7 [8]) seems quite different from his attitude toward Absalom ("Be gentle with the young man Absalom for my sake" [2 Sam. 18:5]). This tension can be resolved in a number of ways. Perhaps the psalm reflects David's attitude toward Absalom's men but not Absalom himself. Perhaps David's attitude changed from the time he was fleeing in 2 Samuel 17 to the time he was fighting in 2 Samuel 18. Perhaps there are other explanations. Whatever explanation we conceive, however, seems to undermine the connection between the *context* given in the title and the *content* given in the text.

It is difficult, then, to connect in any specific way psalms that have historical information in their titles to the events mentioned. We are thus on even shakier ground if we try to correlate psalms without historical information in the titles to events in the life of David. While it is possible, for example, that Psalm 24 arose in the context of David bringing the ark of the covenant to Jerusalem (2 Sam. 6:12–19), this psalm could have been composed for a regular liturgical procession after victory in battle[12] or for some more general occasion.[13]

Therefore, we seem to be left with a certain ambivalence toward the historical information in the titles: it is canonical but cannot play much of a role in the interpretive process other than illustrating in a general way the kind of situation in which a given psalm arose.[14] That is, a noticeable difference is found between the historically specific language in the titles and the very general—even vague—language in the psalms themselves. Or, put yet another way, the historical information in the titles gives the impression that the psalms are time-bound, while the psalms themselves seem rather timeless.[15] To this timeless quality of the psalms we now turn.

The Timelessness of the Psalms

The language of the psalms is typically general and universal.[16] Psalms 3–7 offer some examples. In Psalm 3:1 David refers to his "foes" and to the "many" who "rise up against me." Were it not for the information in the title, we would not know who these "foes" are, because insufficient information is given in the body of the psalm to make this determination. This lack of specific information is typical in the psalms. We do not know who the "men" are in 4:2, or who the "arrogant" are in 5:5 [6], or who the "enemies" are in 6:10 [11], or who is pursuing David in 7:1. Nor, based on the content of Psalm 4, can we determine

---

12. See Wilson, *Psalms Volume 1*, 453.
13. See VanGemeren, "Psalms," 219.
14. This same ambivalence applies to other matters in the titles. For example, Psalm 8 is עַל־הַגִּתִּית ("According to gittith"; Ps. 8:1), yet such information plays no role in our interpretation of the psalm, since we have no certainty as to what עַל־הַגִּתִּית means.
15. On the other hand, the historical information in the title of Psalm 51 matches up quite nicely with the content of the psalm itself.
16. Daniel J. Estes, *Handbook on the Wisdom Books and Psalms* (Grand Rapids: Baker, 2005), 141.

what David's "distress" (v. 1) was. In Psalm 6:2 [3], even though David uses the language of physical illness, we cannot be sure that he is using this language literally rather than as a figure for some other adversity, since he also prays for deliverance from "enemies" in verses 8–10 [9–11]. Not knowing with precision in such cases is actually a blessing in that the general and universal nature of the language makes it all the easier to appropriate the language of a given psalm as applicable to a contemporary reader's own situation. A New Testament example can underscore this point: What was Paul's "thorn," and was his "flesh" his physical body or his sinful nature (2 Cor. 12:7)? We simply do not know.[17] As Philip Hughes has argued, if we knew what Paul's thorn was and we did not suffer from that same problem, we would be inclined to dismiss Paul's experience as one that is not applicable to our own lives.[18] The result of not knowing is that Paul's "thorn in the flesh" becomes a metaphor for all of those situations in life that keep us humble. So the lack of precision in our understanding of the historical context of a given psalm results in increased ease in applying the text to contemporary life.

The Historical Setting of the Psalms

Bruce Waltke has persuasively argued that a psalm can be read in multiple historical contexts given the growing nature of the canon of Scripture.[19] As the canon grew so did the context in which to read a given psalm. We can better understand these contexts by asking a series of questions: (1) What did the psalm mean in the context of the original poet? (2) What did the psalm mean in the context of the editors who finalized the shape and content of the Hebrew Bible in the postexilic community? (3) What did the psalm mean in the context of the authors of the New Testament? The answers to these questions will have a strong thread of continuity, as each stage in the process of canonical growth is organically related to the previous stage(s). To flesh

---

17. See the excursus in Philip Edgcumbe Hughes, *Paul's Second Epistle to the Corinthians*, NICNT (Grand Rapids: Eerdmans, 1962), 442–48, for a full treatment of this question.
18. Ibid., 442.
19. Bruce K. Waltke, "A Canonical Process Approach to the Psalms," in *Tradition and Testament: Essays in Honor of Charles Lee Feinberg*, ed. John S. Feinberg and Paul D. Feinberg (Chicago: Moody, 1981).

out this process of growth, let's look at Psalm 89 and verses 39–45
[40–46] in particular.

> You have renounced the covenant with your servant
>   and have defiled his crown in the dust.
> You have broken through all his walls
>   and reduced his strongholds to ruins.
> All who pass by have plundered him;
>   he has become the scorn of his neighbors.
> You have exalted the right hand of his foes;
>   you have made all his enemies rejoice.
> You have turned back the edge of his sword
>   and have not supported him in battle.
> You have put an end to his splendor
>   and cast his throne to the ground.
> You have cut short the days of his youth;
>   you have covered him with a mantle of shame.

According to the title, this psalm is "A maskil of Ethan the Ezrahite."
Ethan the Ezrahite was a counselor in the court of Solomon (1 Kings
4:31 [5:11]). The description of devastation in the above verses makes
no sense in the context of Solomon's reign but could easily fit into
the reign of his son, Rehoboam, into whose reign Ethan could very
well have lived. In the fifth year of Rehoboam's reign, Shishak king
of Egypt attacked Jerusalem and plundered the temple and the royal
palace (1 Kings 14:25–26). Psalm 89:39–45 can be read in that original
context. The prayer of the psalm would then be for the restoration of
the present king, Rehoboam.

It is not difficult at all, moreover, to imagine how the faithful in
the postexilic community would have heard the words of this text. It
would have been easy and natural for them to connect this text with
the much more radical devastation of Jerusalem at the hands of the
Babylonians in 586 B.C. For those living in postexilic Judah, with neither royal palace nor Davidic monarch, the pain of the question in verse
49 [50] would have been much more intense.

> O Lord, where is your former great love,
>   which in your faithfulness you swore to David?

In this context the prayer of the psalm would have been for the coming of *the absent king.*

In the context of the New Testament, I think we can read this text in two ways. First, the question raised by the psalm and articulated most poignantly in verse 49 [50] is answered in Jesus Christ. God's love for, and faithfulness to, David is realized in the sending of his Son as the true Son of David (see Matt. 1:1 and Rom. 1:3). So this psalm assures present-day believers that God is always faithful to his promises. On the other hand, we neither see King Jesus nor the fullness of his kingdom in the present. In fact, when we look at the church, we too often see broken-down walls and ruins and shame. We, like the ancients, cry out,

> O Lord, where is your former great love,
>   which in your faithfulness you swore to David?

Thus, this psalm gives voice to our anguished perplexities about the present reality of the kingdom. It fills us with hope to continue to pray and to work for God's kingdom to come and his will to be done *on earth* as it is in heaven, "for no matter how many promises God has made, they are 'Yes' in Christ" (2 Cor. 1:20).

THE STATE OF THE TEXT

"What is the text?" With this question I'm actually raising two separate questions: (1) What is the canonical number and order of psalms in the book of Psalms? and (2) What is the original wording of any particular text in the book of Psalms? Related to the second is a third: (3) How does one determine the original wording of any particular text when that wording is in doubt for one reason or another? In this section I will briefly introduce you to these issues and direct you to more detailed resources for further study.

The Nature of the Text

Many readers of Psalms would be surprised to find out that, in both the Greek and Syriac editions, the final psalm is 151, not 150, and that the Syriac edition contains four additional psalms as well.[20] Even more surprising would be the knowledge that at Qumran there existed a scroll of psalms (11QPsᵃ) that approximates Psalms 90–118 but (1) is missing a good number of canonical psalms, (2) contains eleven non-canonical psalms, and (3) arranges the psalms in a different order than the Hebrew Psalter as we know it.[21] So we face the question, "What is the text?"

Bruce Waltke has succinctly traced the history of the text (and its witnesses) from the formative period (ca. 1400–400 B.C.)—and from the fixing of the text (ca. A.D. 100) now called the Proto-Masoretic Text (Proto-MT)—to the production of the authoritative Masoretic Text (ca. A.D. 1000).[22] Between 1400 B.C. and A.D. 100, two tendencies were operative side by side: the tendency to preserve the text and the tendency to revise the text. During this period, the tendency to preserve increased while the tendency to revise decreased. As just one example, the use of vowel letters in the Hebrew language in general increased throughout the years, and their use also increased at this same time in the Hebrew Bible. But the significantly increased use of vowel letters in the Hebrew of Qumran was not incorporated into the spelling system of the Hebrew Bible, reflecting a decrease in the tendency to revise even the spelling of words in the text.

Between the formative period and the fixing of the text, there also existed quite diverse text-types alongside the text-type that would become the Proto-MT. These diverse text-types, according to Waltke, "are best regarded as distinct, literary stages in the development of the text or as distinct compositions."[23] Emanuel Tov also differentiates the

20. For the details, see S. Pigué, "Psalms, Syriac (aprocryphal)," in *ABD*, 5:536–37.

21. For the details, see Gerald H. Wilson, "The Structure of the Psalter," in *Interpreting the Psalms: Issues and Approaches*, ed. David Firth and Philip S. Johnston (Downers Grove, IL: InterVarsity Press, 2005), 242–43. The standard introduction to this topic is Peter W. Flint, *The Dead Sea Psalms Scrolls and the Book of Psalms* (Leiden: Brill, 1997).

22. Bruce K. Waltke, "Textual Criticism of the Old Testament and Its Relation to Exegesis and Theology," in *NIDOTTE*, 1:52–62.

23. Ibid., 61.

period of compositional development from that of the transmission of the finished literary work.

> At the end of the composition process of a biblical book stood a text which was considered authoritative (and hence also finished at the literary level), even if only by a limited group of people, and which at the same time stood at the beginning of a process of copying and textual transmission.[24]

Tov is of the opinion that the diverse text-types that existed prior to the establishment of the final authoritative text would have been received as authoritative along the way. He views, however, the final authoritative copy,[25] containing "the corpus of the Holy Writings of the Jewish people,"[26] as the proper object of study in the textual criticism of the Hebrew Bible.

Waltke agrees with this opinion, adding that this same text became the authoritative text of the church, as well as of the synagogue, as early as the text-critical work of Origen and Jerome.[27] Brevard Childs summarizes the logical conclusion of the history of the text and its witnesses.

> The MT inherently commended itself to both the synagogue and the church. As the canon of the OT emerged in the historical process, so also the MT surfaced as the best text of that canon.[28]

So the answer to our question "What is the text?" is this: The text is the Masoretic Text.

From this perspective, then, we could view 11QPsa^a as a "distinct literary stage" in the development of the MT, a stage that did not become the authoritative text. On the other hand, we could view 11QPsa^a as

---

24. Emanuel Tov, *Textual Criticism of the Hebrew Bible*, 2nd ed. (Minneapolis: Fortress, 2001), 177.
25. Ibid., 177.
26. Ibid., 179.
27. Waltke, "Textual Criticism of the Old Testament," 1:62.
28. Brevard S. Childs, *Introduction to the Old Testament as Scripture* (Philadelphia: Fortress, 1979), 96–97.

a "distinct composition" altogether, which may or may not have been regarded as authoritative in some quarters of ancient Israel. Scholars are divided as to the nature of 11QPsaᵃ; some take 11QPsaᵃ as an alternative canonical tradition, while others take it as a distinct liturgical text.[29] Either way, the existence of 11QPsaᵃ does not, in my opinion, affect the answer to the question "What is the text?" The text of the book of Psalms is the 150 psalms found in the MT.

The Need for Text Criticism

We can illustrate the need for text criticism by examining a particular text, Psalm 104:6a.

$$\text{תְּהוֹם כַּלְּבוּשׁ כִּסִּיתוֹ}$$

A wooden translation would be, "The deep like the garment you covered it." This text, though, contains a grammatical problem and a theological problem. The grammatical problem is in the final form כִּסִּיתוֹ,[30] which is typically translated, "You covered it."[31] There is no masculine singular antecedent for the suffix. The logical antecedent is אֶרֶץ ("the earth") in verse 5, but אֶרֶץ is feminine. The LXX has περιβόλαιον αὐτοῦ ("his garment"), and the Vulgate follows suit with *amictus eius* ("his garment"), providing evidence for the masculine, singular suffix, but apparently reading כְּסוּתוֹ ("his garment") for כִּסִּיתוֹ ("you covered it"). Other witnesses give evidence of a feminine, singular suffix, which the context seems to require.[32]

The theological problem is found in the logic of the passage if we keep the text as is. Verses 5–9 are a strophe that describes God's establishment of dry land by his containment of the sea in its proper place. First, God placed the land (אֶרֶץ)[33] on a solid foundation, so that

29. For a concise overview of the debate and the significant bibliography, see David M. Howard Jr., *The Structure of Psalms 93–100*, Biblical and Judaic Studies, ed. William Henry Propp (Winona Lake, IN: Eisenbrauns, 1997), 5:26–27.
30. The form is a verb, piel, perfect, second person, masculine, singular from כָּסָה, plus the third-person, masculine, singular suffix.
31. So ESV, NASB, NIV, NRSV.
32. Aquila (A.D. second-century Greek), Theodotian (A.D. second-century Greek), Jerome's Old Latin (A.D. fourth-century Greek), and Targums (Aramaic translations).
33. For אֶרֶץ as "dry land" in a creation context, see Genesis 1:10.

it would not "totter" (v. 5 NASB). Then he covered the dry land with "the deep" (תְּהוֹם)[34] to the extent that "the deep" covered even the mountain peaks (v. 6). This is followed by the water's flight from off the dry land at God's "rebuke" (גַּעֲרָתְךָ; v. 7)[35] and their flight to the sea (v. 8), where they were to remain, never again "to cover [לְכַסּוֹת] the dry land" (הָאָרֶץ; v. 9). Why would God cover (כסה) the land with water only to rebuke the water for being there, and then confine the water to the sea so that it can never cover (כסה) the land? Note also that this sequence is at variance with Genesis 1, where the dry land (אֶרֶץ) does not exist/appear until after the waters are removed and placed in the sea (Gen. 1:9).

A minor emendation elegantly solves the grammatical and the theological problems. If we emend כְּסִיתוֹ ("you covered it") to כִּסַּתָּה[36] ("it covered it"), both problems are solved. The feminine, singular subject of the verb is תְּהוֹם ("the deep"), and the referent for the feminine, singular suffix is אֶרֶץ ("the land"). A coherent picture now emerges in Psalm 104 and paints the same picture found in Genesis 1: The deep (תְּהוֹם) covered the land (אֶרֶץ; Gen 1:2; Ps. 104:6); then God removed the deep and confined these waters to the sea (Gen. 1:9; Ps. 104:7–9).

In conclusion, it must be said that no major doctrine is affected by either reading and that this is always the case with text-critical decisions in the book of Psalms. I'm not aware of any major tenet of the Christian faith being affected by any text-critical decision in the book of Psalms. Engaging in the text-critical process, however, will at times provide a better understanding of a particular text and put the preacher in a better position to rightly explain the Word of God.

---

34. This is the same word that is used in Genesis 1:2.
35. The cognate verb (גָּעַר) is used in Psalm 106:9 for God's rebuking the sea at the time of the Exodus. There God rebuked the sea because it stood in opposition to God's redemptive purpose to bring his people into his presence in the land. In Psalm 104:7 God rebuked the sea because it stood in opposition to his creational purpose to have his people live in his presence on the land.
36. Verb, piel, perfect, third-person, feminine, singular with a third-person, feminine, singular suffix.

The Nature of Text Criticism

In coming to the text-critical decision made in the previous section, two principles were at work: (1) never base text-critical decisions on external evidence alone; (2) base text-critical decisions primarily on internal evidence.[37] External evidence refers to other Hebrew manuscripts and other ancient versions. Internal evidence refers to matters within the text itself like morphological, syntactical, and literary factors. My decision above was based primarily on the grammatical and theological factors within the text. The evidence from the versions played a secondary and supportive role. This example models the typical interplay between external and internal evidence.

To engage the text-critical process, though, the interpreter needs more input than the brief discussion provided here. The interpreter should, in fact, apply three levels of introductory treatments that discuss text criticism as it applies in the Hebrew Bible. If you are new to this discipline, I recommend the following sequence of study to develop your text-critical skills.

1. Start with a concise introduction or two. Three good ones that I recommend are,
    - Chisholm, Robert B., Jr. *From Exegesis to Exposition: A Practical Guide to Using Biblical Hebrew*, 19–29. Grand Rapids: Baker, 1999.
      (This is a very concise and helpful introduction.)
    - Chisholm, Robert B., Jr. *Interpreting the Historical Books: An Exegetical Handbook,* 145–49. Grand Rapids: Kregel, 2006.
      (This contains detailed examples of the process.)
    - Waltke, Bruce K. "Textual Criticism of the Old Testament and Its Relation to Exegesis and Theology." In *NIDOTTE*, 1:51–67.
      (This contains an excellent history of the text and its witnesses and a helpful discussion of the interplay between text criticism, exegesis, and theology.)

---

37. See Robert B. Chisholm Jr., *Interpreting the Historical Books: An Exegetical Handbook* (Grand Rapids: Kregel, 2006), 89–90.

2. Move on to an intermediate introduction.
   - McCarter, P. Kyle. *Textual Criticism: Recovering the Text of the Hebrew Bible*. Guides to Biblical Scholarship. Philadelphia: Fortress, 1986.
     (This ninety-four-page book is a thorough yet relatively brief treatment of why text criticism is needed, how errors have crept into the text, and what principles to follow in making text-critical decisions.)
   - Weingreen, J. *Introduction to the Critical Study of the Text of the Hebrew Bible*. New York: Oxford, 1982.
     (This one-hundred-page book is out of print but worth finding for its discussion of common errors that are found in the text.)

3. Deepen your knowledge with one of the major introductions to text criticism.
   - Brotzman, Ellis R. *Old Testament Textual Criticism: A Practical Introduction*. Grand Rapids: Baker, 1994.
   - Tov, Emanuel. *Textual Criticism of the Hebrew Bible*. 2nd ed. Minneapolis: Fortress, 2001.
   - Würthwein, E. *The Text of the Old Testament: An Introduction to Biblica Hebraica*. 2nd ed. Grand Rapids: Eerdmans, 1995.

The primary tool for text criticism is *Biblia Hebraica Stuttgartensia* (*BHS*). Since most of the information in the text-critical apparatus is in the form of abbreviations and sigla, three other tools will be useful. The first two are introductions to *BHS*.
   - Scott, William R. *A Simplified Guide to BHS*. Berkeley: Bibal Press, 1987.
   - Wonnenberger, R. *Understanding BHS: A Manual for the Users of Biblia Hebraica Stuttgartensia*. Rome: Pontifical Biblical Institute, 1984.

The third is a handy list that you can keep in your copy of *BHS* and that interprets the sigla and provides information on each referent.
   - Vasholz, R. I. *Data for Sigla of BHS*. Winona Lake, IN: Eisenbrauns, 1983.

And, of course, any number of commentaries will provide helpful discussions of text-critical issues in specific psalms.

THE CONTRIBUTIONS OF OTHERS

Interpretation is best done in community. One aspect of community is interacting with the writings of other interpreters. Below you will find recommendations for additions to your library on all the topics covered in this volume.

Introductions

A number of general introductions provide clear entrées into the book of Psalms.
- Bullock, C. Hassell. *Encountering the Book of Psalms*. Grand Rapids: Baker, 2001.
- Crenshaw, James L. *The Psalms: An Introduction*. Grand Rapids: Eerdmans, 2001.
- Estes, Daniel J. *Handbook on the Wisdom Books and Psalms*. Grand Rapids: Baker, 2005.
- Futato, Mark D. *Transformed by Praise: The Purpose and Message of the Psalms*. Phillipsburg, NJ: P & R Publishing, 2002.
- Longman, Tremper, III. *How to Read the Psalms*. Downers Grove, IL: InterVarsity Press, 1988.
- Lucas, Ernest C. *Exploring the Old Testament: A Guide to the Psalms and Wisdom Literature*. Downers Grove, IL: InterVarsity Press, 2003.
- McCann, J. Clinton. *A Theological Introduction to the Book of Psalms: The Psalms as Torah*. Nashville: Abingdon, 1993.
- Miller, Patrick D., Jr. *Interpreting the Psalms*. Philadelphia: Fortress, 1986.

Poetry

For additional introductory level reading on Hebrew poetry, several good options are available. The first two are quite brief; the third is one hundred pages.

- Berlin, Adele. "Reading Biblical Poetry." In *The Jewish Study Bible*, 2097–2104. New York: Oxford, 2004.
- Fitzgerald, Aloysius. "Hebrew Poetry." In *The New Jerome Biblical Commentary*, 201–8. Englewood Cliffs, NJ: Prentice Hall, 1990.
- Petersen, David L. and Kent Harold Richards. *Interpreting Hebrew Poetry*. Minneapolis: Fortress, 1992.

Two studies are seminal on what I have called "a new understanding" of Hebrew poetry.[38] Both are essential reading for deepening your understanding of Hebrew poetry.

- Alter, Robert. *The Art of Biblical Poetry*. New York: Basic Books, 1985.
- Kugel, James L. *The Idea of Biblical Hebrew Poetry: Parallelism and Its History*. New Haven: Yale, 1981.

One book devoted to parallelism is, in my estimation, must reading.

- Berlin, Adele. *The Dynamics of Biblical Hebrew Parallelism*. Bloomington: Indiana University, 1985.

Three works are key for helping you analyze the imagery of Psalms. In addition, the two articles by Elmer Smick will broaden your understanding of the use of mythopoeic imagery in Hebrew poetry.

- Brown, William P. *Seeing the Psalms: A Theology of Metaphor*. Louisville: Westminster John Knox, 2002.
- Keel, Othmar. *The Symbolism of the Biblical World: Ancient Near Eastern Iconography and the Book of Psalms*. Winona Lake, IN: Eisenbrauns, 1997.
- Ryken, Leland, James C. Wilhoit, and Tremper Longman III, eds. *Dictionary of Biblical Imagery*. Downers Grove, IL: InterVarsity Press, 1998.
- Smick, Elmer B. "The Mythological Elements in the Book of Job." *WTJ* 40 (1977–1978): 213–28.
- ———. "Mythopoeic Language in the Psalms." *WTJ* 44 (1982): 88–98.

---

38. See chapter 1 (pages 23–56).

Two works will serve you well as reference tools on the wide variety of techniques used by Hebrew poets.
- Alonso Schökel, Luis. *A Manual of Hebrew Poetics*. Subsidia Biblica. Rome: Pontifical Biblical Institute, 1988.
- Watson, Wilfred G. E. *Classical Hebrew Poetry: A Guide to Its Techniques*. JSOTSup. Sheffield: JSOT, 1986.

Shape

Listed here are several works on the topic of the shape and shaping of the book of Psalms as a literary whole.
- Creach, Jerome F. D. *Yahweh as Refuge and the Editing of the Hebrew Psalter*. JSOTSup. Sheffield: Sheffield Academic Press, 1996.
- deClaissé-Walford, Nancy L. *Reading From the Beginning: The Shape of the Hebrew Psalter*. Macon, GA: Mercer University, 1997.
- Futato, Mark D. *Transformed by Praise: The Purpose and Message of the Psalms*. Phillipsburg, NJ: P & R Publishing, 2002.
- Howard, David M., Jr. *The Structure of Psalms 93–100*. Biblical and Judaic Studies. Vol. 5. Edited by William Henry Propp. Winona Lake, IN: Eisenbrauns, 1997.
- ———. "Recent Trends in Psalms Study." In *The Face of Old Testament Study: A Survey of Contemporary Approaches*, 329–90. Grand Rapids: Baker, 1999.
- McCann, J. Clinton, ed. *The Shape and Shaping of the Psalter*. JSOTSup. Sheffield: JSOT, 1993.
- Wilson, Gerald H. *The Editing of the Hebrew Psalter*. SBLDS. Chicago: Scholars, 1985.
- ———. "The Structure of the Psalter." In *Interpreting the Psalms: Issues and Approaches*, edited by David Firth and Philip S. Johnston, 229–46. Downers Grove, IL: InterVarsity Press, 2005.

Theology

Most commentaries will have at least a brief introduction to the theology of Psalms. In addition to these, you will want to read other works along the way.

- Firth, David G. "The Teaching of the Psalms." In *Interpreting the Psalms: Issues and Approaches*, edited by David Firth and Philip S. Johnston, 159–74. Downers Grove, IL: InterVarsity Press, 2005.
- Kraus, Hans-Joachim. *Theology of the Psalms*. Minneapolis: Augsburg, 1979.
- Mays, James L. *The Lord Reigns*. Louisville: Westminster John Knox, 1994.
- McCann, J. Clinton. *A Theological Introduction to the Book of Psalms: The Psalms as Torah*. Nashville: Abingdon, 1993.
- Waltke, Bruce K. "Psalms: Theology of." In *NIDOTTE*, 5:1100–15.
- Wenham, Gordon. "The Ethics of the Psalms." In *Interpreting the Psalms: Issues and Approaches*, edited by David Firth and Philip S. Johnston, 175–94. Downers Grove, IL: InterVarsity Press, 2005.

Categories

A variety of resources are available on the various categories of Psalms. Some of these treat a single category, while others are more comprehensive.

- Allender, Dan B., and Tremper Longman III. *Cry of the Soul: How Our Emotions Reveal Our Deepest Questions About God*. Colorado Springs: NavPress, 1994.
- Barker, Kenneth L. "Praise." In *Cracking Old Testament Codes: A Guide to Interpreting the Literary Genres of the Old Testament*, edited by D. Brent Sandy and Ronald L. Giese, 217–32. Nashville: Broadman & Holman, 1995.
- Brueggemann, Walter. *The Message of the Psalms*. Minneapolis: Augsburg, 1984.
- Futato, Mark D. *Joy Comes in the Morning: Psalms for All Seasons*. Phillipsburg, NJ: P & R Publishing, 2004.
- Gerstenberger, Erhard S. *Psalms: Part 1 with an Introduction to Cultic Poetry*. FOTL. Vol. 14. Grand Rapids: Eerdmans, 1988.

- ———. *Psalms: Part 2 and Lamentations*. FOTL. Vol. 15. Grand Rapids: Eerdmans, 2001.
- Hutchinson, James Hely. "The Psalms and Praise." In *Interpreting the Psalms: Issues and Approaches*, edited by David Firth and Philip S. Johnston, 85–100. Downers Grove, IL: InterVarsity Press, 2005.
- Johnston, Philip S. "The Psalms and Distress." In *Interpreting the Psalms: Issues and Approaches*, edited by David Firth and Philip S. Johnston, 63–84. Downers Grove, IL: InterVarsity Press, 2005.
- Longman, Tremper, III. "Lament." In *Cracking Old Testament Codes: A Guide to Interpreting the Literary Genres of the Old Testament*, edited by D. Brent Sandy and Ronald L. Giese, 197–216. Nashville: Broadman & Holman, 1995.
- Westermann, Claus. *Praise and Lament in the Psalms*. Atlanta: John Knox, 1981.

Proclamation

In addition to the standard introductions to preaching, a number of books and articles focus on proclaiming Psalms or have material in them that is significant for this topic.

- Achtemeier, Elizabeth. *Preaching from the Old Testament*. Louisville: Westminster/John Knox, 1989.
- ———. "Preaching from the Psalms." *RevExp* 81 (1984): 437–49.
- Bettler, John F. "Application." In *The Preacher and Preaching: Reviving the Art in the Twentieth Century*, 331–49. Phillipsburg, NJ: P & R Publishing, 1986.
- Doriani, Daniel. *Putting the Truth to Work: The Theory and Practice of Biblical Application*. Phillipsburg, NJ: P & R Publishing, 2001.
- Goldsworthy, Graeme. *Preaching the Whole Bible as Christian Scripture*. Grand Rapids: Eerdmans, 2000.
- Long, Thomas G. *Preaching and the Literary Forms of the Bible*. Philadelphia: Fortress, 1989.

Commentaries

Commentaries on the book of Psalms abound. I have listed here those that I find most useful.

- Allen, Leslie C. *Psalms 101–150*. WBC. Rev. ed. Nashville: Thomas Nelson, 2002.
- Calvin, John. *Commentary on the Book of Psalms*. Grand Rapids: Baker, 1979.
- Clifford, Richard J. *Psalms 1–72*. AOTC. Nashville: Abingdon, 2002.
- ———. *Psalms 73–150*. AOTC. Nashville: Abingdon, 2003.
- Craigie, Peter C. *Psalms 1–50*. WBC. Waco: Word, 1983.
- Kidner, Derek. *Psalms 1–72*. TOTC. Downers Grove, IL: InterVarsity Press, 1973.
- ———. *Psalms 73–150*. TOTC. Downers Grove, IL: InterVarsity Press, 1975.
- Kraus, Hans-Joachim. *Psalms 1–59: A Commentary*. Minneapolis: Augsburg, 1988.
- ———. *Psalms 60–150: A Commentary*. Minneapolis: Augsburg, 1989.
- Limburg, James. *Psalms*. Westminster Bible Companion. Louisville: Westminster John Knox, 2000.
- Mays, James L. *Psalms*. *Int*. Louisville: John Knox, 1989.
- McCann, J. Clinton. "Psalms." In *NIB*. Vol. 4. Nashville: Abingdon, 1996.
- Tate, Marvin E. *Psalms 51–100*. WBC. Dallas: Word, 1990.
- VanGemeren, Willem. "Psalms." In *EBC*.
- Wilson, Gerald H. *Psalms Volume 1*. NIVAC. Grand Rapids: Zondervan, 2002.

4

INTERPRETING THE CATEGORIES

Let the word of Christ dwell in you richly
as you teach and admonish one another with all wisdom,
and as you sing psalms, hymns *and* spiritual songs
with gratitude in your hearts to God.
(Col. 3:16)

MUSIC COMES IN A WIDE variety of styles. Radio stations are devoted to one kind of music or another: rock, country, classical, smooth jazz, alternative, pop, etc. Without any musical training and because of our exposure to American culture, most of us can readily distinguish blues from classical, or country from jazz, even if we can't label them. The styles are noticeably different. So is the content, to one degree or another. For example, the patriotic themes found in country music are not at all characteristic of rap.

This variety is also true of writings. The different styles of a history textbook and a magazine article are immediately recognizable. The style of Dr. Seuss's *Cat in the Hat* is quite different from John Steinbeck's *Grapes of Wrath*. Again, the differences can be a matter of content as well as style. While we are not surprised to hear Lucy talking with a beaver in C. S. Lewis's *The Lion, the Witch, and the Wardrobe*, we would not tolerate such a conversation in F. Scott Fitzgerald's *The*

Great Gatsby. On the other hand, at times the content of two writings can be quite similar while the style is different. The content of this chapter, for example, overlaps considerably with that of a chapter in a previous book I wrote, but the style of the earlier work is much more popular and homiletical.[1]

Different types of literature fall into different categories.[2] The style and content we encounter in Psalms is strikingly different from that of Leviticus or Ezekiel. Psalms, Leviticus, and Ezekiel represent three different categories of literature. Moreover, the style and content of Psalms 45 and 119 are not the same. Within the general category of psalmic literature there are more specific categories. This chapter describes what categories are, why they are important for reading Psalms, what basic categories we find in Psalms, and how these categories help us read Psalms in relation to Christ.

WHAT ARE CATEGORIES?

From a literary point of view, a **category** is a group of writings that have characteristics in common with each other.[3] Without thinking much about it, we group similar writings together. We recognize all stories that begin with "Once upon a time" as fairy tales. We could collect writings that begin with "I am writing in response to last week's article" into a category called "letters to the editor." A fairy tale and a letter to the editor are quite different. We would be surprised to read about talking trees in a letter to the editor or about someone's political opinion in a fairy tale. Why? Because each category of literature follows its own rules or conventions. Knowing these rules helps us read with greater understanding.

What is true of literature in general is true of the Bible: the Bible contains different categories of literature. We can divide the Bible into two main categories—prose and poetry. We can then divide the poetry

---

1. Mark D. Futato, *Joy Comes in the Morning: Psalms for All Seasons* (Phillipsburg, NJ: P & R Publishing, 2004), chap. 1. Other material, too, in this chapter is a modified version of material that appears in said book. Published by permission.
2. What I am calling categories here is often referred to as **genre**.
3. Richard N. Soulen and R. Kendall Soulen, *Handbook of Biblical Criticism*, 3rd ed. (Louisville: Westminster John Knox Press, 2001), 66.

into a number of different kinds of poetry such as psalms, proverbs, and prophetic sermons. Each of these categories has its own "once upon a time," its own set of rules or conventions. Knowing the conventions, that is, understanding how the different categories in Psalms work, enriches our understanding and use of individual psalms.

WHY ARE CATEGORIES IMPORTANT?

Why do you need to know about the various categories in Psalms? Before answering this question, I need to discuss two related considerations. First, as mentioned earlier, we make literary identifications every time we read a newspaper article or any book in our culture. We make these identifications fluently, although unconsciously, just as first-grade children use English fluently, although they have no self-conscious understanding of grammar. In this chapter we become aware of what we've always been doing but weren't aware we were doing it.

A related consideration is the gap between our culture and the ancient culture(s) of the Bible. While we intuitively identify the category of a piece of literature we read in our own culture, the same intuitions do not work when reading literature from cultures not our own, like those of the Bible. This is true because literary conventions (rules for writing) change from culture to culture. In our culture, for example, quoting what someone wrote must be done with great precision. If Author A is quoting Author B and if Author B's work contains a typographical error that has important implications, our conventions require Author A to pass on the misspelling, followed by [sic], so that we know *precisely* who is responsible for the error.[4] The ancient world in general and the Bible in particular were not concerned with such precision in regard to quotations. Their quoting was much more like our "giving the gist" of what someone said.

This explains many differences between parallel texts in the Bible, like Matthew 6:25 and Mark 8:35, where the recorded words of Jesus are not precisely the same in both texts:

---

4. *Sic* means "thus" in Latin and is used in this way to show that the error is in the source cited.

Matthew 16:25	Mark 8:35
If you try to hang on to your life, you will lose it. But if you give up your life for my sake, you will save it. (NLT)	If you try to hang on to your life, you will lose it. But if you give up your life for my sake *and for the sake of the Good News,* you will save it. (NLT)

Mark includes the words "and for the sake of the Good News," while Matthew leaves them out. Both authors *truly* give the gist of what Jesus said without giving us *precisely* what he said.[5]

With these two considerations in mind, let's answer the question as to why categories are important.

Categories Guide Our Expectations

First of all, categories guide our expectations.[6] When, for example, you open a book and read the words "Once upon a time" you're not surprised if on page 2 you encounter a tree talking to a little girl. Why no surprise? Why no disbelief? Because the words "Once upon a time" guide your expectations. Categories determine what you will and will not expect on the following pages. "Once upon a time" indicates that you are reading a fairy tale, and trees talking to little girls is perfectly acceptable in this category.

Conversely, if you read the words, "I'm writing in regard to the article that was in the paper last week," and this piece goes on to describe a conversation between a tree and a little girl, you are quite surprised or perplexed or incredulous. Why? Because the opening words have guided your expectations. These words determine what you will and will not allow as believable in what you are reading. "I'm writing in regard to the article that was in the paper last week" indicates that you are reading a letter to the editor, and talking trees are not expected in this category.

---

5. Rarely do the authors of the Gospels record Jesus' exact words. Most of the time they give us his words in translation. Jesus taught in Aramaic, but his words are recorded in Greek. When we read Jesus' words in English, we are reading an English translation of a Greek translation of what Jesus said in Aramaic. See Mark 5:41 and 15:34 for two places where Jesus' words are not translated into Greek but are passed on in the original Aramaic.

6. See Tremper Longman III, *How to Read the Psalms* (Downers Grove, IL: InterVarsity Press, 1988), 21–23.

Let's look at how categories affect our reading of two related stories in the Bible. The first is Judges 9:8–15.

> One day the trees went out to anoint a king for themselves. They said to the olive tree, "Be our king." But the olive tree answered, "Should I give up my oil, by which both gods and men are honored, to hold sway over the trees?" Next, the trees said to the fig tree, "Come and be our king." But the fig tree replied, "Should I give up my fruit, so good and sweet, to hold sway over the trees?" Then the trees said to the vine, "Come and be our king." But the vine answered, "Should I give up my wine, which cheers both gods and men, to hold sway over the trees?" Finally all the trees said to the thornbush, "Come and be our king." The thornbush said to the trees, "If you really want to anoint me king over you, come and take refuge in my shade; but if not, then let fire come out of the thornbush and consume the cedars of Lebanon!"

Although this story is recorded in the Bible, few if any readers would believe that this conversation actually took place in real time and space between real trees and other plants. Why the disbelief? The category. The *New Living Translation* correctly discerns the presence of the fable category here and clues in the English reader with "Once upon a time." The talking plants are not characters in the narrative itself but are characters in a story being told by a character in the historical narrative. Jotham is telling a fable to make a point—much like Jesus told parables to make a point.

A second text is Numbers 22:28–30, where we read the following conversation between a donkey and a man:

> Then the LORD opened the donkey's mouth, and she said to Balaam, "What have I done to you to make you beat me these three times?" Balaam answered the donkey, "You have made a fool of me! If I had a sword in my hand, I would kill you right now." The donkey said to Balaam, "Am I not your own donkey, which you have always ridden, to this day? Have I been in the habit of doing this to you?" "No," he said.

Unlike our take on the previous story, as evangelicals we affirm that this donkey talked to Balaam in real time and real space. Why this affirmation? The category. Rather than being a character in a fable being told by a character in the narrative, this donkey is actually one of the characters in the narrative itself. The story of the talking donkey is a historical narrative, not a fable.

Why we believe that the talking trees are not historical and the talking donkey is can be answered in one word: category. Categories are important because in guiding our expectations they determine what can and cannot be found in a particular piece of literature.

Categories Provide Another Level of Context

Categories also are important because they provide an additional level of context. Context is essential for interpretation. To put it simply, context determines meaning. The same words in different contexts can have completely different meanings.

What, for example, does the following sentence mean? "That's a bad board." The answer depends on the context in which these words are spoken. Imagine that you are at the local lumberyard and you overhear a customer say to a sales representative, "That's a bad board." Here "board" means lumber and "bad" means not good, as in cracked or crooked. Now imagine that you're at the beach and you overhear one of my sons say to a fellow surfer, "That's a bad board." In this context "board" means surfboard (made out of Styrofoam and fiberglass, not wood) and "bad" means very good. Same words but different meanings. Why? Different contexts. Because context determines meaning, it is thus essential for interpretation. The better we understand the context, the better we understand the text. Categories provide a kind of context and, therefore, help us understand the text.

What does "interpreting in context" mean? It means a number of things, because there are a number of levels of context. Let's take Psalm 47 as an example. First is the literary context, provided by the surrounding psalms. In Psalm 46 the nations are in an uproar as they rage against Israel (v. 6). Psalm 47 celebrates the subduing of these nations (v. 3). And Psalm 48 recounts how the nations were turned back when they attacked Israel (vv. 4–5).

Second is the historical context of the conquest of Canaan, referred to in Psalm 47:3–4. The reference to the enemies being put "under our feet" (v. 3) must be read in the context of Joshua 10:24: "Joshua told the captains of his army, 'Come and put your feet on the kings' necks.' And they did as they were told" (NLT 1.0).

Third is the cultural context of the ancient Near East. In the ancient Near East there were many kings, and they related to each other in a variety of ways. Sometimes kings were on the same level and related as equals. At other times, one king held a dominant position in the relationship. The dominant king was the suzerain, known as the "Great King," and the subordinate king was the vassal. So Psalm 47:2 is not saying that the God of Israel is "a great king." Rather, the psalm affirms that the Lord is the supreme king, "the Great King" of all the earth.

Fourth is the theological context of the entire Bible. When Psalm 47 celebrates God's reign as the Great King over the nations, it anticipates the reign of King Jesus. Jesus was born into the royal family of David (see Matt. 1:1; Rom. 1:3). He was crucified as "King of the Jews" (Luke 23:38), and as the risen Lord he is now the "King of kings" who comes to rule the nations (Rev. 19:11–16).

Fifth is the context provided by the category. Psalm 47 is a hymn, so it is helpful to study this psalm in the context of other hymns. Psalm 47, however, is a particular kind of hymn, one that celebrates the kingship of God. Psalms 93 and 95–99 also are hymns that celebrate the kingship of God and are, therefore, helpful in giving us a better understanding of Psalm 47.

Categories, then, guide our expectations and provide another level of context to deepen our understanding of the text. Let's turn now to the basic categories we find in Psalms.

WHAT ARE THE BASIC CATEGORIES?

All the songs in the book of Psalms fall into one category—they are all psalms. But these songs can be subdivided into a number of subcategories based on certain characteristics they share. Six basic subcategories (hereafter referred to as "categories") make up the book of Psalms, the first three of which are the primary. The other three are not as frequent but are nonetheless quite important.

Hymns

Hymns were composed for times when all is well. They are songs for those trouble-free times in life, times when our lives are well ordered, well oriented.[7] The hymns typically celebrate God as Creator and God as Redeemer.

Creation hymns often praise God for the orderliness of his creation (see Ps. 104). When our lives are well ordered, they are a microcosm of the well-ordered universe. By celebrating God's good creation, we celebrate the goodness of God that we are currently experiencing.

When the hymns extol God as Redeemer, they are typically celebrating what God has done for us in *the history of his redemptive work*, rather than what God has done for us in our own *personal history*. In Old Testament terms, these psalms celebrate events in the distant past like the exodus from Egypt (see Ps. 105) or the conquest of the Promised Land (see Ps. 47). For Christians, hymns would celebrate events like the death and resurrection of Christ or the outpouring of the Holy Spirit at Pentecost. By celebrating God's redemptive work in the distant past, we celebrate the faithfulness and reliability of God as the foundation of the good life we are currently experiencing.

The hymns usually fall into three sections: an opening invitation to praise God, a central delineation of the praiseworthy character and actions of God, and a concluding affirmation of faith or a renewed invitation to praise and worship.

Hymns invite all to the concert of praise. On the smallest scale, David in Psalm 103:1-2 invites himself to praise the Lord.

> Praise the LORD, *I tell myself*;
> with my whole heart, I will praise his holy name.
> Praise the LORD, *I tell myself*,
> and never forget the good things he does for me.
> (NLT 1.0)

---

7. Walter Brueggemann, *The Message of the Psalms* (Minneapolis: Augsburg, 1984), chap. 2, refers to the hymns as "psalms of orientation."

Sometimes the psalmist broadens the invitation to all Israel, as in Psalm 118:1–2:

> Give thanks to the LORD, for he is good!
>   His faithful love endures forever.
> Let *all Israel* repeat:
>   "His faithful love endures forever."
>
>   (NLT)

At other times, the psalmist expands the invitation even farther to include all the nations. Thus Psalm 117, the shortest psalm, begins,

> Praise the LORD, *all you nations*;
>   extol him, *all you peoples*.

On several occasions, Psalm 29 being one, the psalmist transcends the earth to enlist the angels of heaven in the praise of God.

> Give honor to the LORD, you *angels*;
>   give honor to the LORD for his glory and strength.
> Give honor to the LORD for the glory of his name.
>   Worship the LORD in the splendor of his holiness.
>
>   (vv. 1–2 NLT 1.0)

In unmatched exuberance, Psalm 148 calls the whole created realm to join the chorus. Verses 1–6 address heaven and its countless hosts.

> Praise the LORD from *the heavens* . . .

And verses 7–14 summon every part of the terrestrial globe—animate and inanimate—to worship the God who has created and maintains this wonderful world.

> Praise the LORD from *the earth* . . .

The central section of a hymn provides motivation to praise or the actual substance of praise by recalling who God is and what he has done. Praise is the acknowledgement or confession of God's attributes and actions.[8] The closest thing to a definition of "praise" is found in Psalm 34:1–3, where David says,

> I will *praise* the LORD at all times. . . .
> Come, let us *tell* of the LORD's greatness.
>
> (NLT)

To praise is to tell others just how great the Lord is in terms of who he is and what he has done. Psalm 34 amplifies the greatness of God in terms of how God answers prayer (v. 4) because God is so good (v. 8).

> I sought the LORD, and he answered me;
>   he delivered me from all my fears. . . .
> Taste and see that the LORD is *good*.

This central section frequently takes up most of the space in the hymns of praise and brings into focus various themes relating to God's attributes and actions. Psalmists often introduce these themes with the Hebrew word כִּי, which can be translated "for" or "because." Following are just a few examples. Psalm 30:1–2 [2-3] draws our attention to the healing mercy of God.

> I will exalt you, LORD, *for* [כִּי] you rescued me. . . .
> O LORD my God, I cried to you for help,
>   and *you restored my health*.
>
> (NLT)

Psalm 47:1–2 [2-3] highlights the kingship of God.

> Come, everyone! Clap your hands!
>   Shout to God with joyful praise!
> *For* [כִּי] the LORD Most High is awesome.
>   He is *the great King* of all the earth.
>
> (NLT)

---

8. Mark D. Futato, *Transformed by Praise: The Purpose and Message of the Psalms* (Phillipsburg, NJ: P & R Publishing, 2002), 7–10.

Psalm 117:1–2 focuses on the unfailing love of God.

> Praise the LORD, all you nations;
>> extol him, all you peoples.
> *For* [כִּי] great is his love toward us.

God's delight in us is the theme of praise in Psalm 149.

> Sing to the LORD a new song,
>> his praise in the assembly of the saints. . . .
> *For* [כִּי] the LORD takes delight in his people.
>> (vv. 1, 4)

In the central section, then, the hymns provide us with an abundance of reasons for giving praise to the Lord.

In keeping with the positive tone of the first two sections, the hymns come to a conclusion on an equally positive note. Quite frequently, the conclusion contains a repeated call to praise, as in Psalm 103:20–22.

> Praise the LORD, you his angels,
>> you mighty ones who do his bidding,
>> who obey his word.
> Praise the LORD, all his heavenly hosts,
>> you his servants who do his will.
> Praise the LORD, all his works
>> everywhere in his dominion.
> Praise the LORD, O my soul.

Matching the first two lines of this song of praise, the last line calls David himself to praise the Lord.[9] This conclusion, however, extends beyond David and invites the angels, and in fact the whole created realm, to join the concert of praise.

The hymns also may come to a close with a strong affirmation of faith and confidence in the Lord, as is the case in Psalm 29:10–11,

---

9. The Hebrew is actually a command addressed to the self, and the first four words of verse 1 and last four words of verse 22 are identical in Hebrew (בָּרֲכִי נַפְשִׁי אֶת־יהוה).

which affirms that the Lord is in control of the world and this control
will result in great blessing.

> The LORD sits enthroned over the flood;
>   the LORD is enthroned as King forever.
> The LORD gives strength to his people;
>   the LORD blesses his people with peace.

As we have seen, a bright, positive mood characterizes the hymn.
The chaotic side of life lies in the distant background in these psalms.
The foreground, on the other hand, is filled with faith—faith in the
goodness and faithfulness of God, faith that the world in which we live
will be experienced as good day after day because God governs all. So
the key word of the hymn is "praise." The hymns exalt God for this
life, for the life of all creation, for life that is good.

Laments

We do not always experience life as well ordered or well oriented.
"Disorientation" better describes life at times.[10] The **laments**, or songs
of disorientation, were written for such times.

These are times when you may feel tremendously perplexed or ut-
terly forsaken or paralyzed by fear or overwhelmed with anger or lost
in despair. These are times when you cry out, "My God, my God, why
have you forsaken me? Why are you so far from saving me, so far from
the words of my groaning?" (Ps. 22:1) or "How long, O LORD? Will
you forget me forever? How long will you hide your face from me?
How long must I wrestle with my thoughts and every day have sorrow
in my heart? How long will my enemy triumph over me?" (Ps. 13:1–2)
or "You have taken my companions and loved ones from me; the darkness is my closest friend" (Ps. 88:18).

The laments are the psalms composed for what some have called
"the dark night of the soul," for times when "weeping may last through
the night" (Ps. 30:5 NLT), perhaps even night after night after night

---

10. Brueggemann, *Message of the Psalms*, chap. 3, refers to the laments as "psalms of
    disorientation."

(Ps. 6:6). The psalms of disorientation give us permission, and show us how, to let the tears flow.

While the dominant note in the lament is a sad one, the final note is typically upbeat. The laments almost always move from negative to positive, from plea to praise. There are only two laments that do not exhibit this movement—Psalms 44 and 88. Psalm 88 is the darkest lament, ending with no hope.

> You have taken my companions and loved ones from me;
>   the darkness is my closest friend.
>
> (v. 18)

But such despair is the exception rather than the rule in the laments. Instead, movement from plea to praise is expected.[11]

Laments typically answer three questions in the plea section: "Who?" "Why?" and "What?"

"Who is there to hear the psalmist pray?" Language like "O God" and "O LORD" regularly punctuates the beginning of laments.

> O LORD, how many are my foes!
>   (3:1)

> Answer me when I call to you, O God.
>   (4:1 NLT)

> Give ear to my words, O LORD, consider my sighing.
>   (5:1)

> O LORD, do not rebuke me in your anger.
>   (6:1)

> Keep me safe, O God.
>   (16:1)

---

11. The book of Psalms as a whole exhibits this same movement from plea to praise, from suffering to glory, as does the life of Christ. For more on this, see chapter 2, and Futato, *Transformed by Praise*, 11–25.

God translates the Hebrew word אֱלֹהִים and refers to God as transcendent, as far above us, as the God of the universe. In keeping with this, *God* is the way the Creator is referred to in Genesis 1, where we read of God's creation of the universe. "*LORD*," on the other hand, is the English rendering of God's personal name, the name by which God relates intimately with people.[12] "*LORD*" is appropriately the way the Creator is referred to in Genesis 2, where we read of God's personal relationship with humans in the garden of Eden. This personal relationship is at the heart of God's revealing to Moses the significance of God's personal name in Exodus 3:12–14.

> And God said, "I will be with you. And this will be the sign to you that it is I who have sent you: When you have brought the people out of Egypt, you will worship God on this mountain."
> Moses said to God, "Suppose I go to the Israelites and say to them, 'The God of your fathers has sent me to you,' and they ask me, 'What is his name?' Then what shall I tell them?"
> God said to Moses, "I AM WHO I AM. This is what you are to say to the Israelites: 'I AM has sent me to you.'"

The point is, the psalms teach us to call out to the One who is at the same time the Almighty God of the universe and the ever-so-close and personal LORD. Psalm 109:26 captures both of these perspectives with these words: "Help me, O LORD my *God!*"

A second question the plea section answers is "Why?" "Why am I experiencing trouble?" Here we discover the nature of the trouble the psalmist is in and the reason(s) for the lament. The psalmist provides answers to the "why" question in the form of complaint and confession.

The complaint is not a rebellious complaining like that of Israel in the wilderness (see, e.g., Num. 11:1; 14:2; 16:11). The complaint is

---

12. The English tradition of using *LORD* (written in small capitals) to render God's personal name (יְהוָה) is rooted in the ancient Greek tradition, which uses the word κύριος ("lord") to render יהוה. The Greek tradition is itself rooted in the ancient Hebrew tradition, which substituted the Hebrew word אֲדֹנָי ("my lord") for God's personal name in order to avoid misusing the name, as required by the third commandment: "Do not misuse the name of the LORD your God" (Exod. 20:7 NLT 1.0). The Greek word κύριος is also used in the New Testament in reference to Jesus Christ. Thus to confess that Jesus is κύριος ("Lord") is to confess that Jesus is the God of Israel.

simply the psalmist spelling out with great emotion the struggles being experienced. This complaint can go in three directions. The complaint may be directed toward other people, toward the self, or toward God.

> O LORD, I have *so many enemies*.
> (Ps. 3:1 NLT)

> O LORD, hear me as I pray;
> pay attention to *my groaning*.
> (Ps. 5:1 NLT)

> O LORD, why do *you* stand so far away?
> (Ps. 10:1 NLT)

Honesty is the operative word here. Through the laments the Holy Spirit gives us great encouragement and great freedom to express *all* that we are thinking and feeling, whether those thoughts and feelings are about ourselves, others, or even God.

The confession may go in one of two directions. Often the psalmist confesses his sin. Psalm 38:3–5 contains a good example.

> Because of your wrath there is no health in my body;
>   my bones have no soundness because of my sin.
> My guilt has overwhelmed me
>   like a burden too heavy to bear.
> My wounds fester and are loathsome
>   because of my sinful folly.

As this psalm illustrates, there is often a connection in the Bible between character and consequence. Living in keeping with God's instruction enhances life,[13] while violating divine principles diminishes

---

13. This connection is a frequent theme in the book of Proverbs and in the psalms that share wisdom themes, like Psalm 112: "Happy are those who fear the LORD. Yes, happy are those who delight in doing what he commands. Their children will be successful everywhere; an entire generation of godly people will be blessed. They themselves will be wealthy. . . . All goes well for those who are generous. . . . Such people will not be overcome by evil circumstances. . . . They will have influence and honor" (vv. 1–3, 5, 6, 9 NLT 1.0).

life. When reading the laments, therefore, we often hear a confession of sin in the context of the experience of trouble.[14]

On the other hand, the confession may be of the psalmist's innocence. Psalm 26:1–3 provides one of the best examples of such a confession.

> Declare me innocent, O LORD,
>   for I have acted with integrity;
>   I have trusted in the LORD without wavering.
> Put me on trial, LORD, and cross-examine me.
>   Test my motives and my heart.
> For I am always aware of your unfailing love,
>   and I have lived according to your truth.
>
> (NLT)

This is not the prayer of a misguided and self-righteous person, because the David who in Psalm 26 confesses his innocence is the same David who just confessed his sin in Psalm 25.

> Remember not the sins of my youth.
>
> (v. 7 KJV)

> Forgive my iniquity, though it is great.
>
> (v. 11 TNIV)

> Take away all my sins.
>
> (v. 18)

Rather, Psalm 26 is the prayer David offered in a particular situation in which he was accused of some wrongdoing but was, in fact, innocent. David experienced the pain of false accusations a number of times in his life, and when he did, his lamentation included a confession of his innocence (see, e.g., Pss. 4:1–3 and 7:1–9). Through the laments the Holy Spirit teaches us to confess our sin, when appropriate, and to say, "I am innocent," when we are in the right.[15]

---

14. This is not to say that life has no mysteries, as in the story of Job. It is to say that not all times of trouble are Job-like in character.

15. For a fuller discussion, see the material in chapter 5 on reading the text in literary context (pages 186–89).

The third question the plea section seeks to answer is "What?" "What does the psalmist want God to do?"

Concreteness characterizes the psalmist's pleas at this point in the lament. The psalmist makes very specific requests of God, requests that correspond to the nature of the trouble. Has the psalmist sinned? The request is then for forgiveness.

> *Forgive* the rebellious sins of my youth;
>   look instead through the eyes of your unfailing love,
>   for you are merciful, O LORD.
>
> > (Ps. 25:7 NLT 1.0)

> Help us, O God our Savior,
>   for the glory of your name;
> deliver us and *forgive* our sins
>   for your name's sake.
>
> > (Ps. 79:9)

Is the psalmist ill? The request is then for healing.

> Be merciful to me, LORD, for I am faint;
>   O LORD, *heal* me, for my bones are in agony.
>
> > (Ps. 6:2 [3])

> I said, "O LORD, have mercy on me;
>   *heal* me, for I have sinned against you."
>
> > (Ps. 41:4 [5])

Has the psalmist been falsely accused? The request is then for vindication.

> *Declare me innocent*, O LORD,
>   for I have acted with integrity;
>   I have trusted in the LORD without wavering.
>
> > (Ps. 26:1 NLT)

> *Declare me innocent*, O God!
>   *Defend* me against these ungodly people.
>   Rescue me from these unjust liars.
>   (Ps. 43:1 NLT)

Is the psalmist under attack by adversaries? Then the request is for deliverance.

> Rise up, O LORD, confront them, bring them down;
>   *rescue* me from the wicked by your sword.
>   (Ps. 17:13)

> My times are in your hands;
>   *deliver* me from my enemies
>   and from those who pursue me.
>   (Ps. 31:15 [16])

Is the psalmist weak? The request then is for support.

> *Sustain* me according to your promise, and I will live;
>   do not let my hopes be dashed.
> *Uphold* me, and I will be delivered;
>   I will always have regard for your decrees.
>   (Ps. 119:116–117)

In all of these requests the psalmists are very much concerned with experiencing the help of God *in this life*. This is not to say that Psalms has no interest in the life to come. Rather, through the psalms the Holy Spirit teaches us that we can expect God's salvation to affect our lives now in concrete ways. This confident expectation comes to expression perhaps nowhere more clearly than in Psalm 27:13.

> Yet I am confident that I will see the LORD's goodness
>   while I am here in the land of the living.
>   (NLT)

The plea is usually the larger of the two movements of a lament. Characteristically the praise movement is shorter and is positive in tone. For example, the praise movement may contain a statement of trust or confidence.

> I will lie down and sleep in peace,
>> for you alone, O LORD, make me dwell in safety.
>>> (Ps. 4:8)

> My enemies will retreat when I call to you for help.
>> This I know: God is on my side.
>>> (Ps. 56:9 NLT)

The psalmist also may express a deep assurance that God will answer prayer and grant the request made in the plea movement.

> The LORD has heard my plea;
>> the LORD will answer my prayer.
>>> (Ps. 6:9 [10] NLT)

> You hear, O LORD, the desire of the afflicted;
>> you encourage them, and you listen to their cry.
>>> (Ps. 10:17)

The praise movement also may contain a vow or promise to give God thanks and offer sacrifice at the temple after God answers the psalmist's prayer. Psalm 66:13–14 refers to the making of such a vow.

> I will come to your temple with burnt offerings
>> and fulfill my vows to you—
> vows my lips promised and my mouth spoke
>> when I was in trouble.

Laments record such vows.

> I will praise you in the great assembly;
>   I will fulfill my vows in the presence
>   of those who worship you.
>   (Ps. 22:25 NLT)

> I will fulfill my vows to you, O God,
>   and will offer a sacrifice of thanks for your help.
>   (Ps. 56:12 NLT)

Most of us have experienced trouble—to one degree or another, for long or shorter periods of time. The journey of life may at times take us over some very difficult terrain. Adversity replaces prosperity. Turmoil swallows up tranquility. Chaos obliterates order. Doubt replaces faith. God has given us the laments for times such as these.

Songs of Thanksgiving

Although "weeping may last through the night," says Psalm 30, "joy comes in the morning" (v. 5 [6] NLT). The time eventually comes when you look back at the troublesome days and say to God, "You have turned my mourning into joyful dancing. You have taken away my clothes of mourning and clothed me with joy" (Ps. 30:11 [12] NLT). You experience God parting the heavens and coming down (see Ps. 144:5) to deliver you from the disorienting trouble you are in. The **songs of thanksgiving** express joy and gratitude to God for this deliverance.

Like the hymns, the songs of thanksgiving celebrate God's redemptive work, but they celebrate that redemptive work in your own personal history. These psalms thank God for lifting you personally "out of the pit of despair, out of the mud and the mire" and for setting your "feet on solid ground" once again (Ps. 40:2 [3] NLT), for eliminating the chaos and reestablishing good order in your life.

The songs of thanksgiving thus functioned as one key component of grateful worship that celebrated the goodness of God in delivering people from trouble in this life. Thus, these songs are sequels to the laments. This is clear from their basic content as well as from part of their basic structure.

The songs of thanksgiving often can be divided into three sections. The opening section typically begins with the psalmist's intention to thank or praise God.

> I will praise the LORD at all times.
>   I will constantly speak his praises.
>   (Ps. 34:1 NLT)

> We give thanks to you, O God,
>   we give thanks, for your Name is near.
>   (Ps. 75:1)

The songs of thanksgiving also may begin on a note of loving gratitude for divine intervention.

> I love the LORD, for he heard my voice;
>   he heard my cry for mercy.
>   (Ps. 116:1)

> I love you, O LORD, my strength.
>   (Ps. 18:1)

The central section mirrors the song of lament, as the psalmist here recounts his trouble, his petition, and his deliverance. Sometimes this recounting is fairly extensive. In Psalm 18 David recounts his past experience twice, in verses 4–19 and 31–45. At other times the recounting of the past is much briefer.

> I prayed to the LORD, and he answered me.
>   He freed me from all my fears.
> Those who look to him for help will be radiant with joy;
>   no shadow of shame will darken their faces.
> In my desperation I prayed, and the LORD listened;
>   he saved me from all my troubles.
>   (Ps. 34:4–6 [5–7] NLT)

The concluding section typically is characterized by renewed thanksgiving. The thanksgiving may be continued praise and thanks offered by the psalmist.

> Praise be to God,
>   who has not rejected my prayer
>   or withheld his love from me!
>   (Ps. 66:20)

Or the thanksgiving may come in the form of a promise to praise God in the future.

> Therefore I will praise you among the nations, O LORD;
>   I will sing praises to your name.
>   (Ps. 18:49 [50])

Or the psalmist may conclude by inviting others to join in the thanksgiving.

> Give thanks to the LORD, for he is good;
>   his love endures forever.
>   (Ps. 118:29)

In the preceding three categories of the psalms, we find songs for various stretches on the path of life. There may be stretches when all is well; at other times the going may be pretty rough; but the rough road eventually gives way once again to the smooth. For each of these stretches, respectively, God has given songs to us: hymns, laments, and songs of thanksgiving.

While these three are the primary categories of psalms, there are others as well. We will now look at three other significant categories.

Songs of Confidence

Somewhere between the laments and the songs of thanksgiving lie the **songs of confidence**. While some scholars see the songs of confidence as a development of the expressions of confidence that often bring a lament to conclusion, others associate the songs of confidence more with the songs of thanksgiving.[16] Reasons can be given for both of these connections.

Like laments, the songs of confidence often have some kind of personal trouble in view. This trouble does not seem quite as painful as in the laments. The trouble feels a bit farther away, but it is nonetheless felt. Like the songs of thanksgiving, on the other hand, the songs of confidence express undoubted assurance in God's power to save. This confident mood is the dominant theme and defining characteristic of this category.

As I will explain, the psalms of confidence are, however, neither laments nor songs of thanksgiving. They lack the anguish and the structural elements that characterize the laments. And although confident in God's power to save, the poets who wrote the songs of confidence had not yet experienced that salvation at the time of composition. While these poets seemingly have moved beyond the deep agony of the lament, they are still waiting for the day when a song of thanksgiving for salvation gained can be sung.[17]

Given these fuzzy boundaries, we should not be surprised that scholars differ to some degree over which psalms belong to this category. Tremper Longman, for example, includes Psalms 11, 16, 23, 27, 62, 91, 121, 125, and 131,[18] whereas C. Hassell Bullock lists Psalms 4, 16, 23, 27, 62, 73, 90, 115, 123, 124, 125, and 126.[19] My own analysis yields the following as songs of confidence: Psalms 16, 23, 27, 62, 73, 91, 115, 121, 125, and 131.

While the songs of confidence have no unifying structural shape, several characteristics nonetheless hold this category together.[20] As the name indicates, the distinguishing characteristic of this category is their unwavering confidence or trust in God's ability and willingness to deliver from adverse circumstances. Psalm 27 is an example.

---

16. Ernest C. Lucas, *Exploring the Old Testament: A Guide to the Psalms and Wisdom Literature* (Downers Grove, IL: InterVarsity Press, 2003), 9.

17. C. Hassell Bullock, *Encountering the Book of Psalms* (Grand Rapids: Baker, 2001), 166.

18. Longman, *How to Read the Psalms*, 31.

19. Bullock, *Encountering the Book of Psalms*, 168.

20. Ibid., 168–70.

> The LORD is my light and my salvation—
> whom shall I fear?
> The LORD is the stronghold of my life—
> of whom shall I be afraid? . . .
> Though an army besiege me,
> my heart will not fear;
> though war break out against me,
> even then will I be confident. . . .
> I am still confident of this:
> I will see the goodness of the LORD
> in the land of the living.
> (vv. 1, 3, 13)

The basis for this confidence is rooted in the character of God and often comes to expression through the images that are used for God in these psalms. The most frequent image is God as refuge.

> Keep me safe, O God,
> for in you I take *refuge*.
> (Ps. 16:1)

> The LORD is the *stronghold* of my life—
> of whom shall I be afraid?
> (Ps. 27:1)

> My soul finds rest in God alone;
> my salvation comes from him.
> He alone is my *rock* and my salvation;
> he is my *fortress*, I will never be shaken.
> (Ps. 62:1–2 [2–3])

> I will say of the LORD, "He is my *refuge* and my *fortress*,
> my God, in whom I trust."
> (Ps. 91:2)

Arguably the best known and most loved image of God in the Bible occurs in a song of confidence.

The LORD is my shepherd;
I have all that I need.
(Ps. 23:1 NLT)

Implicit in another psalm of confidence is perhaps the most tender image for God found in the Psalms, God as mother of a weaned child.

But I have stilled and quieted my soul;
like a weaned child with its mother,
like a weaned child is my soul within me.
(Ps. 131:2)

Psalm 121 uses the image of God as guardian six times (vv. 3, 4, 5, 7 [2x], 8), and Psalm 125 likens God's surrounding protection to that of the mountains that surround Jerusalem.

Just as the mountains surround and protect Jerusalem,
so the LORD surrounds and protects his people,
both now and forever.
(v. 2 NLT 1.0)

In these psalms the poets not only articulate their own confidence in God but also invite others to share their confidence.

Wait patiently for the LORD.
Be brave and courageous.
Yes, wait patiently for the LORD.
(Ps. 27:14 NLT)

While it's possible that in the above, the psalmist is addressing himself, or that a priest is addressing the psalmist, it's more likely that the psalmist is addressing another.[21] This conclusion is reached though interpreting the above line in the context of similar lines that are found in other psalms in this category. The following lines demonstrate the similarity:

---

21. Gerald H. Wilson, *Psalms Volume 1*, NIVAC (Grand Rapids: Zondervan, 2002), 487.

> Trust in him at all times, O people;
>   pour out your hearts to him,
>   for God is our refuge.
>   (Ps. 62:8 [9])

> O house of Israel, trust in the LORD . . .
> O house of Aaron, trust in the LORD . . .
> You who fear him, trust in the LORD . . .
>   (Ps. 115:9–11)

> O Israel, put your hope in the LORD
>   both now and forevermore.
>   (Ps. 131:3)

The expressions of confidence in this category are "expressions of faith, not cries of victory."[22] These psalms articulate a confidence that has moved the psalmist away from the deep anguish of the lament and toward the joy of the song of thanksgiving. While the psalmist is confident that help is on the way, that help has not yet arrived. This is clear from the oblique allusions and references to present trouble, as well as from the petitions, that are found in the psalms of confidence.

> Keep me safe, O God,
>   for in you I take refuge.
>   (Ps. 16:1)

> Hear my voice when I call, O LORD;
>   be merciful to me and answer me.
>   (Ps. 27:7)

> So many enemies against one man—
>   all of them trying to kill me.
> To them I'm just a broken-down wall
>   or a tottering fence.
>   (Ps. 62:3 [4] NLT)

---

22. Bullock, *Encountering the Book of Psalms*, 168.

> I lift up my eyes to the hills—
>   where does my help come from?
>   (Ps. 121:1)

> The wicked will not rule the land of the godly,
>   for then the godly might be tempted to do wrong.
>   (Ps. 125:3 NLT)

While bringing great comfort, the songs of confidence also bring a great challenge. It is one thing to sing a hymn when all is well, or a lament when trouble is on all sides, or a song of thanksgiving when God has delivered us from distress. In each of these cases our song and our circumstances match. To express profound confidence in God when help has not yet come is quite another matter. In this case we experience a disconnect between our song and our situation. As we have seen, however, our confidence is not rooted in our situation but in the character of God. He is our refuge, our shepherd, our "mother," our guardian, and our surrounding mountain.

And, of course, he is our King who reigns over our lives and the world he has made. It is fitting at this point, then, to look at a category of psalms that celebrate God's kingship.

Divine Kingship Songs

Like the songs of confidence, the **divine kingship songs** have no common structure. The primary characteristic that holds this category together is the focus on the kingship of God.[23] Other frequent themes that occur in this category are God's works of creation, redemption, and judgment,[24] God's supremacy over the gods of the nations, and God's universal care for the nations.[25]

Also, the boundaries of this category, as for the songs of confidence, are a bit fuzzy. We might think of this category of psalms in terms of concentric circles. Some are at the core, while others move away

---

23. Another group of psalms, the "royal psalms," focus on the human king. See the excursus at the end of the chapter.
24. See chapter 2, pages 90–91 for the meaning of *judge* in these psalms.
25. J. D. W. Watts "YHWH-Malak Psalms," *TZ* 21 (1965): 341–48.

toward the periphery. Certainly at the core of this group are Psalms 93, 97, and 99, each of which opens with the affirmation יְהוָה מָלָךְ.[26] Psalm 96 also employs this affirmation, albeit within the body of the psalm and not in the opening line.

Scholars have debated how best to translate the phrase יְהוָה מָלָךְ. All major English translations use a present tense, "the LORD reigns" or "the LORD is king." This is a bit odd, however, since this verb form in Hebrew is elsewhere typically translated with a past tense (e.g., "has become king" or "was king" or "reigned"). Here are just two examples:

> Go in to King David and say to him, "My lord the king, did you not swear to me your servant: 'Surely Solomon your son shall be king after me, and he will sit on my throne'? Why then has Adonijah *become king* [מָלָךְ]?" (1 Kings 1:13)

> Rehoboam son of Solomon *was king* [מָלָךְ] in Judah. He was forty-one years old when he became king, and *he reigned* [מָלַךְ] seventeen years in Jerusalem. (1 Kings 14:21)

Contrary to the often-repeated claim that the grammar of this phrase allows for either a present or a past rendering, "is king" in an ongoing sense is not attested anywhere in the Hebrew Bible.[27] When the ancients wanted to affirm God's ongoing reign, they used a nominal clause, e.g., כִּי מֶלֶךְ כָּל־הָאָרֶץ אֱלֹהִים, "For God *is the king* of all the earth" (Ps. 47:7 [8]). Moreover, whether the personal name comes before or after the verb in Hebrew does not matter. Both word orders are used in Hebrew for "has become king."

> Then Nathan asked Bathsheba, Solomon's mother, "Have you not heard that Adonijah, the son of Haggith, has become king מָלַךְ אֲדֹנִיָּהוּ—verb + name] without our lord David's knowing it? (1 Kings 1:11)

---

26. C. John Collins, *Introduction to the Hebrew Bible* (Minneapolis: Fortress, 2004), 464.
27. John Day, *Psalms*, OTG (Sheffield: Sheffield Academic Press, 1995), 76.

"But now Adonijah has become king [מָלַךְ אֲדֹנִיָּה—name + verb], and you, my lord the king, do not know about it." (1 Kings 1:18)

The bottom line is that whether or not we translate יְהוָה מָלָךְ "is king" or "has become king," it is clear that יְהוָה מָלָךְ has an event in view in the immediate past, not a general state of sovereignty. So, for example, when the NIV translates מָלַךְ אַבְשָׁלוֹם with "Absalom is king" (2 Sam. 15:10), it is still clear from the context that the crowd is proclaiming that Absalom *has just now become king*. We will consider the theological implications of this interpretation shortly.

Psalm 47 also belongs to the divine kingship psalms, although it is slightly removed from the core. Psalm 47:8 [9] has a modified version of the יְהוָה מָלָךְ formula: מָלַךְ אֱלֹהִים ("God has become king" [author's translation]).[28] This expression in this context lends support to rendering יְהוָה מָלָךְ with "The LORD has become king." In verse 3 [4] God defeats the nations. In verse 5 [6] God returns to the city in triumphal procession. In verse 7 [8] God is proclaimed king over the nations. In verse 8 [9] God takes his seat on his throne and begins his new reign. In verse 9 [10] the rulers of the newly subjected nations assemble before their new king. Here, God has become king in a new sense, because he has won a new victory that has brought his kingdom to realization in a new way.[29]

Also fitting into this category are Psalms 95 and 98. Although lacking the acclamation "the LORD has become king," these psalms are clustered with the core (Pss. 93; 96; 97; 99) and celebrate the Lord's kingship.

> For the LORD is the great God,
> the great King above all gods.
> (Ps. 95:3)

---

28. This shift is understandable given that Psalm 47 is part of the Elohistic Psalter, a group of psalms (Pss. 42–83) that refers to God as אֱלֹהִים (204x) more frequently than as Yahweh (46x). See Willem VanGemeren, "Psalms," in *EBC*, 20.

29. See Richard J. Clifford, *Psalms 73–150*, AOTC (Nashville: Abingdon, 2003), 108: "Kingship was understood concretely as resulting from specific victory."

> With trumpets and the blast of the ram's horn—
> shout for joy before the LORD, the King.
>
> (Ps. 98:6)

Psalms 24 and 29, too, although not customarily included in this category, are part of this group even if they lie at the periphery. Like Psalms 47 and 93, Psalm 24 celebrates the "King of glory" ascending into the royal city, having shown himself victorious in battle.

> Who is this King of glory?
> The LORD strong and mighty,
> the LORD mighty in battle.
>
> (v. 8)

The victory in this case is alluded to in the opening lines of the poem.

> The earth is the LORD's, and all it contains,
> The world and those who dwell in it.
> For he founded it upon the seas
> and established it upon the rivers.
>
> (vv. 1–2 NASB)

The "seas" and "rivers" are typical parts of the mythopoeic picture of God's defeat of chaos and his establishment of cosmic order on these defeated foes.[30]

Psalm 29 likewise alludes to God's vanquishing of the sea. Verse 3 refers to the Lord as one who "thunders over the mighty waters" (מַיִם רַבִּים). These "mighty waters" are the forces of chaos[31] defeated by the Lord, as proclaimed in the shortest of the songs of divine Kingship, Psalm 93.

> The seas have lifted up, O LORD,
> the seas have lifted up their voice;
> the seas have lifted up their pounding waves.

---

30. Richard J. Clifford, *Psalms 1–72*, AOTC (Nashville: Abingdon, 2002), 134. See my excursus on mythopoeic imagery at the end of chapter 1.

31. See Wilson, *Psalms Volume 1*, 506; and Clifford, *Psalms 1–72*, 155.

Mightier than the thunder of the great waters [מַיִם רַבִּים],
    mightier than the breakers of the sea—
the LORD on high is mighty.

(Ps. 93:3–4)

This defeat of the "mighty waters" in Psalm 29:3 is coupled with the Lord manifesting himself in a powerful thunderstorm that signals the onset of the rainy season, the *sine qua non* of cosmic order for the ancient Israelite (vv. 4–9). The establishment of cosmic order is then followed by the Lord's enthronement as king in verse 10.[32]

The LORD sits enthroned over the flood;
    the LORD is enthroned as King forever.

Now that we have surveyed the psalms that compose this category, we can synthesize the overarching message of these particular psalms. First, the divine kingship psalms proclaim God's victory over the forces that oppose a well-ordered and abundant life for his people. Sometimes these forces are cosmic (Pss. 24; 29; 93), and the order established is cosmic as well. This is part of the reason why the theme of God as Creator and Sustainer of the universe is a regular feature in this group.[33] At other times the opposing forces are human (Pss. 47; 97; 99), and God's order is established among the nations.[34] The victory God wins is in some sense a new victory, which is why it is the occasion for singing a "new song."

Sing to the LORD a new song;
    sing to the LORD, all the earth.
Sing to the LORD, praise his name;
    proclaim his salvation day after day.

(Ps. 96:1–2)

---

32. See Wilson, *Psalms Volume 1*, 506–7.
33. See Psalms 24:1–2; 29:3–9; 93:1–2; 95:4–5; 96:5, 10–13; 98:7–9.
34. See Psalms 47:9–10; 96:3; 97:1; 98:2; 99:1–3.

> Sing to the LORD a new song,
>   for he has done marvelous things;
>   his right hand and his holy arm
>   have worked salvation for him.
>   (Ps. 98:1)

This new victory is the occasion, and the new song is a celebration, of a new realization of the Lord's kingship. So these psalms celebrate the Lord's ascension to his throne and announce the inauguration of a new phase of his reign with the acclamation: "The LORD has become King!" (author's translation).[35]

These psalms thus instruct us to affirm God's sovereign reign over the affairs of the world he has made and to anticipate the coming of his kingdom in greater and greater ways until he begins to reign in a consummate way and we can say,

> We give thanks to you, Lord God Almighty,
>   the One who is and who was,
> because you have taken your great power
>   and *have begun to reign*.
>   (Rev. 11:17)

Moreover, these psalms may have been in the back of Jesus' mind when he taught us to pray, "your kingdom come, your will be done on earth as it is in heaven" (Matt. 6:10). Wherever we see chaos in this world, we can hope for the in-breaking of God's order that issues in life in all of its abundance.

> Say among the nations, "The LORD reigns."
>   The world is firmly established, it cannot be moved;
>   he will judge the peoples with equity.
> Let the heavens rejoice, let the earth be glad;
>   let the sea resound, and all that is in it;
>   let the fields be jubilant, and everything in them.

---

35. Psalms 93:1; 97:1; 99:1 (and 47:8 [9] in modified form).

> Then all the trees of the forest will sing for joy;
>   they will sing before the LORD, for he comes,
>   he comes to judge the earth.
> He will judge the world in righteousness
>   and the peoples in his truth.
>
> (Ps. 96:10–13)

Because God is king over all the earth, this well-ordered, abundant life can be a vibrant hope for all the nations of the earth. As we learned in chapter 2, a concomitant element of such an abundant life is a life lived in keeping with God's instruction (תּוֹרָה). This is the life of wisdom that the nations are invited to live out in the presence of the "One enthroned in heaven" (Ps. 2:4): "Therefore, you kings, be wise" (Ps. 2:10). The promise to all who follow this wisdom and submit to the divine King is a blessed life: "Blessed are all who take refuge in him" (Ps. 2:12). It is natural, therefore, to follow our discussion of the divine kingship songs with a look at one final category, the wisdom songs.[36]

Wisdom Songs

Of all the categories studied in this chapter, that of **wisdom songs** is perhaps the most elusive. Some scholars go as far as to deny the existence of the category altogether,[37] but this is surely an unwarranted claim. On a pop quiz, who would not assign the following line to Ecclesiastes or Job?

> For all can see that wise men die;
>   the foolish and the senseless alike perish
>   and leave their wealth to others.

---

36. For more on the interfacing of the royal and wisdom motifs in the book of Psalms, see Gerald H. Wilson, "Shaping the Psalter: A Consideration of Editorial Linkage in the Book of Psalms," in *The Shape and Shaping of the Psalter*, JSOTSup, ed. J. Clinton McCann (Sheffield, England: JSOT, 1993), 78–81. See also the excursus on royal psalms at the end of this chapter.

37. J. Luyten, "Psalm 73 and Wisdom," in *La sagesse de l'Ancien Testament*, BETL, ed. M. Gilbert (Leuven: Leuven University Press, 1979), 63–64.

Yet this line is from Psalm 49:10. Some psalms, then, have an obvious affinity with the wisdom literature.[38]

In his book *The Tree of Life: An Exploration of Biblical Wisdom Literature*, Roland Murphy devotes a chapter to "Echoes of Wisdom" found in the Hebrew Bible outside of Job, Proverbs, and Ecclesiastes. In that chapter Murphy sets out two characteristics of the wisdom category of psalms: the presence of wisdom diction and wisdom themes.[39] By wisdom diction Murphy refers to such things as the אַשְׁרֵי formula ("O the joys"), numerical sayings, "better than" sayings, alphabetic structuring, and admonitions. A convergence of such diction, together with representative wisdom themes—such as the way of the righteous and the way of the wicked, the contrast between the wise and the foolish, practical advice, retribution, and the fear of the Lord—suffices to warrant the placing of given psalms in the wisdom category. To Murphy's two characteristics we could add the reflective and explicitly didactic tone found in the wisdom songs.[40] The result is the following list of Psalms that I would include in the wisdom category: 1, 19, 32, 34, 37, 49, 73, 112, 119, and 128.

Life often confronts us with choices that we could call "the way of the righteous" and "the way of the wicked" (Ps. 1:6). Through the wisdom songs, God invites us to make choices that lead to a truly happy life (Pss. 1:1; 34:13–14 [12–13]) rather than a life that in the end amounts to nothing (Pss. 1:6 and 112:10). Two keys are necessary to attaining such a truly happy life. One is trusting the Lord. The wisdom songs steer us away from trusting in ourselves (Ps. 49:13 [14]) or our own resources (Ps. 49:6 [7]) and encourage us to place our trust in the Lord.

> Trust in the LORD and do good.
> Then you will live safely in the land and prosper.
>
> (Ps. 37:3 NLT)

---

38. Longman, *How to Read the Psalms*, 33.
39. Roland E. Murphy, *The Tree of Life: An Exploration of Biblical Wisdom Literature* (Grand Rapids: Eerdmans, 1996), 103.
40. Collins, *Introduction to the Hebrew Bible*, 468; and Wilson, *Psalms Volume 1*, 72.

Commit your way to the LORD;
> trust in him, and he will act.
>> (Ps. 37:5 ESV)

They do not fear bad news;
> they confidently trust the LORD to care for them.
>> (Ps. 112:7 NLT)

Many sorrows come to the wicked,
> but unfailing love surrounds those who trust the LORD.
>> (Ps. 32:10 NLT)

The other key is trusting the Lord's instruction. "I trust in your word," says the sage in Psalm 119:42. The reason we can trust the Lord's instruction is because it is trustworthy.

The statutes of the LORD are trustworthy.
> (Ps. 19:7)

All your commands are trustworthy.
> (Ps. 119:86)

Trusting in the Lord's instruction entails putting it into practice (see Pss. 1:1–3; 19:7–14; 119:1–8). The wisdom songs teach you how to put God's instruction into practice in many of the major areas of life, like how you relate to your money and how you face death (Ps. 49), how you handle your sin (Ps. 32) and how you use your tongue (Ps. 34), how you wrestle with the perplexities of life (Pss. 37; 73) and how you hope for a better tomorrow (Ps. 112).

The bottom line is this question: "Do any of you want to live a life that is long and prosperous?" (Ps. 34:12 [13] NLT I.0). The wisdom songs show you the way.

WHAT DO THE CATEGORIES HAVE TO DO WITH CHRIST?

Let's return for a moment to the text with which I began this chapter:

> Let the word of Christ dwell in you richly as you teach and ad-
> monish one another with all wisdom, and as you sing psalms,
> hymns and spiritual songs with gratitude in your hearts to God.
> (Col. 3:16)

The apostle Paul encourages us to let "the word of Christ" saturate
our lives by singing "psalms, hymns and spiritual songs." The Greek
words Paul uses for "psalms," "hymns," and "songs" are all used in the
ancient Greek translation of the Old Testament that Paul would have
used. These three words are used in the titles to various psalms.[41] So
while "the word of Christ" includes more than Psalms, the book of
Psalms certainly is "the word of Christ." Some take the "the word of
Christ" as a **subjective genitive**, so that Christ is the speaker, while
others understand it as an **objective genitive** with Christ as the one
spoken about. Arguments can be made for either interpretation. Perhaps
it is better to take "the word of Christ" as a **pregnant expression**,
meaning both "the word spoken by Christ" and "the word spoken
about Christ."

When reading a psalm, it is helpful to read that psalm both as being
spoken by Christ and as speaking about Christ.[42] Each of these perspectives will yield different insights into any given psalm. Both perspectives can be used for the simple reason that Christ is the Lord of the
covenant and the Servant of the covenant. As the Lord of the covenant,
Christ is the one to whom the psalms are addressed *by us*; and as the
Servant of the covenant, Christ is the one by whom the psalms are
voiced *for us*.

Each of the categories studied in this chapter provides a different
window through which the interpreter can look to gain perspective
on who Jesus is and what he has done for us. While the "by Christ"
and "about Christ" perspectives help with each of these categories, the
laments, the songs of thanksgiving, and the wisdom songs lend themselves to the "by Christ" perspective, while the hymns and the divine
kingship songs lend themselves to the "about Christ" perspective.

This study of categories, therefore, is not a sterile exercise. By learn-

---

41. See Psalm 3:1 for "psalm" (ψαλμός), Psalm 6:1 for "hymn" (ὕμνος), and Psalm 4:1 for "song"
(ᾠδή).

42. Longman, *How to Read the Psalms*, 68.

ing to read the various psalms in keeping with their categories, you will see more of the richness of Christ, and this richness will fill your life more and more.[43]

Christ and Our Hymns

Two major themes in the hymns are the praise of God as our Creator and the praise of God as our Redeemer. Psalm 104:1, 24, for example, praises God as our Creator.

> Praise the LORD, I tell myself;
>   O LORD my God, how great you are! . . .
> O LORD, what a variety of things you have made!
>   In wisdom you have made them all.
>   The earth is full of your creatures.
>   (NLT 1.0)

And Psalm 107:1–2 praises God as our Redeemer.

> Give thanks to the LORD, for he is good!
>   His faithful love endures forever.
> Has the LORD redeemed you? Then speak out!
>   Tell others he has redeemed you from your enemies.
>   (NLT)

The New Testament presents Christ as both our Creator and our Redeemer. The apostle John says of Jesus,

> Through him all things were made; without him nothing was made that has been made. (John 1:3)

And the apostle Paul says,

---

43. For a complementary approach to this kind of Christological reading of the Psalms, see Bruce K. Waltke, "A Canonical Process Approach to the Psalms," in *Tradition and Testament: Essays in Honor of Charles Lee Feinberg*, ed. John S. Feinberg and Paul D. Feinberg (Chicago: Moody, 1981), 3–18.

Christ *redeemed* us from the curse of the law by becoming a curse for us, for it is written: "Cursed is everyone who is hung on a tree." (Gal. 3:13)

So when we sing or read the songs of praise, we are singing and reading about Christ, our Creator, our Redeemer, our Shepherd, our King, our God.

Christ and Our Laments

David once cried out in agony, saying,

> My God, my God, why have you forsaken me?
>   Why are you so far from saving me,
>   so far from the words of my groaning?
> (Ps. 22:1)

Many of us have shared David's thoughts and feelings along the path of life. While we may have felt terribly alone, we were never truly alone in those times, because Jesus was there with us. Jesus no doubt prayed the laments throughout his journey on this earth. As the author of Hebrews says,

> While Jesus was here on earth, he offered prayers and pleadings, with a loud cry and tears, to the one who could deliver him out of death. (Heb. 5:7 NLT 1.0)

And, as Matthew records, Jesus prayed the laments most intensely on the cross.

> At about three o'clock, Jesus called out with a loud voice, "*Eli, Eli, lema sabachthani?*" which means, "My God, my God, why have you forsaken me?" (Matt. 27:46 NLT 1.0)

So, when we sing or read the laments, we are singing and reading about Christ, who has gone before us and sung the laments for us.

Christ and Our Songs of Thanksgiving

Hebrews 5:7 in its entirety says,

> While Jesus was here on earth, he offered prayers and plead-ings, with a loud cry and tears, to the one who could deliver him out of death. *And God heard his prayers* because of his rever-ence for God. (NLT 1.0)

God heard Jesus' agonizing cry on the cross and redeemed him from death and hell by raising him from the dead. Jesus no doubt celebrated this deliverance with songs of thanksgiving. The author of Hebrews leads us to this conclusion, when he quotes Jesus as saying to the Father,

> I will declare the wonder of your name
> to my brothers and sisters.
> I will praise you among all your people.
> (Heb. 2:12 NLT 1.0)

Here Jesus is reciting words of thanksgiving first recorded in Psalm 22:22. From this text we learn not only that Jesus sang the songs of thanksgiving for us, but also that he now leads us as we too thank God for all that he has done and continues to do for us in answer to our prayers.

Christ and Our Songs of Confidence

Living confidently before God is, no doubt, the aspiration of all believers. Especially when we find ourselves in those in-between times—between the agony of the lament and the joy of the song of thanksgiving—we hope to have a profound confidence in God that sees us through to the experience of God's full victory. Christ lived such a life of confidence for us.

We have seen that Christ sang the laments for us when he was on the cross and that he sang the songs of thanksgiving for us after his resur-rection. But what did he sing "in between"? He sang the songs of con-fidence. In the first sermon recorded in the book of Acts, the apostle Peter speaks of the death and resurrection of Christ (Acts 2:23–24).

Peter goes on to speak of the great confidence Christ had in his Father during this ordeal with these words:

> I saw the Lord always before me.
>   Because he is at my right hand,
>   I will not be shaken.
> Therefore my heart is glad and my tongue rejoices;
>   my body also will live in hope,
> because you will not abandon me to the grave,
>   nor will you let your Holy One see decay.
> You have made known to me the paths of life;
>   you will fill me with joy in your presence.
>   (Acts 2:25–28)

These words are taken from the first song of confidence, Psalm 16:8–11. Christ knew what it was to be "in between," and when he was "in between" he sang the songs of confidence for himself and for us. Christ's confidence that his Father would not ultimately abandon him was proven true through his resurrection from the dead. Peter goes on to say,

> Brothers, I can tell you confidently that the patriarch David died and was buried, and his tomb is here to this day. But he was a prophet and knew that God had promised him on oath that he would place one of his descendants on his throne. Seeing what was ahead, he spoke of the resurrection of the Christ, that he was not abandoned to the grave, nor did his body see decay. (Acts 2:29–31)

We can have this same confidence when we are "in between," whatever that may look like.

The author of Hebrews, after listing a number of real-life situations, encourages us with these words:

> Never will I leave you;
>   never will I forsake you.
>   (Heb. 13:5)

And then by his own example, he invites us to sing from Psalm 118 with great confidence,

> The Lord is my helper, so I will not be afraid.
> What can mere mortals do to me?
> (Heb. 13:6 NLT 1.0)

It is through Christ that we can live with confidence before God. As the apostle Paul says, "Such confidence as this is ours through Christ before God" (2 Cor. 3:4).

Christ and Our Divine Kingship Songs

In Psalm 2 we read of the divine King, "the One enthroned in heaven" (v. 4) and of a human, messianic king through whom the divine King rules the earth: "I have placed my chosen king on the throne in Jerusalem" (v. 6 NLT). When we turn to the pages of the New Testament, the two become one. Jesus is the Son of David, the messianic King.

> This is a record of the ancestors of Jesus the Messiah, a descendant of David. (Matt. 1:1 NLT)

Jesus is also the divine King. In 1 Timothy 6:15 Paul refers to "God, the blessed and only Ruler, the King of kings and Lord of lords." And in Revelation 19:16 Jesus bears the twin title King of kings and Lord of lords. If God is the "*only* Ruler, the King of kings and Lord of lords," and if Jesus is the "King of kings and Lord of lords," then Jesus is the divine King, as well as the human King.

As we have seen, at the center of the divine kingship songs is the celebration of God's vanquishing of chaotic forces, be they cosmic or human. This role in the New Testament belongs to King Jesus. You will recall that occasion when the disciples were caught in a tumultuous storm at sea, while Jesus was asleep in the boat (Luke 8:22–24). In the face of this grave danger "the disciples went and woke him, saying, 'Master, Master, we're going to drown!'" Then Jesus "got up and rebuked [ἐπετίμησεν] the wind and the raging waters; the storm subsided, and all was calm." The Greek verb translated "rebuked" (ἐπιτιμάω) is cognate with the noun "rebuke" (ἐπιτίμησις) that is used in Psalm 104:7 (103:7 LXX) to describe the action of the divine King in quelling the chaotic sea at the time of Creation. Jesus is the divine King. His coming to establish cosmic order and bring abundant life was what the ancients and all of creation longed for (Pss. 96:10–13; 98:7–9). As Old Testament saints celebrated his procession into the city of God as the "King of glory" (Ps. 24:7), so the saints in the New Testament celebrated the triumphal procession of King Jesus into Jerusalem, shouting, "Blessed is he who comes in the name of the Lord! Blessed is the King of Israel!" (John 12:13).

What few if any understood at that moment was that the divine King would conquer chaos and bring abundant life through his own suffering and death. On the cross Jesus was not defeated by, but *defeated*, all the forces that oppose the ordered and abundant life God intends, for on the cross he was still the King.

> A sign was fastened to the cross above Jesus' head, announcing the charge against him. It read: "This is Jesus, the King of the Jews." (Matt. 27:37 NLT)

Through his resurrection from the dead, he now reigns and will continue to reign until the last force that opposes the ordered and abundant life God intends, death itself, is placed under his feet (1 Cor. 15:25–26). Although forces of chaos may still threaten, "the Lamb will overcome them because he is Lord of lords and King of kings" (Rev. 17:14).

Christ and Our Wisdom Songs

The life of wisdom set forth in the book of Psalms is an ideal life that we do not live out in reality. There is someone, however, who has lived this ideal life every day and everywhere, Jesus Christ. Luke tells us that, as a young boy, Jesus "grew and became strong; he was filled with wisdom, and the grace of God was upon him" (Luke 2:40) and that "Jesus grew in wisdom and in stature and in favor with God and all the people" (Luke 2:52 NLT).[44] Christ not only lived this life of wisdom for himself, but he also lived it for us. Paul tells us that Christ "has become for us wisdom from God—that is, our righteousness, holiness and redemption" (1 Cor. 1:30). Christ lived the perfect life of wisdom for us so that as we trust in him, the Father views us as perfectly wise (justification) and is in the process of making us perfectly wise (sanctification). Christ lived God's wisdom for us and is now producing that wisdom in us. So as we reflect on the wisdom songs, we are reflecting on who Christ is and who we are and are becoming in him.

Understanding the categories of the Psalms guides the interpreter's expectations, provides an additional level of context, and gives multiple windows through which to look more deeply into who Jesus is and what he has done and continues to do for his people. This emphasis on Christ by no means excludes the Father and the Spirit. Rather, our focus on the Son in Psalms is to the glory of the Father through the power of the Spirit. As the New Testament says,

> Don't be drunk with wine, because that will ruin your life. Instead, *be filled with the Holy Spirit, singing psalms and hymns and spiritual songs* among yourselves, and making music to the Lord in your hearts. And *give thanks for everything to God the Father* in *the name of our Lord Jesus Christ.* (Eph. 5:18–20 NLT)

EXCURSUS: THE ROYAL PSALMS

Like the psalms of confidence, divine kingship psalms, and wisdom psalms, another group of psalms are united by a common theme without sharing a common structure. A focus on the human king unites these psalms into one category, customarily called "royal psalms." A fairly strong consensus[45] affirms the following as royal psalms: Psalms 2, 18, 20, 21, 45, 72, 89, 101, 110, 132, and 144.

---

44. Compare Proverbs 3:4: "Then you will find favor with both God and people" (NLT).

45. See Collins, *Introduction to the Hebrew Bible*, 468; Lucas, *Exploring the Old Testament*, 7; Michael D. Coogan, *The Old Testament: A Historical and Literary Introduction to the Hebrew Scriptures* (Oxford: Oxford University Press, 2006), 465; and Wilson, *Psalms Volume 1*, 66.

A variety of subthemes are evident in the royal psalms. Psalms 2, 72, 101, and 110 are arguably related to the king's coronation and enthronement. Psalms 78, 89, and 132 focus on the ideology of the monarchy. Psalms 20, 21, and 144 seem to be prayers for divine help in battle. Psalm 18 apparently is a song of thanksgiving for victory in battle. Psalm 45 is a song for a royal wedding.

The number and variety of the royal psalms, along with the number of psalms that have "of David" in the title, are indicators of the centrality of the human king in Israel's life in general and in worship in particular.[46] The centrality of the Davidic king is the corollary to the centrality of the divine King in the life of ancient Israel. The Israelites lived under the rule of the divine King enthroned in heaven (Ps. 2:4) and the rule of his "Son" enthroned on the earth (Ps. 2:7). The close connection between these two thrones is seen in 1 Chronicles 28:5.

> Of all my sons—and the LORD has given me many—he has chosen my son Solomon to sit on the throne of the kingdom of the LORD over Israel.

Solomon sits on the throne over Israel, which is the same as the Lord's own throne. It is for this reason that the apparent demise of the Davidic covenant (Ps. 89:38–45 [39–46]) was such a deep crisis of faith for the community (Ps. 89:46–51 [47–52]). It is also for this reason that hope for the future lay in the coming of the divine King (Ps. 96:10–13) and his anointed Son (Pss. 118:26 and 132:17).[47]

---

46. Wilson, *Psalms Volume 1*, 67.
47. See chapter 2, pages 80–95.

5

PROCLAIMING THE PSALMS

Sing a new song to the LORD!
Let the whole earth sing to the LORD!
Sing to the LORD; bless his name.
Each day proclaim the good news that he saves.
Publish his glorious deeds among the nations.
Tell everyone about the amazing things he does.
(Ps. 96:1–3 NLT)

THE BOOK OF PSALMS ITSELF *proclaims* the good news that God saves, *publishes* God's glorious deeds, and *tells* everyone about the amazing things that God does. So why would some professors of preaching counsel against preaching the Psalms?[1] The primary reason is category. Since the psalms are poetry, so the argument goes, the psalms resist being analyzed for the purpose of serving as instructional material. But this misses, as I have argued, the primary purpose of the book of Psalms, and that is, in one word, instruction.[2] The focus of this current chapter, then, is how to proclaim the psalms.

---

1. See the discussions in Elizabeth Achtemeier, "Preaching from the Psalms," *RevExp* 81 (1984): 437; and Thomas G. Long, *Preaching and the Literary Forms of the Bible* (Philadelphia: Fortress, 1989), 43.
2. See chapter 2 of this book and chapters 3 and 4 of Mark D. Futato, *Transformed by Praise: The Purpose and Message of the Psalms* (Phillipsburg, NJ: P & R Publishing, 2002). In addition, Long argues that there is no reason why literature from one category cannot be transformed for use in another, as in transforming a poetic text into sermonic form (*Preaching*, 44).

A number of approaches can be used to preach from the book of Psalms. It is quite common to preach from single psalms that fit special occasions. At how many funerals has Psalm 23 been preached? How many preachers have chosen Psalm 22 as their text for a Good Friday service? No doubt Psalm 45 has been preached at countless weddings. Moreover, the message of a particular psalm often has been just what a congregation has needed to hear on a particular Sunday morning. The Psalms have and will continue to serve as texts for such occasional preaching.

Given the ground we've covered in this current volume, we can readily see that the book of Psalms is also suitable for preaching series of sermons in a variety of ways.[3] One approach might be preaching a series introducing the congregation to the various categories of the Psalms. Such a series could be presented in three parts that trace the ebb and flow of life through the lens of the hymn, the lament, and the psalm of thanksgiving.[4] Or the series could be expanded to include sermons on a psalm of confidence, a divine kingship psalm, and a wisdom psalm. Such a series not only would illuminate particular psalms but also would have the added value of guiding congregants in how to read Psalms more profitably on their own.

A second approach might be a series that not only would illuminate particular texts but also would instruct the listeners on the shape of the book of Psalms, thereby aiding them once again in their own reading of Psalms. Such a series might start with several sermons on the laments at the front of the book of Psalms before concluding with several sermons on the songs of praise found at the end of Psalms. Another series might follow the unfolding drama of the Five Books as sketched out in chapter 2. In this case, the series might begin with a sermon on the inauguration of kingship (Ps. 2), followed by sermons on the confirmation of kingship (Ps. 41), the transference of kingship (Ps. 72), the apparent failure of kingship (Ps. 89), the affirmation of kingship (Ps. 96), and the coming of kingship (Ps. 132).

---

3. Graeme Goldsworthy, *Preaching the Whole Bible as Christian Scripture* (Grand Rapids: Eerdmans, 2000), 211.

4. See Mark D. Futato, *Joy Comes in the Morning: Psalms for All Seasons* (Phillipsburg, NJ: P & R Publishing, 2004) for sequential expositions of Psalm 104 (hymn), Psalm 13 (lament), and Psalm 30 (thanksgiving).

A third kind of series might cover a group of integrated contiguous psalms. For example, in chapter 2 we saw how the book of Psalms contains numerous batches of psalms that articulate the theme of God's plan to bless the nations. Psalms 46–49 would make a marvelous series on the missionary mind of God. Similarly, Psalms 93–100 focus on the kingship of God.[5] And Psalms 121–134 could serve for a series on the journey of life. The added value of this type of sermon series is how it would instruct the listeners in the art of reading psalms in their immediate literary context.

Whether one is preaching an occasional sermon on a psalm or preparing a series of sermons from the book of Psalms,[6] four key steps should be followed in the preparation of each sermon, and these steps are the focus of this current chapter.

STEP 1: GETTING ORIENTED

Before heading out on a trip, I typically look over a map to get oriented to my journey. The trip itself may involve large highways and small city streets, cloverleaf interchanges and four-way stops. Getting oriented right at the beginning can keep me from getting lost in the proverbial forest because of all of the trees. I find preaching to be quite similar. Before diving into the details of **exegesis**, I find it helpful to get oriented to the text. There are two aspects to getting oriented: reading the text and asking questions.

Reading the Text

There's no substitute for knowing your text well. Not only must you get a grasp of the text, but the text must get a grasp on you. This happens by spending time reading and rereading the text. A combination of the

---

5. See David M. Howard Jr., *The Structure of Psalms 93–100*, Biblical and Judaic Studies, vol. 5, ed. William Henry Propp (Winona Lake, IN: Eisenbrauns, 1997).

6. While it will often be the case that the text for a sermon from the book of Psalms will be an entire psalm, this will not always be the case. Longer psalms, like Psalm 104, might be better handled as a short series with each sermon focusing on a different strophe. Moreover, a portion of a psalm might contain the message that the congregation needs to hear, given its situation. See Elizabeth Achtemeier, *Preaching from the Old Testament* (Louisville: Westminster/John Knox, 1989), 159–60.

length of the psalm and your proficiency in Hebrew will determine how much of this is done in the original language and how much in translation. Either way, immersing yourself in the text is a key step in proclaiming the text.

As you are reading and rereading the psalm, you should be seeking the answer to a couple of questions. But before we get to those questions, I'll expand on what I mean by reading the text. Narrowly conceived, reading the text starts with the first verse and ends with the last. There's more to it than that, however. In the previous chapter we discussed reading the text in context on a number of different levels. Here, I want to illustrate reading in context by focusing on just two of those levels: literary context, and in context of its category.

It's important to read a psalm in its literary context, that is, in the context of the surrounding psalms. For example, Psalm 26:1–3 could be interpreted as the prayer of a very self-righteous person.

> Vindicate me, O LORD,
>   for I have led a blameless life;
> I have trusted in the LORD
>   without wavering.
> Test me, O LORD, and try me,
>   examine my heart and my mind;
> for your love is ever before me,
>   and I walk continually in your truth.

And verses 9–11 of the same psalm could have been quoted by the Pharisee (although in a self-righteous way) in the parable Jesus taught with regard to confidence in one's own righteousness (Luke 18:11–12).

> Do not take away my soul along with sinners,
>   my life with bloodthirsty men,
> in whose hands are wicked schemes,
>   whose right hands are full of bribes.
> But I lead a blameless life;
>   redeem me and be merciful to me.

Reading this text in its literary context, though, will help us to avoid misinterpreting it, because the author of these words—David—is the author of the previous psalm (Ps. 25), where we read,

> Remember not the sins of my youth
> and my rebellious ways;
> according to your love remember me,
> for you are good, O LORD. . . .
> For the sake of your name, O LORD,
> forgive my iniquity, though it is great. . . .
> Look upon my affliction and my distress
> and take away all my sins.
>
> (Ps. 25:7, 11, 18)

How then are we to understand the language of Psalm 26? Several possibilities present themselves, one of which finds support from the following psalm, in which David says,

> Do not turn me over to the desire of my foes,
> for false witnesses rise up against me,
> breathing out violence.
>
> (Ps. 27:12)

It is quite likely that in Psalm 26 David has been subjected to false accusations similar to those referred to in Psalm 27:12. Psalm 7 below has a protestation of innocence similar to the one in Psalm 26.

> Judge me, O LORD, according to my righteousness,
> according to my integrity, O Most High.
>
> (Ps. 7:8 [9])

And verses 3–5 [4–6] of Psalm 7 make clear that this is not a general protestation of absolute innocence in every area of life but of innocence with regard to the false accusations being leveled by Cush the Benjaminite (v. 1).

> O LORD my God, if I have done this
>   and there is guilt on my hands—
> if I have done evil to him who is at peace with me
>   or without cause have robbed my foe—
> then let my enemy pursue and overtake me;
>   let him trample my life to the ground
>   and make me sleep in the dust.

So, read in the literary context of Psalms 25 and 27, Psalm 26, like Psalm 7, is not the prayer of a self-righteous person but the prayer of an innocent person who has been falsely accused.[7]

The second level of context is that of context within its category. Psalm 15, for example, begins with a question (v. 1), which is followed by a detailed answer (vv. 2–5a). The psalm concludes with a promise (v. 5b). Some scholars take this psalm as a wisdom psalm that instructs the young on the moral implications of worship.[8] The majority, however, understand Psalm 15 to be an "entrance psalm," a psalm that functioned as part of a liturgy used for entering the temple for worship.[9] The language of Psalm 15:1 is quite similar to that of Psalm 24:3.

> LORD, who may dwell in your sanctuary?
>   Who may live on your holy hill?
>   (15:1)

> Who may ascend the hill of the LORD?
>   Who may stand in his holy place?
>   (24:3)

And as Psalm 15:1 is followed by an answer to the question posed, so too is Psalm 24:3.

---

7. The appeal to Psalm 7 illustrates the need to read each psalm in the theological context of the book of Psalms as a whole, as well as that of the entire Scriptures.

8. Peter C. Craigie, *Psalms 1–50*, WBC (Waco: Word, 1983), 150.

9. Richard J. Clifford, *Psalms 1–72*, AOTC (Nashville: Abingdon, 2002), 92.

He who has clean hands and a pure heart,
who does not lift up his soul to an idol
or swear by what is false.

(24:4)

And just as the answer given in Psalm 15:2–5a is followed by a promised blessing in verse 5b, so too the answer given in Psalm 24:4 is followed by a promised blessing in verse 5.

He will receive blessing from the LORD
and vindication from God his Savior.

Thus, reading Psalm 15 in the context of Psalm 24 provides a richness to our reading that we would otherwise not have were it not for
reading the psalm as an entrance psalm.

By reading and rereading a psalm, both narrowly conceived and in
its various contexts, we get a big-picture grasp of the text, and we can
hope that the text is beginning to get a grasp on us. And as you'll recall,
grasping and being grasped through reading and re-reading is the first
aspect of getting oriented.

This initial step on the journey toward proclamation naturally leads
us to the second aspect of getting oriented—asking questions. We
should, in fact, be searching for answers to two key questions.

Asking the Questions

The first question pertains to structure: What are the main divisions of the text? The second question pertains to meaning: What is
the message of the text? While these are separate questions, they are
interdependent, for in practice you will be answering them at the same
time. Although your focus may be on one more than the other at any
particular moment in the process, seeing the structure and grasping the
meaning go hand in hand.

As we learned in chapter 1, when looking at the structure of a psalm
most of the time we are asking about strophic divisions. It's easy for
teachers and preachers to lose their audience in all the details of exegesis. Often this is because expositors themselves get lost in the details.

The key to avoiding getting lost and losing others is to have a clear grasp of the psalm's structure, which entails a clear grasp of the overall message and the flow of thought from one strophe to another.

Several primary factors are involved in analyzing the structure of a psalm. The first, as discussed in chapter 1, is sense. To say *sense* is to refer to *meaning*, so we're looking for meaning with our first consideration of structure. Biblical poems are not simply a **concatenation** of unrelated lines. Rather, a given psalm possesses an overall sense and, typically, groups of lines contain similar content that holds them together and at the same time separates them from the surrounding lines. In Psalm 24, for instance, verses 1–2 are a strophe, held together by their focus on the Lord as Creator. The topic changes in verses 3–6, which addresses the qualifications for entering the temple for worship. The focus shifts again in verses 7–10, which describe the Lord's entrance into the city as the King who has been victorious in battle. Thus we have a text with a threefold strophic structure: The Lord's victory at Creation (vv. 1–2), the Lord's requirements for worshipers (vv. 3–6), and the Lord's entrance as victorious warrior (vv. 7–10).

Closely related to strophic shifts in topic are shifts in imagery. Psalm 23 naturally falls into two strophic images. In the first (vv. 1–4), the Lord is imaged as Shepherd, and we as his sheep are on the move. In the second (vv. 5–6), the Lord is imaged as Host, and we as his people are at rest in his house.

Whether or not we call them strophes is not as important as seeing the sections. Psalm 133, for example, has four sections. Verse 1 is an opening exclamation that makes the first key point of the psalm: unity is a wonderful corporate virtue.

> How good and pleasant it is
> when brothers live together in unity!

Verse 2 employs the image of anointing oil.

> It is like precious oil poured on the head,
> running down on the beard,
> running down on Aaron's beard,
> down upon the collar of his robes.

The first half of verse 3 uses the image of dew.

> It is as if the dew of Hermon
> were falling on Mount Zion.

Finally, the second half of verse 3 is a concluding affirmation that the Lord bestows his blessing where unity exists.

> For there the LORD bestows his blessing,
> even life forevermore.

Psalm 133 is also an example of another factor involved in analyzing a psalm's structure, that is, patterning. You were introduced to the concept of structural patterning in chapter 1. Here we will illustrate patterning for the purpose of demonstrating the role it plays in proclaiming the text. Psalm 133 manifests a symmetrical pattern.

A   Unity is good and pleasant (v. 1)
    B   Unity is like anointing oil (v. 2)
    B   Unity is like dew (v. 3a)
A   Unity is blessed by God (v. 3b)

Analyzing the structure helps us to see in brief that Psalm 133 is about the blessings of living in harmony with others. We'll return to this psalm shortly to add more detail to our understanding of the meaning when we focus on the details of the imagery.

Psalm 1 provides another example of the symmetrical pattern.[10]

A   The righteous are blessed (vv. 1–2)
    B   Like a tree (vv. 3a–b)
        C   The righteous prosper (v. 3c)
        C   The wicked don't (v. 4a)
    B   Like chaff (v. 4b)
A   The way of the wicked perishes (v. 5)
Concluding summary (v. 6)[11]

---

10. For more details on the structure of this psalm, see David L. Petersen and Kent Harold Richards, *Interpreting Hebrew Poetry* (Minneapolis: Fortress, 1992), 89–97.

11. For a somewhat different, although still symmetrical, analysis of Psalm 1, see David A. Dorsey, *The Literary Structure of the Old Testament* (Grand Rapids: Baker, 1999), 175–76.

Again the structure helps us grasp the message. Psalm 1 is about the contrast between the righteous, who are blessed and prosperous, and the wicked, who perish.

You will find good grist for the mill in analyzing the structure of psalms by working through the material in David Dorsey's *The Literary Structure of the Old Testament*.[12] In this volume, Dorsey analyzes the structures of some three dozen psalms.

One other factor brings this discussion to a close: **grammatical mood**. At times movement from one strophe to another will be marked by a shift in grammatical mood. Psalm 13 is a clear example. The opening strophe (vv. 1–2) is marked by the **interrogative mood**: "How long?" is repeated four times. The middle strophe (vv. 3–4) is marked by the **imperative mood**: "Look," "answer," "give light." The final strophe (vv. 5–6) is marked by a shift to the **indicative mood**, "I trust," followed by verbs in the **volitive mood** used to express firm resolve: "my heart rejoices," "I will sing."[13] Paying attention to the shifting grammatical mood yields a threefold structure for Psalm 13.

Having read and reread the text and having answered the basic questions pertaining to structure and message, you are now ready to focus on the second step of sermon preparation—the details of exegesis.

STEP 2: FOCUSING ON THE DETAILS

Since this volume is not a handbook on interpretation in general but on poetry and Psalms in particular, we will at this point give our attention to only two aspects of detailed exegesis: parallelism and imagery.

Parallelism

In chapter 1 you learned that Hebrew poems are comprised of parallel lines that are typically formed with two half lines or cola, have a correspondence of some sort between these cola, and exhibit movement from the first colon to the second. At this stage in the exegetical

---

12. Ibid., 173–86.
13. For a discussion of this point and the structure and message of the whole psalm, see Futato, *Joy Comes in the Morning*, 58–73.

process, you will do a close reading of the lines with a view to ferreting out the movement within each line. Let's look at a few examples.

In Psalm 24:1 we read,

לַיהוָה הָאָרֶץ וּמְלוֹאָהּ
תֵּבֵל וְיֹשְׁבֵי בָהּ

To the Lord belongs the earth and its fullness,
The world and its inhabitants.

(author's translation)

First, note the correspondences: הָאָרֶץ ("the earth") corresponds with תֵּבֵל ("world"), and וּמְלוֹאָהּ ("and its fullness") corresponds with וְיֹשְׁבֵי בָהּ ("and its inhabitants"). While אֶרֶץ ("earth") and תֵּבֵל ("world") are at times synonymous (having interchangeable meanings in at least some contexts[14]), they do not always have the exact same sense. Both words can have the sense "the global mass called earth, including the atmosphere or heaven."[15] Yet תֵּבֵל ("world") also has the more specific sense "inhabited and cultivated areas of the mainland."[16] So Psalm 24:1 contains movement from the general "earth" (= "global mass including the atmosphere") to the specific "world" (= "inhabited and cultivated areas of the land"). Joined to this is movement from "its fullness" (i.e., everything that fills the global mass including the atmosphere) to "its inhabitants" (i.e., the humans who live in the inhabited areas of the land). What is the point of the parallelism? The poet is underscoring the universal scope of the Lord's authority. His authority is over not only the globe but also all of the contents of the globe, and over not only the inhabited areas but also all of the inhabitants. With rhetorical power the poet affirms the absolutely universal scope of the Lord's authority. As you grasp the power of the line and it grasps you, you will be in a position to proclaim this text with a corresponding power of your own.

Let's now look at Psalm 30:4 [5] where we read,

---

14. Moisés Silva, *Biblical Words and Their Meaning: An Introduction to Lexical Semantics* (Grand Rapids: Zondervan, 1994), 122.
15. R. Alexander, "יָבַל," in *TWOT*, 1:359.
16. So *HALOT*, 4:1682. See also C. Wright, "תֵּבֵל," in *NIDOTTE*, 4:273; and R. Alexander, "תֵּבֵל," in *TWOT*, 1:359.

זַמְּרוּ לַיהוָה חֲסִידָיו
וְהוֹדוּ לְזֵכֶר קָדְשׁוֹ

The verb זַמְּרוּ ("sing") corresponds with הוֹדוּ ("give thanks" NASB) and thus ties the two cola together. While we might be tempted to assert that there is movement from the general "sing" to the specific "give thanks," the fact that this pair of words typically occurs in the reverse order gives us pause.[17] The movement here is of a different sort. Note that each colon has three words. The first colon tells us who is to do the singing, חֲסִידָיו ("His godly ones" NASB). The second colon has no corresponding term. To make up for the absence of a corresponding term, the poet uses two words in the second colon, לְזֵכֶר קָדְשׁוֹ ("to His holy name" NASB), to correspond to one in the first colon, לַיהוָה ("to the LORD"). The use of these two words provides focus on the *holiness* of the Lord. While this may not be an earthshaking insight, observing it shields against a flat reading of the text and provides color that will enrich the proclaiming of the text.

This same shift from "the LORD" to "his holy name" is also found in Psalm 103:1:

בָּרֲכִי נַפְשִׁי אֶת־יהוָה
וְכָל־קְרָבַי אֶת־שֵׁם קָדְשׁוֹ

Here יהוָה ("the LORD") corresponds with שֵׁם קָדְשׁוֹ ("his holy name"), and נַפְשִׁי ("my soul") corresponds with כָּל־קְרָבַי ("all that is within me"). It is possible that נַפְשִׁי here refers to the immaterial aspect of the human being and is well translated "soul." If this is the case, there is no discernible movement from נַפְשִׁי ("my soul") to כָּל־קְרָבַי ("all that is within me"). On the other hand, נַפְשִׁי could refer here to the whole person,[18] and thus there would be movement from the whole to the part, the preacher could make the point that God desires praise from our whole being and especially from our hearts. Certainty on this is not possible, in my estimation, and so I would advise against making a point of the shift in language in cases like this. If movement

---

17. See Psalms 7:17 [18]; 18:49 [50]; 33:2; 57:9 [10]; 71:22; 92:1 [2]; 108:3 [4]; 138:1. Psalm 30:12 [13] is the only other text using the order of Psalm 30:4 [5].
18. Ibid., 2:589.

can be discerned, excellent! If not, do not make the text say more than can be demonstrated.[19]

Imagery

In chapter 1 you learned that images work by creating associations. Unpacking these associations is a key to richly proclaiming the poetic texts. Let's look at two images in Psalm 133 as examples.

The first image is that of oil. In verse 2, brothers living in harmony is likened to oil.

> It is like precious oil poured on the head,
>> running down on the beard,
> running down on Aaron's beard,
>> down upon the collar of his robes.

Since in the dry climate of ancient Israel oil was used to refresh travelers once they reached their destination,[20] we might be tempted to say that harmonious relationships are a source of great refreshment on life's journey. While that is true, in all likelihood it is not the point our poet is making. Note that the poet does not refer to oil in general but to the anointing oil used for the consecration of Aaron and Aaronic priests. So to unpack this image, we need to read the description of this oil as recorded in Exodus 30:22–33.

> Then the LORD said to Moses, "Collect choice spices—12½ pounds of pure myrrh, 6¼ pounds of fragrant cinnamon, 6¼ pounds of fragrant calamus, and 12½ pounds of cassia—as measured by the weight of the sanctuary shekel. Also get one gallon of olive oil. Like a skilled incense maker, blend these ingredients to make a holy anointing oil. Use this sacred oil to anoint the Tabernacle, the Ark of the Covenant, the table and all its utensils, the lampstand and all its accessories, the incense altar, the altar of burnt offering and all its utensils, and the washbasin

---

19. See Robert Alter, *The Art of Biblical Poetry* (New York: Basic Books, 1985), 22, for a brief discussion of what he calls "static synonymity," lines with no apparent movement.
20. See Psalm 23:5; and "Oil," in *DBI*, 603.

with its stand. Consecrate them to make them absolutely holy. After this, whatever touches them will also become holy.

"Anoint Aaron and his sons also, consecrating them to serve me as priests. And say to the people of Israel, 'This holy anointing oil is reserved for me from generation to generation. It must never be used to anoint anyone else, and you must never make any blend like it for yourselves. It is holy, and you must treat it as holy. Anyone who makes a blend like it or anoints someone other than a priest will be cut off from the community.'" (NLT)

Notice two things about this oil. First, it was aromatic, being made from myrrh, cinnamon, sweet cane, and cassia. This oil was like the finest perfume in our culture. Second, it was holy. This oil was used only for anointing the sacred and was never to be used for common purposes, such as anointing travelers at the end of a long journey. So what associations is the poet creating with this image in Psalm 133? At a minimum the poet is saying that living in harmony with others is wonderfully, even extraordinarily, "good and pleasant" (v. 1), like the extraordinarily fragrant perfumelike oil used to anoint Aaron. Maximally the poet is saying that such harmony is not to be taken for granted as something quite common. Rather, such harmony is to be deeply appreciated as a "sacred" part of life.[21] It is the locus, after all, where God bestows the blessing of life (v. 3b).

The second image is that of dew.

> It is as if the dew of Hermon
> were falling on Mount Zion.
> (Ps. 133:3a)

In ancient Israel there was very little rain from May to October, but there was much dew. This dew was essential for the flourishing of vegetation during the dry season. In addition, dew was the primary source of water in the drier areas of the country. "Because dew is a source of

---

21. See J. Clinton McCann, "Psalms," in *NIB* (Nashville: Abingdon, 1996), 4:1214.

the very water on which life depends, it symbolizes blessing, favor or prosperity."[22] In keeping with this, the poet in Psalm 133 is saying that living in harmony with others is a source of blessing and prosperity in our lives. What's more, the dew that is evoked in this image is that of Mount Hermon, to the north of Israel. Mount Hermon was known for its copious moisture (see Jer. 18:14), so the image is not just of blessing and prosperity but of superabundant blessing and prosperity.

Patient and thoughtful analysis of the images in the Psalms will yield much fruit for one wishing to proclaim the message of the text.

STEP 3: SHAPING YOUR PRESENTATION

Someone once said, "If there is a mist in the pulpit, there is a fog in the pew." Clarity is essential in proclaiming the psalms. And there must be clarity on two levels: clarity in the mind of the preacher as to the flow of thought in the text and clarity in the presentation of the message. If the flow of thought is fuzzy in the mind of the preacher, the message will be garbled in the ears of the listener. Clarity in thought and clarity in presentation are, then, at the heart of effective communication. One surefire way to test clarity in thought is to produce an outline. A logical outline gives evidence of clear thinking. A logical outline also enhances clear communication. Thus, in discussing how to shape your presentation, it will be helpful to consider some of the basics of outlining your thoughts so that you can proclaim the text with clarity.

Outlining: The Approach

There are two basic approaches to outlining your understanding of a text. One we could call the **analytical approach** and the other the **topical approach**. An analytical outline follows the flow of thought straight from the beginning to the end of the text. A topical outline reorganizes the thoughts of the text based on key concepts embedded in the text. Both work well, although some texts lend themselves more to one approach than to the other. Let's look at some examples.

---

22. "Dew," in *DBI*, 207.

We have seen how Psalm 13, a lament, falls naturally into three strophes: verses 1–2 [1–3] are interrogative, verses 3–4 [4–5] are imperative, and verses 5–6 [6] are indicative and volitive. In this psalm David moves from articulating his agonizing questions (vv. 1–2 [1–3]) to making his specific request (vv. 3–4 [4–5]) to affirming his steadfast faith (vv. 5–6 [6]). Having a clear grasp on the flow of David's thought in this psalm naturally suggests presenting his thought under three main headings, which for now we can simply articulate as questions, requests, and affirmations.

Psalm 29 has a similar tripartite flow. Verses 1–2 are held together by the imperative mood and the threefold repetition of הָבוּ ("ascribe"). The sevenfold repetition of קוֹל יְהוָה ("the voice of the LORD") provides cohesiveness to verses 3–9. And verses 10–11 are united by the fourfold use of the divine name serving as the subject of a verb, a grammatical structure found nowhere else in the psalm. In verses 1–2 we encounter an invitation to worship. Verses 3–9 provide the motivation for worship. And verses 10–11 show us the outcome of worship.

Certainly we could organize Psalms 13 and 29 in other ways, but two benefits are inherent in using an analytical outline for these texts and others like them. One, you will make it easy for the congregation to follow your **exposition** as you make your way straight through the text from beginning to end. Two, you'll make it easy for your audience to conclude, even if unconsciously, that your message is coming from the text rather than from your own imagination.

Let's think for a moment about preaching on Psalm 119. One might try to follow the example left by the Rev. Thomas Manton, who preached a series of 119 sermons on this one psalm.[23] I think it would take an extraordinary preacher coupled with an extraordinary congregation to pull off such a series in our sound-bite generation. Even a mere twenty-two-part series, with one sermon for each strophe, would be more than the average congregation could bear these days. If the analytical approach—working your way through the text from beginning to end—is not a practical option, how could you effectively communicate the message of this marvelous psalm? For a number of psalms the topical approach will work much better.

---

23. Thomas Manton, *One Hundred and Nineteen Sermons on the Hundred and Nineteenth Psalm* (London: William Brown, 1842).

One key to interpreting Hebrew literature in general and poetry in particular is to pay attention to repeated vocabulary and themes. It will often be better to use a topical arrangement to communicate the message of a psalm that employs a high level of repetition. Repetition helps us to quickly discern the central theme of Psalm 119: תּוֹרָה ("instruction"). The Hebrew word תּוֹרָה occurs twenty-five times in this twenty-two-strophe poem. The poet also employs seven other synonyms of תּוֹרָה to underscore his focus on the Lord's instruction.[24] As I've studied this psalm, I see the poet repeating throughout the text five subthemes: (1) our attitude toward the Lord's instruction; (2) our desire for the Lord's instruction; (3) our resolve to live in keeping with the Lord's instruction; (4) our benefits from following the Lord's instruction; (5) our Lord's heart revealed in his instruction. A sermon that covers these five topics will, I believe, accomplish the purpose that is inherent in the psalm itself. (On the other hand, these five headings could be the titles for a five-part series on Psalm 119.)

Psalm 30 is another example of a psalm with a high level of repetition. The overarching theme is thanksgiving and praise, as is clear from the opening line, "I will exalt you, O LORD," and the threefold repetition of the verb יָדָה in the Hiphil ("give thanks") in verses 4 [5], 9 [10], and 12 [13]. Note that the order of events as narrated in the poem is not the same as the order of events as experienced: intention to praise/give thanks (v. 1 [2]), plea for deliverance and deliverance recounted (vv. 1–3 [2–4]), reversal of circumstances recounted (v. 4–5 [5–6]), situation prior to the trouble described (vv. 6–7 [7–8]), plea for deliverance recounted again (vv. 8–10 [9–11]), reversal of circumstances recounted again (v. 11 [12]), intention to praise/give thanks (v. 12 [13]). For a contemporary audience, the preacher could reorder this text, resulting in a sermon that follows the order of events in David's experience: situation prior to the trouble, the trouble, the plea for deliverance, the reversal of circumstances, and the response of thanksgiving.[25]

Both the analytical and topical approaches to outlining your thoughts and your presentation serve to bring clarity. The choice, I believe, will

---

24. The synonyms are דָּבָר ("word"), מִשְׁפָּטִים ("laws"), עֵדוּת ("decrees"), מִצְוָה ("command"), חֻקִּים ("principles"), פִּקּוּדִים ("commandments"), and אִמְרָה ("promise").

25. For an analytical treatment of this psalm, see Futato, *Joy Comes in the Morning*, 84–99.

be dictated largely by the characteristics of each text. Once you have determined your general approach, you can then move to filling in the details of your outline in a logical and clear way.

Outlining: The Logic

There are two keys to formulating a logical outline of your thoughts about, and your presentation of, the text: coordination and subordination. Some thoughts are coordinate, while others are subordinate. Coordinate thoughts will end up on the same level in the presentation, while subordinate thoughts will appear on a lower level. As a rather simple illustration, analyze the following list: doves, dogs, birds, animals, boxers, Dalmatians, hawks. Which terms are coordinate, and which are subordinate? Doves and hawks are coordinate with each other and subordinate to birds. Likewise, boxers and Dalmatians are coordinate with each other and subordinate to dogs. Finally, birds and dogs are coordinate categories that are subordinate to the most general term in the list, animals. Were this list a text, the results of our analysis could result in the following presentation:

Animals
   I.   Birds
        A.   Doves
        B.   Hawks
  II.   Dogs
        A.   Boxers
        B.   Dalmatians

How would you analyze and present the following list: teaching, fruits, peace, preacher, studying, love, functions? What is the main idea, or the most general term? What are the main points, that is, what terms are coordinate with each other and subordinate to the most general term? What are the subpoints, those terms that are coordinate with each other and subordinate to the main points. The logic of the terms results in the following outline:

Preacher
  I.   Functions
        A.   Studying
        B.   Teaching
  II.   Fruits
        A.   Love
        B.   Peace

Let's return to Psalm 13, which we have seen falls into three strophes based on the shifting grammatical mood in the verses. Without
concern at this point for poetic flair of presentation, but with a focus
on the logic of your thoughts about the text and your presentation of
the text, how might you outline this psalm? Before reading on, try your
own hand at it.

One thing that serves to coordinate all three strophes is that they
are expressing David's feelings and thoughts in a time of deep distress.
Verses 1–2 [2–3] express David's agonizing questions, questions about
God (note the "you" in verse 1 [2]), about self (note the "I" and "my"
in v. 2a [3a]), and about others (note the "enemy" in v. 2b [3b]). Verses
3–4 [4–5] express David's requests, what he wants God to do ("look"
and "answer" in v. 3a [4a]) for him ("my eyes" and "I will sleep" in v.
3b [4b]) in relation to others ("enemy" and "foes" in v. 4 [5]). Verses
5–6 [6] express David's resolve to trust the Lord's love and goodness
and his resolve to praise the Lord. A simple analytical outline that manifests the logical coordination and subordination of ideas in this poem
could look as follows:

David's Dealing with Distress
  I.   David's Questions (vv. 1–2 [2–3])
        A.   About God (v. 1 [2])
        B.   About self (v. 2a [3a])
        C.   About others (v. 2b [3b])
  II.   David's Requests (vv. 3–4 [4–5])
        A.   In relation to God (v. 3a [4a])
        B.   In relation to self (v. 3b [4b])
        C.   In relation to others (v. 4 [5])

III.   David's Affirmations (vv. 5–6 [6])
    A.   His resolve to trust the Lord (v. 5 [6a])
    B.   His resolve to praise the Lord (v. 6 [6b])

While you might think that your work is done once you've produced a logical outline, you need to consider one final step, and that is the language of your outline.

Outlining: The Language

There's a difference between what I call exegetical language and expository language. Exegetical language is typically text specific and third person, while expository language is universal[26] and second person.[27] The above outline of Psalm 13 is exegetical, thus the language is tied closely to the text, and it is third person. The benefit of using such language is that it "brings the contours, structure, and content, and therewith the meaning of the text into sharp focus."[28] The downside is that such language tends to put immediate distance between the text and the contemporary audience. The above outline says that Psalm 13 is about David, not about you. Using exegetical language suggests that application is something that the preacher adds on to exposition.[29] The use of expository language, however, presumes that "exposition is indeed application."[30]

Expository language is universal. This simply means that the message embedded in the text is applicable to all people in all times and places, and can be expressed as such. We could say, for example, that Genesis 14 is about Abraham and the kings of the east, or we could say that it is about action rooted in the promise and motivated by love.[31] The for-

---

26. On the use of universal language in preaching, see Hendrik Krabbendam, "Hermeneutics and Preaching," in *The Preacher and Preaching: Reviving the Art in the Twentieth Century* (Phillipsburg, NJ: P & R Publishing, 1986), 239–45.

27. On the use of second-person language in preaching, see John F. Bettler, "Application," in *The Preacher and Preaching: Reviving the Art in the Twentieth Century* (Phillipsburg, NJ: P & R Publishing, 1986), 331–49.

28. Krabbendam, "Hermeneutics and Preaching," 239.

29. Bettler, "Application," 332.

30. Krabbendam, "Hermeneutics and Preaching," 239.

31. Ibid., 241.

mer says the story is about a distant time and place, while the latter says the story impacts how people live now. We could say that Psalm 121 gives promises to Israelite pilgrims on the journey to Jerusalem, or we could say that it gives promises to all believers on their journey through life. Expository language engages the heart and mind from the outset.

Expository language is also second person. Second-person language is personal, and immediately engages the audience and applies the text to the listeners. We could say that Philippians 1:1–11 is about how the Holy Spirit encourages unity through service, or we could say that it's about how the Holy Spirit encourages you to build unity in the church through mutual service.[32] Even if no other "applications" are made, you've already applied the text by communicating what the Holy Spirit wants your audience to do. We could say that Psalm 29 invites the angels to worship in response to God's theophanic presence, or we could say that it invites you to worship God when you perceive God's power and glory in creation. Saying that expository language is second person is not to say there's no room in preaching for first- or third-person speech. Mixing first-person address ("I" and "we") with second-person address has the benefit of identifying the preacher with the audience and thereby avoids "preaching down to" the congregation. The point here is that a balanced use of second-person address, especially in the upper levels of the outline, immediately engages the audience and applies the text.

With expository language in mind, our outline of Psalm 13 might look like the following:

How to Deal with Distressing Situations in Life
    I.   Ask Your Questions (vv. 1–2)[33]
        A.   About the way God is treating you (v. 1)
        B.   About the struggle in your own soul (v. 2a)
        C.   About your frustration occasioned by others (v. 2b)
    II. Make Your Requests (vv. 3–4)

---

32. Bettler, "Application," 340.

33. Note that I have removed the Hebrew verse references (normally indicated in brackets) in the expository outline. Including them would, in my estimation, detract from the clarity of presentation without adding value to any measurable degree.

     A.   For God to pay attention to you (v. 3a)
     B.   For God to deliver you (v. 3b)
     C.   For God to vindicate you (v. 4)
III. Affirm Your Intentions (vv. 5–6)
     A.   To trust the Lord (v. 5)
     B.   To praise the Lord (v. 6)

There certainly are other ways to proclaim the message of Psalm 13, but a presentation like the one above has the advantages of walking your audience straight through the flow of thought in the text and addressing your audience in clear, memorable language that immediately "applies" the text to them. Let us now turn our attention to some final reflection on the text and life.

STEP 4: REFLECTING ON YOUR TEXT AND LIFE

Elizabeth Achtemeier has clearly articulated the need to avoid what I've called "exegetical language" in proclaiming the message of a psalm, and she challenges the preacher to ask questions of the text, the answers to which will aid in bringing the text home to a contemporary audience. Permit a rather extensive quotation that summarizes the previous section and introduces the importance of this final section.

> Having discovered the intricacies of the thought in a psalm . . . probably the worst thing a preacher can do in the sermon is simply to describe the thought and experience of the psalmist, as objects "out there" to be considered by the congregation. Such sermons contain phrases such as "the psalmist feels," "the psalmist learns," "the psalmist realizes." The experience of the singer with God remains an event unconnected with the life of the listening congregation, an experience that happened to someone long ago but that has not happened to them. The point of a sermon from the psalms is so to appropriate the language of the psalm for the congregation that what happened long ago for the psalmist happens in the immediate now for the congregation. Israel's experience with its God becomes their experience. The psalmist's journey in the relation with God

becomes their journey. This means that exegetical and commentary work with a psalm to uncover its meaning does not suffice. A preacher may have a very clear idea, after doing exegesis, of what a psalm text meant originally, but the principal questions to be answered by the preacher are: What does this text mean for my people? How is it the mirror of their life? Where are they in this psalm's words, and how can I show them that is their position? And then how can I lead them through the experience of all that the psalmist has experienced, that they may grow in the faith and knowledge of their Lord? The way the preacher answers those questions in shaping a sermon will determine whether or not the word of God in the psalm comes home to the hearts of the congregation.[34]

The interpreter can ask of the text several questions that will aid in this process of bringing the message of the psalm "home to the hearts of the congregation."

Ask the Big Question

The big question simply put is, "So what?" Does what you are planning to say in your sermon make any difference in the lives of those listening, and are you clear on what that difference is? James 1:26–27 says,

> If you claim to be religious but don't control your tongue, you are just fooling yourself, and your religion is worthless. Pure and lasting religion in the sight of God our Father means that we must care for orphans and widows in their troubles, and refuse to let the world corrupt us. (NLT 1.0)

Our religion is not simply a set of ideas. Ideas are, of course, central to our faith, but these ideas must translate into action in our lives. What we believe must shape how we live.[35] When you have a clear answer

---

34. Achtemeier, *Preaching from the Old Testament*, 148–49.
35. The best monograph on application I have read is Daniel Doriani, *Putting the Truth to Work: The Theory and Practice of Biblical Application* (Phillipsburg, NJ: P & R Publishing, 2001). In my estimation this book is must reading for those who teach and preach the Bible.

to "So what?" you are ready to preach. But how do you get that clarity? No doubt there are any number of paths you can take.[36] I've found that asking the "covenant questions" provides a wonderful balance in answering the "So what?"

Ask the Covenant Questions

At the heart of biblical religion is relationship. Jesus taught that the primary relationship is between God and people (Matt. 22:37). According to Exodus 6:7 redemption has this relationship as its goal: "I will take you as my own people, and I will be your God. Then you will know that I am the LORD your God, who brought you out from under the yoke of the Egyptians." This relationship the Bible calls *covenant*. As God said to Abraham, "I will establish my covenant as an everlasting covenant between me and you and your descendants after you for the generations to come, to be your God and the God of your descendants after you" (Gen. 17:7).

How we relate to God can never be isolated from how we relate to other people. As 1 John 4:20 teaches, "If someone says, 'I love God,' but hates a Christian brother or sister, that person is a liar; for if we don't love people we can see, how can we love God, whom we cannot see?" (NLT). This biblical logic lies behind Jesus' teaching that the secondary relationship in our religion is with other people (Matt. 22:39). Covenant, therefore, refers to our relationship with God and others.

All relationships involve thoughts, feelings, and actions. Having a relationship with someone entails knowing at least some things about that person, acting in some ways in relation to that person, and experiencing some emotions in response to that person. So three basic covenant questions to ask the text are, (1) What does this text teach me to believe? (2) What does this text teach me to do? (3) What does this text teach me to feel?

Every text will not yield equal numbers of answers to these questions. The focus of Psalm 104, for example, which is a song of praise to the Creator, is clearly on what we are to believe about God and his

---

36. Ibid., 97–157, uses four questions: (1) What should I do? (2) Who should I be? (3) Where should I go? (4) How can I distinguish truth from error?

creation. But also present are the invitations to praise God (v. 33) and
to feel great joy (v. 34) as we relate to God in creation.

No doubt the laments more than any other category of psalms speak
to our feelings in our relationships with God and others.[37] At a minimum David feels abandoned, perplexed, grieved, and frustrated when
he says,

> How long, O LORD? Will you forget me forever?
>   How long will you hide your face from me?
> How long must I wrestle with my thoughts
>   and every day have sorrow in my heart?
> How long will my enemy triumph over me?
>   (Ps. 13:1–2 [2–3])

Yet this psalm also teaches us to ask God for the things we need (vv.
3-4 [4–5]) and to wait in faith for God to act on our behalf (vv. 5-6 [6]).
On the other hand, Psalm 15 emphasizes what we are to do (vv. 2–5a)
much more than what we are to believe or how we are to feel. Yet even
this psalm reminds us of God's holiness (v. 1) and fills our hearts with
courage (v. 5b).

By reflecting on the text and life in relation to God, self, and others, we bring our preparation to a close. We are now ready to proclaim
the message of the text in a way that does justice to its meaning as first
experienced by the original users of the text and in a way that comes
home to modern hearts.

---

37. Must reading in this regard is Dan B. Allender and Tremper Longman III, *Cry of the Soul:
    How Our Emotions Reveal Our Deepest Questions About God* (Colorado Springs: NavPress,
    1994).

6

PRACTICING THE PRINCIPLES

A psalm of David.
Ascribe to the LORD, O mighty ones,
ascribe to the LORD glory and strength.
Ascribe to the LORD the glory due his name;
worship the LORD in the splendor of his holiness.

The voice of the LORD is over the waters;
the God of glory thunders,
the LORD thunders over the mighty waters.
The voice of the LORD is powerful;
the voice of the LORD is majestic.
The voice of the LORD breaks the cedars;
the LORD breaks in pieces the cedars of Lebanon.
He makes Lebanon skip like a calf,
Sirion like a young wild ox.
The voice of the LORD strikes
with flashes of lightning.
The voice of the LORD shakes the desert;
the LORD shakes the Desert of Kadesh.
The voice of the LORD twists the oaks

and strips the forests bare.
And in his temple all cry, "Glory!"

⌘

The LORD sits enthroned over the flood;
the LORD is enthroned as King forever.
The LORD gives strength to his people;
the LORD blesses his people with peace.
(Ps. 29)

IT IS TIME NOW TO SYNTHESIZE what we've learned and put into practice the principles we've discussed. Our text is Psalm 29. We will follow the steps outlined in the previous chapter, although you'll see that our analysis of Psalm 29 will not be quite as linear as the previous discussion was. As mentioned there, while you are focusing on one step of the process, or even one aspect of one step, you are often working on any number of levels simultaneously. With this in mind, let's get oriented to Psalm 29.

STEP 1: GETTING ORIENTED

As you read and reread Psalm 29, you will note a number of things. First, you'll note some key repetitions: the threefold repetition of הָבוּ ("ascribe") in verses 1–2, the fourfold repetition of לַיהוָה ("to the LORD") in these same verses, the sevenfold repetition of קוֹל יְהוָה ("the voice of the LORD") in verses 3–9, the fourfold repetition of יְהוָה ("the LORD") alone in verses 3–9, the twofold repetition of the verb יָשַׁב ("sits enthroned") in verses 10–11. These repetitions lead to the initial idea of dividing Psalm 29 into three strophes (vv. 1–2, vv. 3–9, vv. 10–11).

Second, you will note the shift in grammatical mood that takes place at verse 3. Verses 1–2 are in the imperative mood, while verses 3–11 are in the indicative mood. A more subtle but nonetheless significant shift takes place at verse 10, where the subject of the verbs is no longer קוֹל יְהוָה ("the voice of the LORD"), as is the case in verses 3–9, but simply יְהוָה ("the LORD"). Thus you will note a shift in content from the summons to worship the Lord in verses 1–2 to a description of "the voice of the LORD" in verses 3–9 to predications about the Lord's reign in verses 10–11.

Third, you will note the symmetry of word counts. Verses 1–2 contain sixteen words in the Hebrew text. Four of the sixteen are the divine name, יְהוָה ("the LORD"). Verses 10–11 also contain sixteen words in the Hebrew text. Again, four of the sixteen are the divine name, יְהוָה ("the LORD"). And the intervening Hebrew verses contain seven (a number used for completion in the Hebrew Bible[1]) occurrences of קוֹל יְהוָה ("the voice of the LORD").

A number of indicators thus converge to confirm that Psalm 29 is, in fact, comprised of three clearly demarcated strophes. The general sense of these strophes is also clear. Verses 1–2 are a summons to worship the Lord. Verses 3–9 provide the context of that worship: worship is a response to the manifestation of "the voice of the LORD" in creation. Verses 10–11 are affirmations about the Lord's reign and the implications of that reign for his people.

Reading and rereading Psalm 29 in the context of Psalms 28 and 30 yields some additional insights. Most striking is the motif of "silence." In Psalm 28:1–2 the psalmist is desperate for God not to be silent.

> To you I call, O LORD my Rock;
> > do not turn a deaf ear to me.
> For if you remain silent,
> > I will be like those who have gone down to the pit.
> Hear my cry [קוֹל] for mercy
> > as I call [בְּשַׁוְּעִי] to you for help,
> as I lift up my hands
> > toward your Most Holy Place.

In Psalm 29 the Lord is anything but silent. His "voice" (קוֹל) is heard seven times in verses 3–9 as he "thunders" over the waters (v. 3), clearly in response to the psalmist's "voice/cry" (קוֹל) in 28:2. In particular the psalmist in 28:2 calls (שָׁוַע) on God for help, lest he join

---

1. "Seven," in *DBI*, 774–75.

"those who have gone down to the pit" (יוֹרְדֵי בוֹר); and in the wake of Psalm 29, the psalmist in 30:2 [3] celebrates how God responded to his call (שִׁוַּע) and in 30:3 [4] how God spared him from "going down into the pit" (מִיוֹרְדִי־בוֹר). So the transcendence of God emphasized in Psalm 29:3–9 must be balanced with the immanence of God articulated in Psalms 28 and 30.

Also of note are the themes of strength and blessing. In Psalm 28 the poet ends his prayer by declaring that the Lord is his own "strength" (עֻזִּי; v. 7) and "the strength of his people" (עֹז לְעַמוֹ[2] v. 8) and by asking the Lord to "bless" (וּבָרֵךְ) his inheritance (v. 9). The psalmist responds in Psalm 29 by concluding his hymn with the twofold affirmation that the Lord will indeed give "strength to his people" (עֹז־לְעַמּוֹ) and will bless (בְּרַךְ) his people with peace (v. 11). These connections remind us that our exposition of Psalm 29 must not be an abstract theological lesson but must be a vehicle of strength and blessing for the daily living of God's people.

Reading and rereading Psalm 29 in the context of other psalms of its category—the **Kingship of Yahweh psalms**—will help us when we turn to some of the details of exegesis. In particular, reading 29:3 with its reference to the "mighty waters" in the context of 93:4 will lead us to conclude that the "mighty waters" in Psalm 29 refer not only to the massive waters of the Mediterranean but also to the chaotic waters that threaten God's well-ordered world. We will also see that, although Psalm 29:1–2 summons the angelic hosts to worship the Lord, this summons is rightly extended to humans, since Psalm 96 does just this. Psalm 96:7–9 is a quotation of Psalm 29:1–2 with several key changes, one of which is the shift from summoning the "angels" to worship to summoning the "families of nations" to worship.

STEP 2: FOCUSING ON THE DETAILS

Now that you are oriented to the text, you can begin to focus on the details of exegesis. In the previous chapter we spoke primarily about parallelism and imagery in this section, so we will consider those di-

---

2. The MT reads לָמוֹ ("to them"), but a few Hebrew manuscripts, the Septuagint, Syriac, and the parallel term "*his* anointed" support the emendation to לְעַמּוֹ ("to *his* people"). See Peter C. Craigie, *Psalms 1–50*, WBC (Waco: Word, 1983), 236.

mensions of the exegetical process here and look at other exegetical details as well.

Verses 1–2

Verses 1–2 are a lovely example of a quatrain.[3] Verses 1–2 are neither two bicola nor a tricolon followed by a **monocolon**. The threefold repetition of הָבוּ ("ascribe") and the fourfold repetition of לַיהוָה ("to the LORD") bind these cola into a single line. The shift from הָבוּ ("ascribe") to הִשְׁתַּחֲווּ ("worship") not only signals the end of the line but also signals the climax of the call to worship the Lord when he appears in holy splendor (see below). The first colon tells us who is to do the ascribing, the second indicates the content of the ascription, the third sharpens the focus on one dimension of the ascription, and the fourth specifies when the worship is to take place.

The worshipers are the בְּנֵי אֵלִים, literally "sons of gods." Who are these "sons of gods"? This exact phrase occurs only one other time in the Hebrew Bible, Psalm 89:6 [7].

> For who in the skies above can compare with the LORD?
> Who is like the LORD among the בְּנֵי אֵלִים?

Occurring between the "assembly of the holy ones" (v. 5 [6]) and the "council of the holy ones" (v. 7 [8]) who surround the Lord in heaven, the בְּנֵי אֵלִים in verse 6 [7] no doubt refer to "angels." The NLT 1.0, therefore, is on solid ground in translating בְּנֵי אֵלִים in Psalm 29:1 with "angels." The worshipers in Psalm 29 are not humans on earth but angels in heaven.[4]

The angels are to ascribe two characteristics to the Lord: glory (כָּבוֹד) and strength (עֹז). When used as an ascription for God, "glory" (כָּבוֹד) has two dimensions. God's glory is visible and royal.[5] Israel *saw*

---

3. Wilfred G. E. Watson, *Classical Hebrew Poetry: A Guide to Its Techniques*, JSOTSup (Sheffield: JSOT, 1986), 185.

4. A similar address to the angels is found in the traditional doxology that the church sings: "Praise God from whom all blessings flow. Praise him all creatures here below. *Praise him above you heavenly host.* Praise Father, Son, and Holy Ghost."

5. See Mark D. Futato, *Creation: A Witness to the Wonder of God* (Phillipsburg, NJ: P & R Publishing, 2000), 2–8.

God's glory on Mount Sinai: "And you said, 'The LORD our God has *shown us his glory*'" (Deut. 5:24). Moses was allowed to *see* God's glory: "When my *glory* passes by . . . you will *see* my back; but my face must not be *seen*" (Exod. 33:22–23). In keeping with this, John tells us that "The Word became flesh and made his dwelling among us. We have *seen his glory*" (John 1:14). And this visible glory is also royal. This is true on the human level as well as the divine. "Glory" is an attribute of the human kings.

> You made him a little lower than the heavenly beings
>   and *crowned* him *with glory* and honor.
>
> (Ps. 8:5)

> O LORD, *the king* rejoices in your strength. . . .
>   Through the victories you gave, his *glory* is great.
> (Ps. 21:1, 5 [6])

"Glory" also is an attribute of the divine king.

> Lift up your heads, O you gates;
>   be lifted up, you ancient doors,
>   that the *King of glory* may come in.
> (Ps. 24:7)

In a psalm that celebrates the kingship of God, we read, "Declare his *glory* among the nations" (Ps. 96:3). This leads us to expect that the angels in Psalm 29 are about to see the royal glory of God in some way or another.

"Strength" (עֹז) is likewise a royal attribute. Psalm 74:12–13 confesses that God as king has conquered the forces of chaos by his "strength."

> But you, O God, are my *king* from of old;
>   you bring salvation upon the earth.
> It was you who split open the sea by your *power* [בְעָזְּךָ];
>   you broke the heads of the monster in the waters.

Psalm 68 celebrates the victory of the divine King and prays for a renewed manifestation of the King's saving strength (עֹז).

> Your procession has come into view, O God,
>> the procession of my God and *King* into the sanctuary.
>>> (v. 24 [25])

> Summon your power [עֻזְּךָ], O God;
>> show us your strength, O God, as you have done before.
>>> (v. 28 [29])

When are the angels to ascribe this royal glory and strength to the Lord? The answer to this question is found in the final colon of the quatrain. The NASB interprets the final phrase, בְּהַדְרַת־קֹדֶשׁ, as referring to the worshiper's attire: "in holy array." Most translations interpret the phrase in reference to the Lord in some more general way, such as, "in the splendor of his holiness" (NIV). Hebrew הֲדָרָה is a "gender doublet" for the more common הָדָר ("splendor").[6] As such it is a synonym of כָּבוֹד ("glory") and shares the "visible" nature of כָּבוֹד. The phrase in Psalm 29:2 thus could be translated, "in the visible splendor of holiness." The "visible splendor" (הֲדָרָה) of the Lord's holiness is about to be witnessed in the "majestic" (הָדָר; v. 4) nature of the storm described in verses 3–9. So the sense of this final colon is "Worship the LORD when his holiness appears in the splendor of the storm that you are about to witness."[7] The opening quatrain thus builds step by step to a climax that leads directly to the second strophe of this psalm.

---

6. Bruce K. Waltke, *The Book of Proverbs: Chapters 1–15*, NICOT (Grand Rapids: Eerdmans, 2004), 581n. 47.

7. For Ugaritic evidence for translating בְּהַדְרַת־קֹדֶשׁ with "when he appears in holiness," see Frank M. Cross, "Notes on a Canaanite Psalm," *BASOR* 117 (1950): 19–21; and for a defense of Cross's view, see Mark D. Futato, "A Meteorological Analysis of Psalms 104, 65, and 29" (Ph.D. diss., The Catholic University of America, 1984), 236–38. For a more recent and confirmatory discussion of this phrase as it is used in Psalm 96:9, see David M. Howard Jr., *The Structure of Psalms 93–100*, Biblical and Judaic Studies, vol. 5, ed. William Henry Propp (Winona Lake, IN: Eisenbrauns, 1997).

Verses 3–9

Verses 3–9 describe a massive rainstorm that traverses the land from west to east. Above all else, this storm manifests the glory and power of the Lord, which are to elicit a response of worship from the angels in heaven.

The opening tricolon sets the stage. The "voice" of the Lord in verse 3a is defined in verse 3b as thunder, and the "waters" of verse 3a are defined in verse 3c as the "mighty waters." Thus we are encountering a thunderstorm brewing over the "mighty waters." The "mighty waters" (מַיִם רַבִּים) are an obvious geographical reference to the Mediterranean. But they have a theological nuance in addition. The phrase מַיִם רַבִּים can simply refer to any large amount of water (e.g., Num. 20:11; 2 Chron. 32:4; Jer. 41:12). But it also can be used as an image of chaos that needs to be quelled. In Psalm 32:6 the מַיִם רַבִּים refers to the troubles that threaten to overwhelm a well-ordered life. In Psalm 93:3–4 the מַיִם רַבִּים are an image of the cosmic forces of chaos that the Lord vanquished at the time of Creation.

> The seas have lifted up, O LORD,
>> the seas have lifted up their voice;
>> the seas have lifted up their pounding waves.
> Mightier than the thunder of the *great waters* [מַיִם רַבִּים],
>> mightier than the breakers of the sea—
>> the LORD on high is mighty.

Psalm 29 thus employs the mythopoeic imagery of the Lord's conquest of the sea.[8]

The grammar of the two cola in verse 4 is identical.[9] The only difference in the line is the substitution in the second colon of the word הָדָר ("splendor") for the word כֹּחַ ("power") in the first. Hebrew הָדָר ("splendor") and כֹּחַ ("power") are synonyms of כָּבוֹד ("glory") and עֹז ("strength") from verse 1. The use of these synonyms in verse 4

---

8. See the excursus on mythopoeic imagery at the end of chapter 1 (pages 53–55).

9. For the use of the preposition *beth* to introduce the predicate of a sentence, see *DCH*, 2:84; and Paul Joüon and T. Muraoka, *A Grammar of Biblical Hebrew* (Rome: Pontifical Biblical Institute, 1991), §133c.

serves to tie the storm (vv. 3–9) to the call to worship (vv. 1–2). The
הָדָר ("splendor") and כֹּחַ ("power") witnessed in the storm are to be
ascribed to the Lord and to no other deity.

The intensity of the storm comes out in the imagery used in verse
5. Notice the shift from "cedars" to "cedars of Lebanon" as you move
from the first colon to the second. This shift does two things. One,
it intensifies the image as the general "cedars" are replaced with the
grand "cedars of Lebanon." Two, it locates the storm as having moved
in off of the Mediterranean and crossed the coastal mountains.

The parallelism in verse 6 serves a similar function. The shift from
"Lebanon" to "Sirion" moves the storm from the Lebanon range to
the Anti-Lebanon range, since "Sirion" is an ancient name for Mount
Hermon, at the southern tip of the Anti-Lebanon range.[10] The imagery also underscores the intensity of the storm. Massive mountains
undulating like calves and young oxen at the sound of thunder is a
hyperbolic description of the power of this storm that manifests the
power of God.

Having passed over the Anti-Lebanon range, the storm heads out to
the desert east of Mount Hermon. Notice the shift from the general
"desert" in verse 8a to the specific "Desert of Kadesh" in verse 8b.
The Desert of Kadesh is neither in the area of Kadesh Barnea to the far
south nor in the area of Kadesh on the Orontes to the far north, since
no storm would have made such a ninety-degree turn to the south or
to the north. The "Desert of Kadesh" is no doubt the Syrian steppe,
which lies just to the east of Mount Lebanon and is the logical terminus
for a storm trekking from the Mediterranean through the Lebanon and
Anti-Lebanon ranges.

With the track of the storm complete, the poet sets the time of year
for us in verse 9a. Any leaves remaining on trees at the end of the dry
season would have been stripped off with the coming of the first storms
in the fall.[11] What is described in verses 3–9, therefore, is the first powerful cyclonic storm of the rainy season, which, as we will see when
we turn to verses 10–11, manifest the kingship of the Lord. The Lord's
coming in the *rain* manifests his coming to *reign*.

---

10. See Deuteronomy 3:9, "Sidonians call Hermon Sirion" (NKJV, NASB).
11. Futato, "Meteorological Analysis," 219–21.

Some understand the "temple" in verse 9b to be the earthly temple,[12] but two factors lead to the conclusion that this "temple" is in heaven. First, the track of the storm does not terminate in Jerusalem. Second, those invited to "ascribe glory" to the Lord in verses 1–2 are in heaven, not on earth. This colon seems to offer a final motivation for the angelic host to comply with the invitation to worship the Lord. The verb form translated "cry" is a participle. Participles are used for continuous action. The point seems to be that crying "Glory!" is what the angelic host has continuously done in past years when the glory of God has been manifested in the powerful storms that start the rainy season.[13] That being said, it is certainly the case that the poet intends for the worshipers who use Psalm 29 in the earthly temple to follow the example of their heavenly counterparts.

Verses 10–11

With the description of the storm complete, the poet is now ready to draw out several implications. Verse 10 affirms that the coming of the rains is evidence that the Lord reigns. The verbs translated "sits enthroned" and "is enthroned" are forms of יָשַׁב ("to sit"). This verb is used to describe the Lord's being "enthroned" between the cherubim in the earthly sanctuary (e.g., 1 Sam. 4:4; 2 Sam. 6:2), from where he reigns over all the earth (2 Kings 19:15). In Psalm 29:10a we are told that the Lord is enthroned, not over the ark of the covenant, but over the "flood." The Hebrew word מַבּוּל is used elsewhere in the Hebrew Bible only in the Flood story (Gen. 6:1–9:17). A reference at this point in the psalm to the Flood in the days of Noah seems quite out of place.

So to what does the poet refer with the word מַבּוּל? Given the use of מַבּוּל in the Flood story—where מַבּוּל refers to the waters that returned the earth to the chaotic state described in Genesis 1:2 ("Now the earth was formless and empty, darkness was over the surface of the deep, and the Spirit of God was hovering over the *waters*")—and given the reference to the waters of chaos in Psalm 29:3 ("the LORD

---

12. Gerald H. Wilson, *Psalms Volume 1*, NIVAC (Grand Rapids: Zondervan, 2002), 507.
13. Futato, "Meteorological Analysis," 223–24.

thunders over *the mighty waters*"), it is best to interpret מַבּוּל as referring to these same waters.[14] The word מַבּוּל evokes the mythopoeic image of the Lord's vanquishing chaotic waters at the time of Creation and ever since. The power and glory of the Lord evident in the rainstorm described in verses 3–9 demonstrate that the Lord reigns over all the forces that threaten a well-ordered life on earth. And this reign, as verse 10b makes clear, is not a brief flash in the pan but is "forever."

If the Lord reigns over the forces that threaten a well-ordered life, there are sure implications for his people. The first implication has to do with power: "The LORD gives strength to his people" (v. 11a). The word translated "strength" is עֹז, the same word used in verse 1 for the "strength" that the angels are to ascribe to the Lord when they witness his power in the storm. The point is that the power of God manifested in the storm is the kind of power that the Lord is able and willing to give to his people. God's power in the storm is a demonstration of the power that is available to his people. The second implication is the blessing of peace: "The LORD blesses his people with peace" (v. 11b). When God is the subject of this verb for "bless"(בָּרַךְ), it means to empower to live at the optimum level,[15] and the noun for "peace" (שָׁלוֹם) is used for complete well-being and prosperity.[16] Since the power of God supersedes the power of chaos, God can empower his people to experience this שָׁלוֹם. For the ancients this would have referred primarily to the agricultural success and prosperity that would have resulted from the coming of the rains described in verses 3–9.

One more overarching "detail" must be considered before we move on to step 3. While it cannot be proven beyond a shadow of a doubt, there is some likelihood that David did not compose Psalm 29 from scratch but rather took an existing hymn to Baal and modified it for polemical reasons.[17] One argument for this view is based on topography. The storm described in verses 3–9 follows a clear path that lies outside the borders of ancient Israel. The storm passes through Phoenicia, where Baal as the storm god was the chief deity. Another argument is that "Sirion" is the Sidonian/Phoenician name for what Israelites called

---

14. See Wilson, *Psalms Volume 1*, 507; and Richard J. Clifford, *Psalms 1–72*, AOTC (Nashville: Abingdon, 2002), 156.

15. M. Brown, "בָּרַךְ," in *NIDOTTE*, 1:759.

16. P. Nel, "שָׁלוֹם," in *NIDOTTE*, 4:131.

17. For detailed bibliography on this issue, see Craigie, *Psalms 1–50*, 243–44.

Mount Hermon. "Sirion" needed to be explained to an Israelite audience in Deuteronomy 3:9 but would have been well known among the Phoenicians. A third argument is based on alliteration. If the name Baal (בַּעַל) is restored to the psalm, a substantial amount of alliteration with the consonants *beth*, *ayin*, and *lamed* is evident.[18]

Anti-Baal polemics abound in the Hebrew Bible. There are narrative polemics like the Creation accounts in Genesis 1–2,[19] Gideon's tearing down of his father's altar to Baal in Judges 6, and the famous "Elijah versus the prophets of Baal" in 1 Kings 18. The author of the latter story uses satire and irony to mock an impotent Baal and to exalt the all-powerful Lord. All the strange gyrations (v. 26) and self-mutilations (v. 28) of the Baal prophets produce no results at all (v. 29), while Elijah's simple prayer to the Lord (vv. 36–37) brings fire (v. 38) and rain (v. 45) from heaven, along with the resounding confession, "The LORD—he is God! The LORD—he is God!" (v. 39).

We also have seen how ancient Israelite poets borrowed the mythological language of their Canaanite neighbors to affirm truth about the God of Israel.[20] Texts like Psalm 74:12–17 polemicize against the Canaanite storm deity by affirming that it was Yahweh who conquered the primordial forces of chaos, not Baal. David's use of an entire Canaanite poem for this same purpose would thus be part of a larger Israelite theological tradition. Whether originally a hymn to Baal or not, Psalm 29 is clearly a polemic against the worship of Baal and for the worship of Yahweh. The ancients were not to ascribe the glory and the power of the storm to Baal but to Yahweh.[21]

STEP 3: SHAPING YOUR PRESENTATION

Having studied the text in some detail, you are now ready to give shape to your presentation. To illustrate the differences discussed in the previous chapter, I will first discuss Psalm 29 from an exegetical perspective and then from an expository perspective. I'll produce two

---

18. See Aloysius Fitzgerald, "A Note on Psalm 29," *BASOR* 214 (1974): 61–63.

19. See Mark D. Futato, "Because It Had Rained: A Study of Genesis 2:5–7 with Implications for Genesis 2:4–25 and Genesis 1:1–2:3," *WTJ* 60 (1998): 1–21.

20. See the excursus on mythopoeic imagery at the end of chapter 1 (pages 53–55).

21. See Craigie, *Psalms 1–50*, 249, who argues for the anti-Baal polemic, even though he argues against the Canaanite origin of Psalm 29.

outlines along the way, one from each perspective, so that you can reflect on the differing uses of language.

Exegesis

Psalm 29 is a hymn. As you learned in chapter 4, hymns usually fall into three sections: an opening invitation to praise God, a central delineation of the praiseworthy character and actions of God, and a concluding affirmation of faith or renewed invitation to praise and worship. In this regard, Psalm 29 is typical.

Verses 1–2, with their triple use of "ascribe" (הָבוּ) and their climactic use of "worship" (הִשְׁתַּחֲווּ), invite the angels to worship the Lord, in particular by ascribing glory and power to him. These verses answer three key questions. What is to be ascribed? Answer: glory and power. To whom is this glory and power to be ascribed? Answer: the Lord (not Baal). When is this ascription to be made? Answer: When this holy glory and power appear for all to see.

Verses 3–9 describe the glory and power of God not in abstract terms but with the concrete image of a glorious and powerful thunderstorm at the beginning of the rainy season as it brews over the Mediterranean, traverses the mountains, and dissipates over the desert. The sevenfold repetition of קוֹל יְהוָה ("the voice of the LORD") rolls through the text just as thunder rolls through the hills and valleys of the land. With this repetition the poet reminds us that this thunder is not just the breaking of the sound barrier by superheated air but is a manifestation of the praiseworthy presence of God.

Verses 10–11 conclude this hymn by affirming that the Lord is King of creation and King over all the forces that threaten a well-ordered life (v. 10). They also affirm that the power of the God manifested in the storm is a power that God grants to his people so that they can experience well-being and prosperity in the land. Whereas the opening strophe addresses the angels, this concluding section explicitly draws out implications of the storm for those living on earth.

The climactic use of the word "worship" in the first strophe justifies our use of this term in articulating the overarching message of Psalm 29. We can say that Psalm 29 is about worshiping the Lord. The second strophe's focus on God's glory and power in the storm allows us to sharpen the message by saying that Psalm 29 is about the angelic worship of the Lord when his glory and power are witnessed in the storms of the fall rainy season. The final strophe brings further clarity with its focus on the Lord's reign, which is evident in the rain. Thus we might title Psalm 29, "The Angelic Worship of the Lord who Reigns/Rains," and outline it as follows:

The Angelic Worship of the Lord Who Reigns/Rains
   I.   The Invitation to Worship (vv. 1–2)
       A.   An invitation to angels (v. 1)
       B.   An invitation to ascribe (vv. 1–2)
           1.   To the Lord (v. 1)
           2.   Glory and power (v. 1)
           3.   When he appears (v. 2)
  II.   The Reasons for Worship (vv. 3–9)
       A.   The glory of the Lord in the storm
           1.   Experienced in the thunder (v. 3)
           2.   Experienced in the lightning (v. 7)
       B.   The power of the Lord in the storm
           1.   Experienced in the creation (vv. 4–6, 8–9)
           2.   Experienced over the chaos (v. 3)
 III.   The Affirmations of Worship (vv. 10–11)
       A.   The Lord is King (v. 10)
           1.   Ruling over the chaos (v. 10a)
           2.   Ruling forever (v. 10b)
       B.   The Lord is benefactor (v. 11)
           1.   Granting power (v. 11a)
           2.   Granting peace (v. 11b)

Note the logic of the outline. Each main point is coordinate with the other main points and subordinate to the title. Each second-level point, or subpoint is subordinate to its main point, and coordinate with the other subpoints. The same holds true at the third level down. Note also that the outline is analytical in sections I and III and topical in section II.[22] Glory and power are the two themes of section II. *Glory* forms

---

22. See chapter 5, pages 197–98 for the distinction between analytical and topical.

an inclusion around the whole, as it is repeated in verses 3 and 9, and the extended image of the storms continues to highlight the Lord's power. So it seems reasonable to make these two themes the subpoints of the section. Finally, note that the language is exegetical, especially that of the main points as they echo the language used to describe the structure of psalms that fall into the hymn category.

Exposition

Now let's reshape this presentation with expository language. Here I will do two things. First, I'll present an expository outline, and then I'll explain the changes from the exegetical outline.

Worship the King Who Reigns/Rains
- I. Accept the King's Invitation (vv. 1–2)
   - A. You are invited to worship with angels (v. 1)
      1. God's invitation to angels (v. 1)
      2. God's invitation to you (v. 1)
   - B. You are invited to ascribe with angels (vv. 1–2)
      1. Glory and power (v. 1)
      2. To the Lord (v. 1)
      3. When he appears (v. 2)
- II. Respond to the King's Motivation (vv. 3–9)
   - A. Experience the King's glory
      1. In the thunder (v. 3)
      2. In the lightning (v. 7)
   - B. Experience the King's power
      1. In the creation (vv. 4–6, 8–9)
      2. Over the chaos (v. 3)
- III. Affirm the King's Bounty (vv. 10–11)
   - A. Your King reigns (v. 10)
      1. Over the chaos of your life (v. 10a)
      2. Over the whole of your life (v. 10b)
   - B. Your King blesses (v. 11)
      1. You with power (v. 11a)
      2. You with peace (v. 11b)

The first change I made is shifting from addressing angels to addressing humans. I accomplished this with a number of changes. Note the shift to second-person address throughout the outline. In keeping with this shift, the title and main points are all in the imperative (second-person) mood, so the listener is being engaged and called upon to respond throughout the entire sermon. Along with the shift to second person, references to angels have been removed from the title and second level of the outline. Only one reference remains, and that is in the third level down. The result is that the sermon is no longer an explanation of how the psalmist summoned and motivated the angels to worship but has become a summons to a contemporary audience to worship the Lord.

Let me say three things about this shift from the angels to humans as the addressees of the text. One, the text makes this shift itself in verses 10–11, where the psalmist shows us that he is interested in the implications for humans of verses 1–9. Two, the activity of the angels in the heavenly temple is an example of the kind of activity in which humans are to be engaged in the earthly temple. In particular, as the ancient Israelites received the benefits of the rains (power and peace in verses 10–11), they were to acknowledge that these benefits came to them from the Lord and not from Baal. Three, I would explain this shift to the congregation, along with the relationship between angels and humans, at subsection A in section I.

A second change is the order of thought in section I subsection B. Instead of following the order of the text (to whom, what, when), I rearranged the material slightly to present the ideas in a way that flows better for a contemporary audience (what, to whom, when). The modified order now flows in a sentence: *Ascribe glory and power to the Lord when he appears*. Although I encourage the use of an analytical order, I do not follow this slavishly, but always ask how best to get the ideas across to today's listeners.

A third change is to the word "experience" in the subsections of section II. This shift is intended to accomplish a specific goal: to facilitate the listener in actually experiencing God's glory and power in creation, in addition to knowing about this glory and power as ideas. The ancients did not read expositions about powerful storms coming in off the Mediterranean to fructify the land; rather, they *experienced* such storms. Today's expositors would do well to recreate this experience for their listeners, so that the next time they experience a powerful storm they too will say, "There is the glory and power of the Lord right before my very eyes," and they will be encouraged to lay hold of such power where they need it in their daily living. And with this we have already begun step 4.

STEP 4: REFLECTING ON YOUR TEXT AND LIFE

In this step you need to reflect on what difference the text should make in the lives of God's people. The beginning of this reflection doesn't occur only now, of course, for you've been doing so all along the way. Now, however, having become oriented to the text, having worked through the details, and having shaped your presentation, you're in a position to sit back and reflect on some of the key ways the text applies to your own life and to that of your listeners.

What Are Your Listeners to Believe?

At a foundational level, Psalm 29 teaches us to believe that God manifests his character in creation.[23] Consider lightning. Lightning is the discharge of electricity that may take place between two parts of the same cloud, between two clouds, or between a cloud and the ground. The average lightning strike is six miles long, reaching more than 50,000 degrees Fahrenheit (four or five times the temperature of the sun at its surface), with a voltage anywhere from 100 million to 1 billion volts. Consider thunder. Thunder is the sound of a shock wave, created when lightning rapidly heats the surrounding air. The heated air expands explosively and compresses the air immediately around the heated area. In the area where the air is compressed, the air pressure is higher; and when the difference in pressure reaches your ear, it is sensed as thunder. That is all true enough from one perspective. Psalm 29 offers a complementary perspective: thunder and lightning are "the voice of the LORD."

When the ancients saw storm clouds moving in they saw more than just clouds. As Psalm 104:3 says,

---

23. For a fuller discussion see Futato, *Creation*.

> He makes the clouds his chariot
> and rides on the wings of the wind.

And Deuteronomy 33:26 adds,

> There is no one like the God of Jeshurun,
> who rides on the heavens to help you
> and on the clouds in his majesty.

In the storm clouds the ancients saw the Lord riding on his chariot. In the thunder and lightning, they heard his voice. The ancient Israelites were not, of course, pantheists or materialists, that is, they neither identified the Lord with the creation nor saw only material clouds. They were biblical theists. They believed that "the heavens declare the glory of God" (Ps. 19:1). They believed that "since the creation of the world God's invisible qualities—his eternal power and divine nature—have been clearly seen, being understood from what has been made" (Rom. 1:20). Psalm 29 invites us to believe this same truth.

Psalm 29 also teaches us to believe that God rules over the creation and intends to bless us as his children. The power and glory manifested in the storm are the royal attributes of the king who sits enthroned, ruling over the whole of his creation, even over the fierce forces that break cedars and strip forests bare. When we look at the apparent chaos in the world around us, we are tempted to conclude that there cannot be a good God who is in control. Ancient Israelites were no different. They, too, had evidence in their world that belied faith in the benevolent reign of God. Yes, there are the "mighty waters" (v. 3) and the "flood" (v. 10). And there is one who sits enthroned above all of this, and he is in control. Psalm 29 invites us to affirm the truth that God rules over the creation he has made and intends to bless us as his children.

The psalmist invites us to believe that the kind of power we witness in the forces of nature are exemplary of the power that God has *for us*. The apostle Paul prays that we might know God's "incomparably great power for us who believe" (Eph. 1:19). The psalmist wants us to believe that God is able and willing to do "more than all we ask or imagine, according to his power that is at work within us" (Eph. 3:20).

What Are Your Listeners to Feel?

Perhaps more than any other portion of Scripture, Psalms evokes an emotional response. A psalm like Psalm 29 intends to stir our emotions in two separate but related settings. One setting is when reading the psalm. Ancient Israelites would not have read or sung Psalm 29 in a dispassionate way but would have experienced a number of emotions when using this psalm in private or in public. The second setting is when experiencing the storm. The same emotions evoked by the psalm would, ideally, have been evoked when the ancients actually experienced the first storms of the rainy season. These two settings, while different, are reciprocal. On the one hand, the experience of reading the psalm would have an effect on one's experience of the storms themselves. This is an aspect of the instructional function of Psalms, as you learned in chapter 2. On the other hand, having experienced actual storms such as the one described in the psalm, one would have a deepened emotional response when reading the text, since the language of the text would have connected with real life experiences.

Anyone who has ever experienced a major electrical storm, such as those we have here in central Florida or those that are typical in the Midwest, has felt a tremendous sense of awe at the power and glory displayed in the storm. One cannot help but be awestruck when lightning strikes every few seconds and thunder follows the lighting almost instantaneously. What child does not run to a parent's lap in fear in the presence of such power and glory? Psalm 29 intends to evoke such feelings as we read of God's power and glory in the text and as we experience such power and glory in the creation itself.

Psalm 29 also intends to evoke a sense of anticipation. In my interpretation, the angels are being summoned to ascribe to the Lord and not to Baal the power and glory *that they are about to witness* in a storm. They are being primed for *what is about to come* and for the response *they are about to have*. Verses 1–2 create feelings of great anticipation. So do verses 10–11. The last two verses affirm that in the wake of the storm described in verses 3–9 the Lord will be present to give power to his people and to bless them with peace.

Thus, the purpose of Psalm 29 was to evoke a deep sense of anticipating the coming of the Lord in the first rains of the season to provide his people with all that they need for life in his presence. For the Israelites, anticipating the coming of the rains and the resultant blessings was anticipating the coming of the Lord to reign in blessing over them. While our geographical settings might be quite different, our theological setting is not. Like the ancients, we, too, need the Lord to show up in the concrete realities of our lives to provide us with all that we need for life in his presence. Psalm 29 is designed to evoke this feeling of great anticipation in the coming of the Lord. Just as Jesus taught us to pray "Your kingdom come . . . on earth as it is in heaven," Psalm 29 intends to fill us with a great sense of anticipation at the coming of the King.

What Are Your Listeners to Do?

The poet expects us to do at least two things in response to this psalm. The first is to worship the Lord. As we have noted, the word *worship* occupies the climatic position in the opening line of the psalm. The poem calls us to worship in response to the message in the text and in response to the manifestation of God's power and glory whenever and wherever we experience that power and glory in nature. The key way in which the psalm envisions this worship coming to expression is by our ascribing to the Lord the power and the glory that we witness in nature.

Few if any of us are tempted to ascribe the power and glory seen in nature to Baal. Our temptation runs in the opposite direction. We are tempted not to ascribe this power and glory to any deity, including the Lord, but simply to the "forces of nature." In other words, we're not tempted to baalism but to materialism or naturalism. We have drunk so deeply at the well of materialism, refilled constantly by our surrounding culture, that even if we are awestruck at an electrical storm, the awe is directed to the storm and not to the Lord who rides on the storm. Psalm 29 instructs us to be theists as we go about our daily lives, to live with an awareness that what we witness in nature is a revelation of divine attributes such as power and glory, and to worship God whenever and wherever we perceive him.

In keeping with the sense of anticipation evoked by the text, the poet also intends for us to respond by living with expectation in our hearts. What situations are you facing, for example, that require great strength of character? Where do you need the power to persevere? Where is there a lack of well-being or prosperity in your life? Psalm 29 intends to speak a word of hope into your heart in these areas. After all, "everything that was written in the past was written to teach us, so that *through endurance* and the encouragement of the Scriptures *we might have hope*" (Rom. 15:4). As the ancients expected the Lord to come in the fall rains and manifest his saving presence in theirs lives, Psalm 29 fills us with hope and encourages us to live with hope that the King will come into our lives with power to bless us with the well-being and prosperity that characterize his *shalom*. And our hope that God will so come into our lives is grounded not in the coming of an electrical storm but in the truth that he has come in the person of his Son. Jesus came that we might have life in all of its abundance (John 10:10). And he has guaranteed this life for us by his perfect life of righteousness lived in our place, his death on the cross, and his resurrection from the dead, which is the ultimate display of God's incomparably great power for us who believe (Eph 1:18–21).

GLOSSARY

analytical approach. An approach to outlining a text that follows the order of the text.

bicolon. A poetic line comprised of two cola.

category. A group of texts with common characteristics; also referred to as a genre.

colon. A colon (plural *cola*) is part, usually the first half, of a poetic line.

concatenation. The state of being linked together as in a chain.

divine kingship songs. A category of psalms composed for celebrating God's kingship; these psalms typically focus on God's universal reign over the nations and the whole of his creation.

eschatological. 1. That which pertains to the proclamation of God's reign in circumstances that seem to deny it. 2. That which pertains to the destiny of the world.

exegesis. The process of interpreting a text.

exposition. The process of explaining a text.

genre. A group of texts with common characteristics; also referred to as a category.

grammatical mood. The use of specific forms of the verb to indicate a speaker's attitude toward the factuality or likelihood of the action or condition expressed.

head linkage. The literary technique of marking the beginning of two sequential sections by repeating grammar or vocabulary.

hymn. A category of psalms composed for times when life is well ordered, well oriented; the hymns typically celebrate what God has done in creation and redemptive history.

imagery. The use of words to paint pictures of concrete actions or things from the fabric of ordinary life; these pictures create associations between a source domain and a target domain.

imperative mood. The grammatical mood used to express commands.

inclusion. The literary technique of marking the beginning and the end of a section by repeating vocabulary; also called "*inclusio*."

indicative mood. The grammatical mood used to express statements.

interrogative mood. The grammatical mood used to express questions.

Kingship of Yahweh psalms. *See* **divine kingship songs**.

laments. A category of psalms composed for times when life is not well ordered, is disoriented; the laments typically articulate the variegated struggles of life.

line. A line is the basic unit of a poem, usually made from two corresponding units/cola, but sometimes from three or four, and expressing one complete parallelistic thought.

linear pattern. A pattern of organization in which the units follow each other in a nonrepeating order: A B C D E (with each letter representing one unit).

monocolon. A poetic line comprised of one colon.

mythopoeic imagery. The figurative use of ancient Near Eastern mythology to communicate truth about the God of Israel.

objective genitive. The grammatical case in which the second word is the object of the verbal idea contained in the first. The genitive case in Greek is used to express the same kinds of relationships between words as the possessive in English (expressed by *of* or *-'s*).

parallel pattern. A pattern of organization in which the units of the second panel parallel or match the units in the first panel: A B C // A' B' C' (with each letter representing one unit).

parallelism. A relationship of correspondence between the cola of a

poetic line, typically manifesting some kind of addition or movement from one colon to the next.

pregnant expression. An expression that is rich in significance, containing more than a single idea.

quatrain. A poetic line comprised of four cola.

songs of confidence. A category of psalms that lies between the lament and the song of thanksgiving; they are united by the dominant thread of trust that runs through the psalm.

songs of thanksgiving. A category of psalms composed for times
when God has delivered one from the disorientation articulated in
the lament, thus reorienting life; the thanksgiving songs typically
express gratitude and praise for what God has done in the psalmist's
personal history.

stanza. A group of closely related strophes.

strophe. A group of closely related poetic lines; analogous to a paragraph in prose.

subjective genitive. The grammatical case in which the second word
is the subject of the verbal idea contained in the first. The genitive
case in Greek is used to express the same kinds of relationships between words as the possessive in English (expressed by *of* or - *'s*).

suzerain. A dominant king who controls a subordinate king known
as a vassal.

symmetrical pattern. A pattern of organization in which the units of
the second panel parallel or match the units in the first panel but in
reverse order: A B C // C' B' A' (with each letter representing one
unit).

synecdoche. A figure of speech that substitutes one idea for another
with which it is associated, as in a part for the whole or the whole
for a part, or the species for the genus or the genus for the species,
or the name of the material for the thing made, etc.

tail linkage. The literary technique of marking the ends of two sequential sections by repeating vocabulary at the tail end of each.

tetracolon. *See* **quatrain**.

theme. A topic of a discourse.

topical approach. An approach to outlining a text that does not follow the order of the text but presents the message of the text in
terms of the dominant themes.

tricolon. A poetic line comprised of three cola.

vassal. A subordinate king who is controlled by a dominant king known as a suzerain.

volitive mood. The grammatical mood used to express the will of the speaker.

wisdom songs. A category of psalms composed for providing instruction on pious living; these psalms typically share themes with the wisdom literature, such as the "blessed" life and the two ways—the way of the righteous/wise and the way of the wicked/foolish—and exhibit an explicit didactic focus.